Cultural Diversity and the Curriculum

Volume 4

Cultural Diversity and the Curriculum

Volume 4

Cross-Curricular Contexts, Themes and Dimensions in Primary Schools

Edited by

G.K. Verma and P.D. Pumfrey

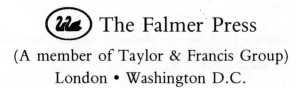 The Falmer Press

(A member of Taylor & Francis Group)
London • Washington D.C.

UK   The Falmer Press, 4 John Street, London WCIN 2ET
USA   The Falmer Press, Taylor & Francis Inc., 1900 Frost Road, Suite 101, Bristol, PA 19007

First published 1994

Library of Congress Cataloging-in-Publication data are available on request

A catalogue record for this book is available from the British Library

ISBN 0 7507 0145 5 (Cased)
ISBN 0 7507 0146 3 (Paperback)

Jacket design by Caroline Archer

Typeset in 10/12pt Bembo by
Graphicraft Typesetters Ltd., Hong Kong

Printed in Great Britain by Burgess Science Press, Basingstoke on paper which has a specified pH value on final paper manufacture of not less than 7.5 and is therefore 'acid free'.

Contents

Contents

Preface

In 1991, twelve refugee families from Somalia came to England. Under the aegis of Sheffield City Council, they were moved into newly-built houses on The Manor estate. The Manor comprises some 6,000 mainly white working-class citizens. The area is characterized by a range of socio-economic difficulties including unemployment, poverty, lack of resources, housing shortages and crime. The arrival into such a situation of a group of about fifty black immigrants provided a focus for the latent racism endemic in most societies. Shortly after their arrival, harassment of the refugees began. It escalated. The all too familiar catalogue of minority group harassment rapidly accumulated including verbal abuse, broken windows, dogs being set on to children, excrement pushed through letter boxes, stoning and attacks in the streets.

'In an attempt to counter harassment, the council installed panic buttons in Somali homes, linking them to a police station. Community workers now tour The Manor after nightfall, checking that the Somali families are safe. Sheffield police have increased their presence on the estate with ten uniformed constables and a sergeant patrolling each night. In perhaps the toughest move, Sheffield council has begun eviction proceeding against four white families it believes to be behind the harassment' (Furbisher, 1993). One man, charged with threatening behaviour towards a Somali, a charge the accused denies, is reported as having his name added to the list of white families facing eviction. Over 200 people signed a petition demanding that this threat of eviction be withdrawn.

One 25 year old male Somali is reported as saying, 'Some of us walked hundreds of miles across desert to escape. Some died. Now many are asking why they came here. I know many white families here are unemployed. They are frustrated. But they seem to take their frustration out on us. Equally tellingly, another Somali spoke of escaping from one form of hatred only to find another. 'My elder daughter, who is thirteen, complained that I had told her that we were going to a European country where there was no war or attacks. She thought there was a war here which had been kept secret. It was hard to explain that not all people in the UK were like this' (ibid).

In April, 1993, the Somalis staged a 'sit-in' at the Sheffield town hall in order to express their soundly-based fears for life and limb, and to request that they be moved.

Is such a case study merely sensationalism and not indicative of latent racist attitudes and behaviours that can arise in virtually any community where resources are limited and resentments readily aroused? Alternatively, is it symptomatic of the animosity and hostilities that all too readily arise in such circumstances?

In October, 1993, in another part of the country, six teenagers from Thorton Heath were charged with beating to death a refugee from Afghanistan. Sadly, it is all too easy to find examples of racial harassment ranging from name-calling to murder. The Chief Commissioner of the Metropolitan Police has stated that reported incidents of racial harassment represent but the tip of an iceberg.

There are neither quick nor easy answers to addressing the appearance and continuation of such anti-social violence against members of minority ethnic groups. The challenge of developing a socially cohesive multicultural society is one requiring the commitment of all citizens. The earlier that this work begins, the greater the likelihood of creating a more tolerant society. In this challenge facing the country, education represents one avenue whereby cultural diversity can be experienced by pupils and their families as enriching rather than threatening. As secondary schools build on what has gone before, the work of the staff of nursery and primary schools is central to the success of this endeavour.

Education for All was the significant and challenging title of the comprehensive report by the Committee of Inquiry into the Education of Children from Minority Ethnic Groups published in 1985. Lord Swann, who chaired that Committee, was the guest of honour of the University of Manchester in 1987 at the inauguration of the Centre for Ethnic Studies in Education (CESE) under the direction of Professor Gajendra K. Verma, based within the University's School of Education. The current series is but one manifestation of the continuing commitment of the CESE, the School of Education and of sixty contributors drawn from organizations across the country, to the ideals of the Swann Report. Fortunately, in developing and implementing the policies and practices demanded if the educational system is to provide an 'Education for All', we are not alone.

> I believe deeply that all men and women should be able to go as far as talent, ambition and effort can take them. There should be no barriers of background, no barriers of religion, no barriers of race. I want . . . a society that encourages each and every one to fulfil his or her potential to the utmost . . . let me say here and now that I regard any barrier built on race to be pernicious. (John Major, 1991)

Thus spoke Prime Minister John Major in an address given in September 1991. It reflects the philosophy and principles embodied in both the Swann report and in Section 1 of the Education Reform Act 1988. The views are ones that provide common ground between political, ethnic, religious and other social groups. Without such an agreed aspiration, social cohesion degenerates into confrontation. Turning comforting political rhetoric into reality in the classroom and community is one of the greatest responsibilities facing the teaching profession. The institutional and individual racism endemic in society must be acknowledged if it is to be alleviated. The school curriculum and the ways in which it is developed, taught and learned represents one of the most promising avenues available to approach this end. As in so many laudable activities, agreement in principle is relatively easy. The devil is in the detail.

This book has two major purposes. The first is to describe and discuss cultural diversity and the curriculum from various curricular perspectives. The second is to consider how the legitimate educational concerns of minority ethnic groups, and those of larger groups, can be constructively addressed within the framework of the National Curriculum and those equally important aspects of the curriculum subsumed under the broader headings of the 'basic' and 'whole' curriculum respectively. To this end, specialists in the key components of the curriculum have considered some of the challenges and describe promising practices in a number of specific subject and cross-curricular fields.

Each contributor in each of the four volumes comments under three headings on that aspect of the curriculum in which the contributor has specialist experience and expertise, in relation to cultural diversity. The headings used by all contributors are identified as 'Context', 'Challenges' and 'Responses'. The views expressed, the analyses of contexts, the identification of challenges and the suggestions for responses represent the considered opinions of the individual contributors.

This is the final volume in a series of four books. All four volumes are concerned with cultural diversity and the curriculum. Volumes 1 and 2 focus on secondary schools. Volumes 3 and 4 consider parallel curricular issues from a primary schools' perspective.

Volumes 1 and 3 address the implications of the National Curriculum foundation subjects and religious education in relation to cultural diversity at the secondary and primary-school levels, respectively. Volumes 2 and 4 consider the implications of cross-curricular themes in relation to cultural diversity at the secondary and primary-school levels respectively.

The Education Reform Act 1988 and the phasing in of its curricular requirements over the past six years has presented many challenges to the teaching profession (NCC, 1992). Six years after the passing of the Education Reform Act 1988, much remains undecided concerning the structure, content, pedagogy and assessment of many components of the school curriculum. The chaos created by numerous ill-considered and hastily implemented changes, followed by even more changes to changes, has detracted considerably from the effective delivery of the 'entitlement curriculum' that had been promised by the ERA (Barber and Graham, 1992).

The National Curriculum Council (NCC) based in York and the School Examinations and Assessment Council (SEAC) located in London were both established as a consequence of the Education Reform Act 1988. The setting up of two separate organizations to develop, respectively, the curricular content and the assessment procedures required to implement the National Curriculum, was criticized from the very start by a considerable body of professional opinion as a recipe for confusion.

By 1993 the problems arising had reached such a magnitude that they could not be ignored. This led to the decision that both organizations would be integrated under the aegis of a new body called the School Curriculum and Assessment Authority (SCAA). Sir Ron Dearing, Chair of the Higher Education Funding Council (HEFC), had successfully managed a relatively trouble-free merging of the previously separate universities and polytechnics funding councils. He accepted the invitation extended by the Secretary of State for Education to undertake a review of the curriculum and its assessment, and to direct SCAA.

Consultation with the teachers charged with the delivery of the curriculum is at the core of Dearing's strategy. At a meeting with heads and teachers from the West Midlands held in May 1993, he is reported as saying:

> I have one master and that is the future of our children and their life chances in the next century, not the Secretary of State nor the many interest groups, but the young people. I care, as you care, very much about them. (Sir Ron Dearing, 1993)

They (teachers) are saying 'We are so committed to covering the National Curriculum that there is no time to respond to the other things.' It is freedom to respond that they want.

A summary of the actions proposed to meet the serious criticisms of the National Curriculum, entitled *The National Curriculum and its Assessment*, was published in September 1993. It was advertised as 'The school report that every teacher should read' (NCC/SEAC, 1993). Will the proposed reductions in the current administrative curricular burdens on teachers and schools provide the profession with freedom to consider the implications of cultural diversity and the whole curriculum in their daily work more effectively than hithertofore? A subsequent joint letter from HM Chief Inspector of Schools, England, HM Chief Inspector of Schools, Wales and the Chairman of the School Curriculum and Assessment Agency is all schools in England and Wales reinforced this point (Sutherland, James and Dearing, 1993). The final version of the Dearing Report appeared in December, 1993 (SCAA, 1993).

Education for All and equality of educational opportunity within an entitlement curriculum are rallying calls that have an appealing simplicity in an age of sound-bites and slogans. Even a cursory consideration rapidly demonstrates that all three involve controversial and complex educational, ethical, moral, legal and financial issues. In our increasingly multicultural and multiethnic community, mutual recognition and acceptance by individuals and groups of the rights and responsibilities of citizenship in a democracy underpins the social cohesion on which our well-being is largely dependent.

The multicultural nature of the population and of schools will develop. Demographic data presented in Volume 3, Chapter 2 and in Chapter 2 of this volume, confirm this point and provide indications of the nature and extent of the demographic changes that are likely to take place in the future. These demographic changes, and their educational implications, must be considered if the state educational system is to respond adequately and equitably.

We deliberately ventured into the controversial field of cultural diversity and the curriculum whilst the 'rules of the curricular game' in state schools, initiated under the Education Reform Act 1988, are still being negotiated in relation to certain aspects of the curriculum. We do so because of the importance with which we view the increasing ethnic diversity of the school population and of the country. Janus-faced, that ethnic diversity represents both problems and opportunities for all parties involved. To deny either would be a disservice to the pupils and the communities that the educational system exists to serve. It would also limit the chances that an education meeting the requirements of the Education Reform Act 1988 would ever be provided.

It has been argued that cross-curricular elements, of which an extensive number can be listed, make a major contribution to the personal and social education of pupils. Such elements 'are ingredients which tie together the broad education of the individual and augment what comes from the basic curriculum' (NCC, 1990, p. 2). The NCC has distinguished three aspects of cross-curricular elements: dimensions; skills; and themes. Dimensions include a commitment to the provison of *equal opportunities* for all pupils, coupled with recognition that 'preparation for life in a multicultural society is relevant to all pupils' and should permeate the entire curriculum (ibid., p. 2). Thus cultural diversity, gender and special educational needs are identified by the NCC as three key considerations. There are others. Because of their salience, we have selected four further dimensions of particular importance in a multicultural school, society and world. There are also many cross-curricular skills. These include:

- communication skills (receptive and expressive aspects of language);
- numeracy skills;
- study skills;
- problem-solving skills;
- personal and social skills; and
- information technology skills.

Cross-curricular themes refer to five major facets of any curriculum that are considered by the NCC to be essential parts of the whole curriculum.

Volume 4 is in three Parts. The first, Part 1, comprises two chapters written to establish the importance to all schools and all pupils, of the context of, challenges to and responses to, cultural diversity in relation to a range of cross-curricular issues. Chapter 1 comprises a consideration of the nature and extent of cultural diversity and its cross-curricular implications. The second chapter summarizes and discusses the cross-curricular elements in more detail and provides demographic information on ethnic diversity based on the latest census information. These two chapters set the scene for subsequent contributions. Part 2 comprises chapters on each of the five major cross-curricular themes specified in the publications of the National Curriculum Council. Thus, Chapters 3 to 7 are concerned with:

- education for economic and industrial awareness;
- careers education and guidance;
- health education;
- education for citizenship; and
- environmental education.

In addition to these important cross-curricular themes, we have identified a further seven cross-curricular dimensions that merit attention. These are presented in Part 3 as Chapters 8 to 14.

- personal and social education;
- gender issues;
- multicultural dimension in the primary National Curriculum;
- children with special educational needs;
- the European dimension;
- information technology; and
- initial teacher education and ethnic diversity.

As in the previous three volumes, our contributors are drawn from various cultural, ethnic and professional backgrounds. Consequently, their respective philosophical and theoretical stances vary. To have sought only individuals operating from a single agreed ideological, philosophical, or theoretical position concerning the nature and curricular implications of cultural diversity in the primary school, would have implied that the editors considered such a position existed and was the most tenable.

Irrespective of the authors' respective ideological, philosophical and theoretical positions, all are clearly concerned with ensuring that the National Curriculum is effectively delivered in our multicultural society. The claim that good practice can help to drive out poor theory, has something to commend it. A belief in the importance of the curricular implications and practices deriving from cultural diversity unites our contributors.

This volume completes the task on which we set out two years ago. It is not the end of our involvement! We acknowledge with appreciation the generous help given to us by our fellow contributors and by the many organizations that have also assisted in providing information, advice and comment. The dissemination and discussion of the ideas contained within the series, their application, development and evaluation within our educational institutions, are eagerly anticipated. Providing *Education for All* is a challenge to which we must rise.

Peter D. Pumfrey and Gajendra K. Verma

References

BARBER, M. and GRAHAM, D. (Eds) (1992) *Sense and Nonsense and the National Curriculum*, London, The Falmer Press.

NATIONAL CURRICULUM COUNCIL (1990) *The Whole Curriculum, Curriculum Guidance No. 3*, York, NCC.

NATIONAL CURRICULUM COUNCIL (1992) *Starting out with the National Curriculum: An Introduction to the National Curriculum and Religious Education*, York, NCC.

NATIONAL CURRICULUM COUNCIL AND SCHOOL EXAMINATIONS AND ASSESSMENT COUNCIL (NCC/SEAC) (1993) *The National Curriculum and its Assessment: Interim Report*, London, SEAC.

SCHOOL CURRICULUM AND ASSESSMENT AUTHORITY (1993) *The National Curriculum and its Assessment: Final Report*, London, SCCA.

SUTHERLAND, G., JAMES, R. and DEARING, R. (1993) Recording Pupils Achievement, Joint letter sent to all schools, 4 November, 1993.

List of Tables and Figures

Tables

Figures

List of Abbreviations

AIMER	Access to Information on Multicultural Education Resources
AIMS	Art and Design in a Multicultural Society
AMA	Association of Metropolitan Authorities
APU	Assessment of Performance Unit
ARE	Anti-Racist Education
AREAI	Association of Religious Education Advisers and Inspectors
ARTEN	Anti-Racist Teacher Education Network
AT	Attainment Targets
ATEM	Association of Ethnic Minority Teachers
BCPE	British Council for Physical Education
BGIN	Black Governors' Information Network
BTEC	Business and Technical Education Council
CARM	Campaign Against Racism in the Media
CATE	Council for the Accreditation of Teacher Education
CCW	Curriculum Council for Wales
CDT	Craft, Design and Technology
CESIE	Centre for Ethnic Studies In Education
CNAA	Council for National Academic Awards
CPD	Continuing Professional Development
CPSA	Curriculum and Parental Support Assistant
CPVE	Certificate of Pre-Vocational Education
CRE	Commission for Racial Equality
CSE	Certificate of Secondary Education
CTA	Caribbean Teachers Association
DES	Department of Education and Science
EBP	Education Business Partnership
EMAG	Ethnic Minority Advisory Groups
ENCORE	European Network for Conflict Resolution in Education
ESRC	Economic and Social Science Research Council
ERA	Education Reform Act 1988
E2L	English as a second language

EFL	English as a foreign language
ESG	Education Support Grant
GCSE	General Certificate of Secondary Education
GEST	Grants for Educational Support and Training
GRIST	Grant Related In-service Training
HEFC	Higher Education Funding Council
HEI	Higher Education Institute
HMI	Her Majesty's Inspectorate
HMSO	Her Majesty's Stationery Office
INSET	In-service Education for Teachers
IRR	Institute for Race Relations
IT	Information Technology
ITE	Initial Teacher Education
ITT	Initial Teacher Training
KS	Key Stages (of the National Curriculum)
LEA	Local Education Authority
LMS	Local Management of Schools
MCE	Multi-Cultural Education
MFLWG	Modern Foreign Languages Working Group
NAHT	National Association of Head Teachers
NAME	National Anti-Racist Movement in Education
NAREC	National Association of Racial Equality Councils
NASA	Northern Association of Section 11 Authorities
NC	National Curriculum
NCCL	National Council for Civil Liberties
NCC	National Curriculum Council
NCDP	National Curriculum Development Plan
NCMT	National Council for the Mother Tongue
NERIS	National Educational Resources Information Service
NFER	National Foundation for Educational Research
NSC	National Science Curriculum
NSG	Non-Statutory Guidance
OPCS	Office of Population Censuses and Surveys
PC	Profile Components
PoS	Programme of Study
PSE	Personal and Social Education
PTA	Parent–Teacher Association
RE	Religious Education
RI	Religious Instruction
RoA	Records of Achievement
RT	Runnymede Trust
SACRE	Standing Advisory Council on Religious Education
SAIL	Staged Assessments in Literacy
SAT	Standard Assessment Task
SCAA	School Curriculum and Assessment Authority

List of Abbreviations

SEAC	School Examinations and Assessment Council
SCIP	School Curriculum Industry Partnership
SCDC	School Curriculum Development Committee
SoA	Statements of Attainment
SSD	Social Services Department
TGAT	Task Group on Assessment and Testing
TVE	Technical and Vocational Education
WGR	Working Group Report

Educational Equality and Cultural Pluralism in Primary Education: Cross-curricular Perspectives

Chapter 1

Cultural Diversity in Primary Schools: Its Nature, Extent and Cross-curricular Implications

Gajendra K. Verma

Context

The papers in the present volume focus on issues related to cross-curricular dimensions, skills and themes. The authors of these papers have analysed the issues from the point of view of cultural, religious and linguistic characteristics of primary schools. It is clear from their analyses that, unless the debate about shared values and different values in society is explicitly acknowledged and resolved, the concept of cultural diversity remains rhetorical and ineffective in the delivery of the curriculum. Many of the pedagogic issues related to plurality in the educational system are still unclear, although the contributors to the present series show that progress has been, and can be made.

Cultural diversity has been a fact of life in the countries of East and West, North and South for many centuries. The implication of this has been the presence within nation states of a number of cultural, ethnic or racial groups. Since the process of migration and the history of different nations vary considerably, the cultural profile of different regions within any particular country also varies. However, contemporary recognition of the value of cultural, linguistic and religious diversity and their educational implications are international and more recent (Lynch, Modgil and Modgil, 1992a,b,c,d).

By the nineteenth century, cultural diversity in European countries was already marked in terms of differences in the religious, linguistic and ethnic profiles of their inhabitants. Political and social forces attempted to acculturate divergent and sometimes conquered cultural groups into the dominant culture and language. Even the post-World War I settlement, which made deliberate efforts to create culturally homogeneous nation states, failed to eliminate diversity and, in some cases, it served to accentuate the diversity. In spite of the fact that certain countries tried to integrate their divergent cultural groups within the dominant culture, many European nation states have allowed ethnic minorities to retain their distinctive cultures which often varied significantly from that of the dominant group. Others have signally failed so to do: to wit, the former Yugoslavia.

It must be acknowledged that in any society it is rare to find that the population is homogeneous. Most societies are now demographically pluralistic (particularly since World War II), characterized by the presence of two or more distinct groups of communities which are differentiated in terms of language, religion, ethnic characteristics and/or cultural heritage. In spite of such diversity, many countries have failed to recognize and support the heterogeneity of its citizens. The aim of 'unity in plurality' represents an ideal more readily espoused in rhetoric than worked towards in reality.

Notwithstanding such tendencies towards homogenization, considerable differences in value orientation can still be found between the European countries. Nationalism, for instance, is still much stronger in some countries than in others. Inglehart (1990) found that in 1985 72 per cent of all Greeks said they were 'very proud to be Greek' and 64 per cent of all Spaniards were 'very proud to be Spanish'. This contrasts quite sharply with only 33 per cent of the Portuguese being 'very proud to be Portuguese' and not more than 20 per cent of all (West) Germans saying that they were 'very proud to be German'. One should keep in mind, however, that important differences in outlook also exist within each of these countries. These differences are aspects of continuing socialization processes.

Inglehart also compared religious and moral attitudes in various countries. 53 per cent of the French describe themselves as a 'religious person' as opposed to 84 per cent of the Italians. In the Netherlands 22 per cent of the population thinks 'homosexuality can never be justified', as opposed to 65 per cent in the United States. Also in the Netherlands 11 per cent of the population think that 'a woman needs children in order to be fulfilled'; in France the corresponding percentage is 71. What common values might enable any country work towards 'unity in plurality'?

The end of World War II was a turning point when ethnic minorities throughout the world started asserting their rights. They became conscious of the fact that their identities were being eroded because of assimilationist educational and social policies. This awareness caused them to challenge the disparity between the declared values of democratic societies and the realities of the operation of such policies. In 1994, the slogan of 'ethnic cleansing' used earlier to justify, for example, the wars in the Balkans, highlights an ever-present challenge to coexistence.

Over the last four decades or so the classical concept of a culturally homogeneous society has been challenged more openly. On the one hand there is the process of European integration — politically, socially and economically — which is likely to affect many of the rules and regulations and consequently citizens' daily lives. On the other hand, cultural, religious and linguistic differences between groups have come under scrutiny. At this point it would be appropriate to consider what we mean by 'culture'.

What is 'culture'? Definition of the term 'culture' is both complex and problematic. A common ambiguity inherent in any discussion of culture is the interchangeable use of other terms when dealing with it, particularly within the educational context. For example, in order to meet the needs of a plural society, educational programmes have adopted certain strategies variously labelled as 'multicultural', 'multiracial', 'intercultural', 'cross-cultural', and 'antiracist' education. Such approaches to teaching have been supported by some and criticized by others. The relationship between cultural diversity and education has become an area of increasing controversy in Britain since the 1960s. It has generated debates and discussions about the nature of society and the functions of schooling. In a culturally diverse society such a debate inevitably involves issues such as value systems, religion, language and ethnic relations.

A review of the literature clearly demonstrates that many writers have not only oversimplified the analysis of the term 'culture' but have often approached it in a stereotypical way (Verma, 1986; Figueroa and Fyfe, 1993). For example, there has often been a tendency to define it primarily in terms of ethnicity, assuming homogeneity in any ethnic community or group. Culture is an evolving, dynamic and ongoing process, and not a static or unidimensional concept. It may be defined as the unique values, symbols, lifestyle, customs and other human-made components that distinguish one social group from another. Such socially determined constructs are themselves amenable to change in a rapidly changing world. It should also be stressed that individuals can belong to more than one social group, and consequently they can develop multiple group affiliations and loyalties.

As Clarke *et al.* (1981) put it:

> A culture includes the 'maps of meaning' which make things intelligible
> to its members. These 'maps of meaning' are not simply carried around
> in the head: they are objectivated in the patterns of social organisation
> and relationship through which the individual becomes a 'social in-
> dividual'. (Clarke *et al.*, 1981)

From this perspective culture is learned, communicated and shaped through individual attempts to master and participate in the life of the group. Thus, culture is constructed and reconstructed through the process of social interaction.

There are many aspects of an individual's identity which develop through the socialization process. This process is influenced by family structures, schooling and experience in the wider society. These forces contribute to the development of an individual's identity which consists of specific behaviours, values, lifestyles, attitudes and world views. Such components of identity may differ and sometimes come into conflict with the mainstream framework or 'norms'. There is sufficient evidence to suggest that many of the conflicts that arise between the school and minority ethnic communities, and many of the cultural disparities that pupils experience, are caused by conflicting values, beliefs and behaviour (Pumfrey and Verma, 1990). Some ethnic and religious groups are socialized in homes and communities in which the sacred is valued more than the secular, and in which traditional cultural beliefs and religious values are strongly held. The attachments that people develop in this process contribute to the formation of cultural in-groups. The attitudes of the in-group towards the out-groups are formed on the basis of experience. The school plays a mediating role in this process.

In Britain, since the introduction of the National Curriculum in 1988, the concern which is taking prominence on the Muslim education agenda is the issue of freedom of religion. Muslims are gaining support from some non-Muslim groups and are pressing for the removal of religious inequalities within the educational framework of the Education Act for religious education and collective worship. At a recent conference, organized by the All-Parliamentary Group for Racial Equality and the Runnymede Trust, the issues of religious discrimination and inequality were discussed. In the conference statement which was published it says that 'the multifaith nature of British society must be firmly anchored and reflected in the planning and development of religious education and collective worship, both locally and nationally' (Yaseen, 1993).

Thus, if we take the word 'culture' to denote the meanings and understandings which are learned, shared and evolve in groups, then the educational system should be constructed to create an environment against a background accepting of other cultures, ethnicities, class, gender and communities. The culture of an educational institution should be a reflection of the culture of society. If a society is a plural one, this ought to be reflected in the culture of the educational environment. In this perspective, culture encompasses almost every aspect of human experience — it represents a more or less consistent pattern of thoughts, feelings and actions, and it is structured.

In Britain, 3.06 million people — approximately 1 in 20 of the population — belong to an ethnic minority. This represents 5.5 per cent of the total population. This also means that these people have different ethnic origins to the majority of British people. Since the 1950s, when the number of people coming to live in Britain from former colonies began to increase, debate has continued about how to ensure that they are accorded the same rights, accept the same responsibilities, and have access to the same opportunities as other people in all aspects of life (see Chapter 2 for ethnic analyses based on the latest census).

The educational responses since the 1960s to the presence of ethnic minorities in British schools have been analysed as movements through three overlapping models based, in turn, upon the concepts of assimilation, integration and cultural pluralism. In this process, many educational strategies and models have been adopted to deal with the disadvantaged position of many ethnic-minority groups within the educational system in general and in schools in particular. None of the models seems to have met the challenges that face the educational system, and consequently they have failed to change the ideological perceptions of British society as a whole.

As early as 1977 a Green Paper, *Education in Schools: A Consultative*

Document (DES, 1977) stressed that the presence of ethnic-minority groups in Britain had implications for the education of all children. It suggested that all schools, whatever their ethnic composition, should give their pupils an understanding both of the multiethnic nature of British society and of Britain's place in an interdependent world. The Green Paper further stated that Britain is a multicultural, multiracial society and that the curriculum of schools should reflect the realities of this new Britain. Despite this, many education authorities in areas where there were few minority pupils turned a blind eye to such suggestions and responded by saying that the wider multiethnic society had little relevance to their local teaching practice.

Two years later, in 1979, the government set up an independent inquiry to look into the education of children from ethnic-minority groups. There were two sets of issues which led to the creation of this inquiry. These were the problem of West-Indian underachievement and that of the presence in British schools of Asian children with distinctly different languages and cultures.

The interim report, produced under the chairmanship of Anthony Rampton, appeared in 1981 entitled *West Indian Children in Our Schools* (DES, 1981). This report had as its focus the circumstances and experiences of West-Indian children in Britain and tended to play down those of children from other ethnic-minority groups. In view of the media headlines that the Brixton, Toxteth and Bristol racial disturbances attracted at the time, the emphasis in the Rampton report was not surprising. Soon after the publication of the interim report, Rampton resigned and Lord Swann was appointed as the new Chairman of the Inquiry.

The interim report (DES, 1981) stated that:

> the curriculum in all schools should reflect the fact that Britain is both multiracial and culturally diverse . . . the intention of multicultural education is simply to provide all children with a balanced education which reflects the nature of our Society . . . all heads should be prepared to develop a multicultural approach towards the curriculum. (DES, 1981)

Critics have always argued that the ethnocentric nature of much of what is taught in the classrooms has an adverse effect on both ethnic-minority and majority children. This restricts the development of the former's self-concepts and reproduces prejudice.

Over the last twenty years there has also been a growing body of opinion that inappropriate assessment procedures are one of the major factors contributing to the disproportionate numbers of black and other minority children assessed as having learning difficulties and placed in special schools (Tomlinson, 1987). It is ironic that the increased per-capita investment in pupils' education that this represented was largely counterproductive.

The Swann Report moved the main focus of the debate about cultural diversity, multicultural education and equal opportunity from issues concerning the education of specific ethnic-minority children to the issues concerning the relevant and good education of *all* pupils for a plural society (DES, 1985). It advocates balance, breadth and equity within a pluralist framework. This would both educate the ethnic majority and make schools acceptable areas for personal development and educational achievement for *all* ethnic groups. The Report comments that:

> The fundamental change that is necessary is the recognition that the problem facing the education system is not how to educate children of ethnic minorities, but how to educate all children — Britain is a multiracial and multicultural society and all pupils must be enabled to understand what this means. (DES, 1985, p. 363)

The Report also asserted that many obstacles lay in the path of ethnic-minority pupils and lessened their chances of fulfilling their educational potential. Among those obstacles were ones created by poor interethnic relationships and by the relative failure of schools to prepare all pupils, of whatever origin, for a life in a multiracial society. The Report pointed out that many school practices related to cultural diversity were harmful and that they reinforced cultural stereotypes and discriminatory practices both inside schools and in the wider society. The question of multicultural education is discussed at some length in the Swann Report, which states that:

> We consider that a multiracial society such as ours would function more effectively and harmoniously on the basis of pluralism which enables, expects and encourages members to participate fully in shaping the society as a whole within a framework of commonly accepted values, practices and procedures whilst also allowing and, where necessary, assisting the ethnic minority communities in maintaining their distinct ethnic identities within their common framework. (DES, 1985)

The Report advocates that the education should combine the cultivation of differences between groups with the maintenance of a core of common national values.

With the introduction of the Education Reform Act (ERA) (DES, 1988), discourse on multicultural and antiracist education, equal opportunity, and cultural diversity was somewhat marginalized despite its explicit guiding principles (see p. 13). The educational debate shifted to the National Curriculum which was conceived of as a list of subjects structured by Attainment Targets and Programmes of Study. The topics such as 'Attainment Targets', 'assessment and testing', 'Key Stages' were given statutory force in the ERA, 1988. However, since 1990 the National Curriculum Council (NCC) has begun to produce booklets and papers which have introduced issues such as equal opportunities, cultural diversity, the multicultural nature of our society and so on. An examination of various documents and guidelines clearly shows that there are ambiguities and often omission of the crucial issues of cultural diversity and the curriculum. One wonders whether the School Curriculum and Assessment Authority (SCAA) which replaced the NCC and SEAC in October 1993, will not make similar mistakes.

The educational experience of ethnic-minority children and adolescents in British schools is affected by a number of factors such as social class, teacher attitudes and expectations against a background of institutional racism. The Swann Report drew attention to one main aspect of institutional racism, namely the Eurocentric/Anglocentric curriculum and the biased assessment procedures, which often bore little relation to the lives and experiences of ethnic-minority pupils (DES, 1985). Similar conclusions have been subsequently reported by Verma (1989), and Tomlinson and Smith (1989) on the basis of extensive research. Studies have also concluded that the educational system has failed to respond adequately to the cultural diversity which is now characteristic of the school population. Minority cultures are all too often undervalued or misunderstood as they are represented in the curriculum.

Ample evidence also exists to show that inequality in educational experiences is a powerful determinant of difference in educational attainment in children (DES, 1985; Barrow, 1988; Tomlinson and Smith, 1989). Social class, ethnicity, gender and disability exert a considerable influence on the life chances of young people. If one accepts its limitations, education remains an important means of social mobility. It contributes towards creating economic and occupational security and acts as a buffer to other forms of social disadvantage. An 'entitlement' curriculum, such as that envisaged by the ERA, represents an important unifying value in a culturally diverse society.

The extent to which a school provides access to the knowledge and experiences children are entitled to, and the consequent improvement in learning that children make, should be the determining factor when judging whether or not a school is effectively offering equality of educational opportunity.

There is evidence to suggest that ethnic-minority communities do accept the importance of a shared framework of educational and societal purposes. Despite this, they find ambiguities and contradictions in the curriculum. The educational system seems to have failed to meet the needs and aspirations of ethnic and cultural minority groups particularly in relation to their identity development.

Challenges

The government has created a state educational system whereby pupils are tested throughout their period of statutory education. The educational content of their courses has been centrally prescribed to an extent unknown in this century. All this has been done in the name of higher standards. Whether these higher standards will be achieved as a result of these changes to the system is more a matter of faith than confident prediction. It may well make for a situation in which personal and societal inequalities will be increased rather than diminished, unless teachers are made keenly aware of the processes in which they are engaged and for which they are, in part, responsible. An educational system based solely on competitive principles leads rapidly to the differentiation between pupils by relative attainments. 'Pecking orders' of individuals and groups are soon established. Cooperative learning is based on a contrasting conceptualization of the educational process. In an ethnically diverse society, the balance between competition and collaboration is analogous to walking a 'high wire'.

The primary purpose of the National Curriculum has been set out as being to:

- promote the spiritual, moral, cultural, mental and physical development of pupils at the school and of society;
- prepare such pupils for the opportunities, responsibilities and experiences of adult life. (DES, 1988)

It is also authoritatively stated that 'the principle that each pupil should have a broad and balanced curriculum which is also relevant to his or her particular needs is now established in law' (DES, 1988).

On the basis of the above principle it is naively assumed that such 'needs' are known, accepted and identified and that all schools will respond to the educational needs of their pupils appropriately. Schools have been and will be responding to the above objectives in different ways, depending on their resources, priorities and characteristics of the school population.

Some observers are of the opinion that the political, economic and social objectives of the Education Reform Act (ERA) are (a) to raise educational standards for all, (b) to secure better education for all, (c) to ensure that future generations are equipped with knowledge, skills and understanding to further their own personal development as well as to make contribution to society by securing the economic success of the country against its 'competitors'.

Under the 1988 Education Reform Act the 'what' i.e., the content of the subjects is, on the whole, controlled centrally. The 'how' i.e., the process is largely in the hands of teachers. Some critics of the ERA suggest that the underlying assumption of this educational model is that by prescribing the content and linking it with statutory assessment arrangements, educational standards can be raised. There is no evidence so far, that by legislating for access and entitlement, the achievement levels of all can be standardized and also raised. Analyses by various practitioners have raised serious questions about the inbuilt assumptions in the new legislation (see also Volumes 1 to 3 in this series). Access and entitlement for *all* pupils cannot be managed unless there is commitment both on the part of teachers who are responsible for the delivery of the National Curriculum and the pupils (and their families) for whose benefit the educational system is provided.

The National Curriculum Council (NCC) has emphasized through its various publications that the cross-curricular aspects of the curriculum are an integral part of what is needed to meet the requirements of the Education Reform Act 1988. It also stresses that different subjects must not be taught in isolation, but should be planned in such a way as to contribute to pupils' learning as a whole, and it should distinguish between cross-curricular dimensions, skills and themes. In Circular No. 6 there is a striking metaphor for the whole curriculum:

> Attainment targets and programmes of study are the bricks with which the curriculum must be built. Cross-curricular strategies bond these bricks into a cohesive structures (NCC, 1989, par. 19).

Cross-curricular elements comprise two major dimensions, six skills and five themes. Cross-curricular aspects explicitly acknowledge the importance of topic work. This is supposed to integrate various aspects of knowledge, understanding and applications that can also be identified as belonging to specific subject domains comprising the National Curriculum foundation subjects and religious education. Circular No. 6 has classified cross-curricular provision under dimensions, skills and themes as being 'helpful for review and organisation of the curriculum and the planning of the content'.

The two dimensions, six skills and five cross-curricular themes are outlined in the introduction and discussed more fully in Chapter 2.

These cross-curricular elements ought to permeate every aspect of the curriculum.

The National Curriculum defines cross-curricular themes as 'elements that enrich the educational experience of pupils'. The themes can be related to all National Curriculum subjects and religious education. Each of these five themes is addressed by specialists in the field of primary education in the present volume. The question often posed by those concerned with the education of *all* children is: 'To what extent are the cross-curricular aspects, and especially those relating to cultural diversity and in general for education for life in a plural society, being addressed in the implementation of the ERA?' If the broad aims of education are to be realized, then cultural diversity must be made creative in school, by weaving together the warp of the interrelated principles of cross-curricular dimensions, skills and themes with the weft of the foundation subjects and religious education.

The Education Reform Act 1988 says that the curriculum should be 'balanced and broadly based' and should promote 'the spiritual, moral, cultural, mental and physical development of pupils' and prepare them for the opportunities, responsibilities and experiences of adult life'. However, pupils come from varying cultural backgrounds, and the society in which they will live their adult lives will be increasingly multicultural. Hence, it is important, as the ERA requires, for the curriculum to address the issues of cultural diversity. The National Curriculum Council (NCC) has approached these issues from a cross-curricular perspective, and stresses the need for whole-curriculum planning and for giving adequate attention in particular to such cross-curricular issues as equal opportunities and education for life in a multicultural society.

The National Curriculum Council (NCC) has stressed that the cross-curricular aspects of the curriculum are an integral part of what is needed to meet the requirements of the Education Reform Act 1988 (ERA). It also stresses that different subjects must not be taught in isolation, but must be planned so as to contribute to pupils' learning as a whole.

Responses

Given the challenges outlined in the preceding section, the questions arise as to what can be done to achieve the stated objectives of the National Curriculum, and how to ensure that cross-curricular dimensions, skills and themes form part of the whole curriculum? It was assumed that the two major dimensions should permeate every aspect of the curriculum, the six skills be systematically and conscientiously fostered across the whole curriculum and that the five themes should be used to enrich educational experiences of pupils.

The introduction of the National Curriculum, the speed of its implementation and the indecisions and revisions in content specification and assessment procedures have caused much strain and tension, not least among teachers. Within the attendant dysfunctionality, it is easy to lose sight of the broad goals that the National Curriculum sets out to meet. Those goals, as suggested in an earlier volume in this series, are ones which have much to commend them and which would seem to be not only equitable but also common sense (Chapter 3, Volume 2). As a starting point to this section, those goals bear repeating:

- the improvement of the quality of the education offered to *all* children and adolescents in the maintained sector of schooling;
- the achievement of a greater balance in the scope of that education;
- the achievement of greater uniformity/continuity in the education offered in different parts of the country, thus not only creating greater equity generally, but also fairness to those children who have to change schools because their families move home.

Whatever the perceived imperfections surrounding the National Curriculum as it is presently, those goals would seem to be a step in the right direction in terms of the equality of opportunity aspect in a culturally diverse society. Against this, however, one has to set the prescriptive nature of its diktat and the Anglocentric orientation of the content. This, as has also been pointed out in other volumes of this series, has tended to undo some of the laudable, albeit rather piecemeal, efforts to move the traditional curriculum towards one that was more empathetic to cultural diversity.

In 1992 the National Union of Teachers issued guidelines showing schools how to maintain antiracist and multicultural teaching and prevent the National Curriculum becoming 'nationalistic and Eurocentric'. It sent advice to all schools that teachers should prepare pupils to be 'citizens of the world' and use every opportunity to widen pupils' awareness of the contributions of non-Europeans to the world's store of knowledge, culture and achievement (NUT, 1992). The National Association of Head Teachers has published *Managing Equality* (NAHT, 1992) which provides all headteachers with a code of practice to ensure that overt and covert forms of racial discrimination are recognized and dealt with.

The requirement to incorporate cross-curricular themes into the education received by children and young people in both primary and secondary schools may not include all the skills and areas of sensitization that might be considered desirable in terms of a *fair* response to cultural diversity in Britain. For example, one might have hoped to see interpersonal relationships more prominently included in the cross-curricular elements. However, as the contributors to this volume show, the cross-curricular elements do not shut the door on issues relating to cultural diversity in our increasingly complex society. These issues cannot be satisfactorily resolved by individual teachers acting alone, although each has an important part to play in the whole process; it is, after all, typically the individual teacher working in his/her classroom. Schools require explicit policies to address the challenges of cultural diversity. Such policies require all teachers to make a joint effort to:

- take a critical stance on the identification of cultural bias, prejudice, sexism, racism and stereotyping whether found in teaching materials or strategies;
- approach all subject matter, whether treating cross-curricular themes or core and foundation subjects, in a way which questions ethnocentrism;
- value teaching which makes an effective response to the aspirations of *all* pupils and which actively seeks to maximize their full potential; and
- seek to keep themselves informed of good professional practice.

Cross-curricular themes are not merely about the transmission of particular skills, and knowledge and understanding. They also have a *value* content; their inclusion is a tacit recognition that the themes are an important 'cement' to the main body content of the National Curriculum. They are included because they are held to be of value to the individual to help equip him/her for life in the modern world, while at the same time being of benefit to society as a whole. Health education, for example, may be of help to the individual in physical terms such as the avoidance of food-poisoning or seeking prompt treatment of an infection through increasing *individual* levels of awareness.

Cross-curricular themes have a *social* benefit, whether to follow the logic of the instanced example, in terms of society being healthier or of fewer working days lost, and so forth.

Examples taken from the primary-school cross-curricular themes will serve to illustrate how cultural diversity issues can permeate such themes.

In *'Economic and Industrial Understanding'* there are many opportunities to raise issues relating to equality of opportunity, both in terms of race and gender (Chapter 3). This could occur in discussion of what children may have seen when on an industrial visit or watching videos treating this topic. The key approach would appear to be in the quality of the illustrations put forward by the teacher in linking children's direct experiences and those arising out of the stimulus material. This theme is well-suited to tackle issues of social justice, race and culture. It is not just the links *per se*, but making children aware of the economic and industrial factors in their lives which shape their communities and their presents and futures.

In the case of *'Careers Education and Guidance'*, it is easy perhaps to fall into the temptation that coverage of such a theme in the primary school is premature. Yet, the early years in school are when children begin to form attitudes about the *value* of particular occupations in terms of their own self-worth and that of others (Chapter 4). Those perceptions are built on what the child picks up from home and neighbourhood, the media, and from the school, both formally through the classroom process, and informally through peer-group interaction. This is therefore a critical phase and teachers need to take particular care in classroom and individual interactions. They need to respond *positively* to early articulations of career aspirations and to try to avoid the often unconscious negative stereotyping about job status. Such discussion also lends itself to drawing attention to the breaking down of the traditional attitude barriers about employment avenues that have been given impetus by the equal-opportunities movement. There are important educational implications for race and gender and for children's perceptions of themselves and others. Careers' education should be presented in such a way as to prepare children for their future in a multiracial society. Appropriate role models are of the essence. Similarly, *'Health Education'*, and *'Education for Citizenship and Environmental Education'* provide illustrations of the possibilities and pitfalls in terms of cultural-diversity treatment.

The complexities of issues surrounding *'Health Education'* make it a delicate theme to treat, not merely from a cultural point of view. There is the inherent danger of over-emphasizing *differences* between one group and another with the risk of adverse stereotypes becoming formed in the minds of children. This is a potential pitfall that can arise out of unguarded or ingenuous remarks or illustrations that may undo progress made elsewhere in sensitizing children to cultural diversity. Health education requires a holistic approach, in that it is a whole-school concern for the whole person and not just the physical aspect (Chapter 5).

'Education for Citizenship' with its implicit emphasis on individual rights

and responsibilities in a democratic society is an important theme in terms of cultural diversity. It is at the heart of all interpersonal contact at the social, cultural and political levels. Fortunately, there is some practical guidance available on the development of material which achieves the combination of precision in assessing progress and ensuring that the curriculum motivates children, increases their self-esteem and engages them as active partners in their own education (Chapter 6).

'*Environmental Education*' is not just about the way in which we treat the planet, it also has implications for the way in which we treat other people. Children and adults must learn to be mindful of the needs and well-being of others now and in the future when seeking solutions to their own immediate environmental problems. It is possible to link environmental education with other cross-curricular themes, ensuring that understanding and awareness contribute to the whole curriculum (Chapter 7).

Given the value-bearing nature of cross-curricular elements and their situation at the nexus of the individual/social matrix, there is every justification for ensuring that the ways in which these are presented make a virtue of cultural diversity while challenging prejudice in all its forms including racism, sexism and ethnocentrism in particular. Children at the primary stage may not be ready for tackling these full on, but it is important that we *start* the process. The evidence of the effects for good or ill of education in the early years and their influence on subsequent attitude formation and behaviours is inescapable.

As far as the translation of theory and policy into practice goes, there are signs that some local education authorities are making efforts to combine the demands of the Education Reform Act (ERA) with policies and practices which promote equality. A good example of this is the 'theme-book series' which has been published by Manchester City Council Education Department (1991). The loose-leaf binders, which make up the series cover the cross-curricular themes, skills and dimensions, offer a range of hints and suggestions to help teachers with the planning and delivery of them (see Chapter 2 for details). Given the overloaded curriculum in schools, teachers need to decide how to fit cross-curricular themes into a crowded timetable. Teachers must not be concerned with factual knowledge only, but with attitudes, under-standing, analytical, personal and social skills.

We must aim to find ways to help young people to become comfortable with diversity and to accept it as a normal part of existence and not as exotic and novel. If, in the primary school, we can start our youngsters out on the path towards treating diversity as part of the cultural norm, we will have made a significant step in the right direction. The differences in various values and beliefs are what make individuals and groups stand apart from others. Were there not such differentiating characteristics, there might well be nothing to distinguish and, therefore, nothing to perceive. The challenge of 'unity in plurality' has been identified as being at the centre of the ERA. The cross-curricular elements in general and the dimensions and themes in particular provide many opportunities to develop the social cohesion essential to all citizens.

References

BARROW, J. (1988) 'The Brent Inquiry: findings and implications', in VERMA, G.K. and PUMFREY, P.D. (Eds) *Educational Attainments Issues and outcomes in Multicultural Education*, London, The Falmer Press.

CLARKE, J., HALL, S., JEFFERSON, T. and ROBERTS, B. (1981) *Resistance Through Rituals*, London, Hutchinson.

DEPARTMENT OF EDUCATION (1977) *Education in Schools: A Consultative Document*, Cmnd. 6869, London, HMSO.

DEPARTMENT OF EDUCATION AND SCIENCE (1981) *West Indian Children in Our Schools*, Committee of Inquiry into the Education of Children from Minority Ethnic Groups (The Rampton Report), Cmnd. 8273, London, HMSO.

DEPARTMENT OF EDUCATION AND SCIENCE (1985) *Education for All*, Report of the Committee of Inquiry into the Education of Children from Ethnic Minority Groups (The Swann Report), Cmnd. 9453, London, HMSO.

DEPARTMENT OF EDUCATION AND SCIENCE (1988) *The Education Reform Act 1988*, London, HMSO.

FIGUEROA, P. and FYFE, A. (1933) *Education for Cultural Diversity: The Challenge for a New Era*, London, Routledge.

INGLEHART, R. (1990) *Culture Shift in Advanced Industrial Society*, Princeton, Princeton University Press.

LYNCH, J., MODGIL, C. and MODGIL, S. (Eds) (1992a) *Cultural Diversity and the Schools; Vol. 1, Education for Cultural Diversity: Convergence and Divergence*, London, The Falmer Press.

LYNCH, J., MODGIL, C. and MODGIL, S. (Eds) (1992b) *Cultural Diversity and the Schools: Vol. 2, Prejudice, Polemic pr Progress?*, London, The Falmer Press.

LYNCH, J., MODGIL, C. and MODGIL, S. (Eds) (1992c) *Cultural Diversity and the Schools: Vol. 3, Equity or Excellence? Education and Cultural Reproduction*, London, The Falmer Press.

LYNCH, J., MODGIL, C. and MODGIL, S. (Eds) (1992d) *Cultural Diversity and the Schools: Vol. 4, Human Rights, Education and Global Responsibilities*, London, The Falmer Press.

MANCHESTER CITY COUNCIL EDUCATION DEPARTMENT (1991) *Cross-Curricular Themes, Skills and Dimensions: Implementing the Whole Curriculum*, Manchester, MED.

NATIONAL ASSOCIATION OF HEADTEACHERS (1992) *Managing Equality*, London, NAHT.

NATIONAL CURRICULUM COUNCIL (1989) *Circular No. 6: The National Curriculum and Whole Curriculum Planning*, York, NCC.

NATIONAL UNION OF TEACHERS (1992) *Anti-Racist Guidelines*, London, NUT.

PUMFREY, P. and VERMA, G.K. (1990) *Race Relations and Urban Education: Promising Practices*, London, The Falmer Press.

TOMLINSON, S. (1987) *Educational Subnormality. A Study in Decision Making*, London, Routledge and Kegan Paul.

TOMLINSON, S. and SMITH, D.J. (1989) *The School Effects, A Study of Multiracial Comprehensions*, London, Policy Studies Institute.
VERMA, G.K. (1986) *Ethnicity and Educational Achievement*, London, Macmillan.
VERMA, G.K. (1989) *Education for All, A Landmark in Pluralism*, London, The Falmer Press.
YASEEN, M. (1993) *Education*, 2 February.

Chapter 2

Cross-curricular Elements and the Curriculum: Contexts, Challenges and Responses

Peter D. Pumfrey

Context

Britain is unquestionably a pluralist society. Inexorably and inevitably, its cultural, ethnic, religious and social composition will continue to evolve. The only aspect of any society that is constant, is change. In an increasingly diverse society, our schools play a central role in educating pupils for life now and in the future.

What will that future be? In what sort of society do we wish our children and their children to live? Is there a common core of values that holds the promise of a cohesive and tolerant pluralist society, or will sectional interests subvert this aspiration? Underpinning such matters lie the nebulous, but extremely potent, concepts of 'fairness' and 'equality of opportunity'.

'From the very earliest days infants are imbibing the implicit assumptions of the society in which they live; and if the social environment is one of racial discrimination it will indeed be difficult for a child to grow up without taking it for granted that such a state of affairs is part of the natural order of things.' Thus wrote the late Dr Cyril Bibby in his book *Race, Prejudice and Education*. The message is of perennial importance. Bibby's book was published in 1959. It follows that nursery and primary schools remain central to the challenges of educating pupils for citizenship, both in the present and for their futures, within a multicultural society. At one extreme, does the racist name-calling that exists within some primary schools lead, via extreme prejudices, to the racist murders of adolescents of one ethnic group by those of others? (see Volumes 1, 2 and 3 in this series).

The establishment of voluntary supplementary schools by a range of ethnic and religious minority groups is indicative of a wish to retain a cultural identity and, in some cases, as a response to what is seen as an inadequate education provided in mainstream schools. A constructive analysis of the work of such schools in Kirklees indicates the nature and extent of this provision,

Table 2.1: Components of the Whole Curriculum

- Religious education
- Subjects additional to the three core subjects and the further seven foundation subjects in the National Curriculum
- A range of cross-curricular elements
- Extra-curricular activities

ways in which it can be improved and its links with mainstream schools developed (Hasnie, 1993). In Kirklees there are some thirty-nine supplementary schools providing eight languages other than English. 5,060 pupils are receiving supplementary education. The oldest of these supplementary schools was established 43 years ago. The schools have very limited resources in terms of teaching staff, materials and equipment (ibid).

The case that shared experiences in education provide a necessary but not sufficient condition for social coherence, is a strong one. The community primary school is a key institution. It faces the challenge of demonstrating a respect for cultural diversity whilst developing communalities across ethnic, religious and cultural differences.

Are the policies explicit in the Education Reform Act 1988, and the many and varied curricular practices steming from the work of the National Curriculum Council (NCC) and the School Examinations and Assessment Council (SEAC), and being continued by their successor organization the School Curriculum and Assessment Agency (SCAA) likely to encourage the provision of an education that encourages social cohesion? The answer to this question will depend largely on the imaginative response of members of the teaching profession. There is considerable evidence that this is being achieved, despite, rather than because of, the denigration to which teachers have all too often collectively been subject over recent years by senior politicians.

In Volume 3, Chapter 3, the objectives, form and content of the whole, basic and National Curriculum in primary schools were considered. The implications of cultural diversity for the teaching of each of the National Curriculum core, foundation subjects and religious education were addressed within the curricular context of the whole curriculum. The 'whole curriculum' comprises four complementary aspects of education.

Here we turn to the cross-curricular elements that permeate all aspects of the whole curriculum. Cross-curricular elements comprise two major dimensions, six skills and five themes. These elements help ensure that the curriculum extends beyond the traditional subject-based practices. They underpin much of primary-school pedagogy. Cross-curricular elements explicitly acknowledge the importance of topic work. This integrates various aspects of knowledge, understanding and applications that can also be identified as belonging to specific subject domains comprising the National Curriculum foundations subjects and religious education (NCC, 1990a).

With reference to dimensions, 'One of the major problems facing societies in almost all parts of the world is the inadequate accommodation of social

Table 2.2: Cross-curricular Elements

Dimensions:

- equal opportunity; and
- multiculturalism.

Skills:

- communication;
- numeracy;
- study;
- problem-solving;
- personal and social; and
- information technology.

Themes:

- economic and industrial understanding;
- careers education and guidance;
- health education;
- education for citizenship; and
- environmental education.

equity with cultural diversity. The lack of discourse between the two systems, cultural and social, means that there are fewer common ideologies on the basis of which accommodations can be negotiated, for ideologies themselves are not static; the very process of discourse for accommodation can generate a greater overlap between the two systems' (Lynch, Modgil and Modgil, 1992a).

The crises emanating from neglect of this issue can be seen in societies as different and wide apart as the republics that have replaced the Soviet Union, in Afghanistan, Angola, Australia, Brazil, Cambodia, Canada, Cyprus, Egypt, Fiji, Iran, Iraq, Nicaragua, India, Israel, New Zealand, Lebanon, Morocco, Nigeria, Pakistan, South Africa, Sri Lanka, the United States, the United Kingdom and the other eleven member states comprising the European community (to mention but a few of the many candidate countries for inclusion). In this respect, the adage 'Let him that is without fault cast the first stone', bears consideration.

The international importance of cultural diversity and education is further developed by Lynch, Modgil and Modgil in *Prejudice, Polemic or Progress?*, *Equity or Excellence? Education and Cultural Reproduction* and *Human Rights, Education and Global Responsibilities* (1992b, 1992c, 1992d).

Pessimists will point to the fact that discourse on any issue can all too easily and rapidly deteriorate into the affirmation of polarized and intransigent positions. Emergent nationalism and religious fundamentalism are potent forces individually: in combination, their social power is significantly increased. Typically, both demand a conformity that further marginalizes minority groups. 'Those who are not for us are against us.' Realists typically accept that compromise can be mutually beneficial. In contrast, many fundamentalists consider compromise unacceptable. Inevitably, tolerance is one of the first victims of such intransigence.

In any society characterized by cultural, ethnic and religious diversities (amongst others), the deeply held moral and political beliefs of individuals and groups are continuing sources of tensions and disagreements. In itself, this is of less significance than the means that society adopts and encourages in addressing and resolving mutually exclusive demands presented by particular pressure groups. The current battles in the Balkans underline the chaos to which nationalist ideological and religious beliefs can rapidly lead. The Balkanization of Britain is not a scenario many citizens would advocate or anticipate with relish.

If our society is not to move towards increasing intolerance, it is essential that divergent opinions are, at the very least, respected. Respecting the opinions of others, even if one disagrees strongly with their views on any of a wide range of topics, is one key characteristic of a democratic society. The models that teachers and other adults present to children are potent determinants of both the current and future behaviours of the younger generation. If we provide models of intolerance, we encourage it. If we choose to sow the wind, we will reap the whirlwind. What teachers demonstrate daily in their work in the classroom and the policies that guide the primary school's development, is of the essence in education for life in a pluralist society (Lynch, 1991).

To assert the importance of tolerance is not to argue that 'anything goes'. Despite the suspicion that there is one law for the 'haves' and another for the 'have nots', the laws of the land apply to all citizens. Many behaviours are proscribed. The behaviours the law demands represent a common cultural context, if not consensus. Within that framework, all citizens live. On its observance, we all depend. We cannot select which of our laws we will obey. In the interests of what we perceive to be 'just', 'fair' and to provide 'equality of opportunity', we can identify and work to change those laws we consider inimical to such aspirations. Laws are neither perfect nor immutable. Means exist whereby perceived weaknesses in the law can be identified and changed without death and destruction (Commission for Racial Equality, 1991). Social evolution is possible. In relation to race-relations law, imperfect as it is, the UK has much to commend its endeavours. However, many challenges remain. The right to a tolerant society is accompanied by the concomitant responsibility of reciprocity. 'Give and take' must be in an acceptable equilibrium between those holding contrasting viewpoints concerning the identification of priorities and the allocation of resources.

The Salman Rushdie issue continues to highlight an important subset of such considerations (MacDonogh, 1993). There is a considerable number of British citizens who profess Islam. The *fatwa*, originally issued by the late Ayatollah Khomeini, called for the execution of Rushdie for blasphemies contained in the book *Satanic Verses*. The day after this pronouncement, the 15th, the Khordad Foundation put a price of two million pounds on Rushdie's head. The Khordad Foundation is an organization run by clergymen. Subsequent to Rushdie's visit to Germany in 1992, the price on his head was increased. In the UK, the Prime Minister has publicly demonstrated his support of Rushdie. In his letter of support to MacDonogh's book, Stoppard argues that Rushdie's freedom of expression is not the central issue: 'We should not be busy standing up for the rights we have accorded ourselves: we should be busy questioning the rights assumed by Iran, beginning with the assumption that Islamic law prevails over all other laws in all other countries.'

In Volume 3, Chapter 3, the activities of Dr Kalim Siddiqui, leader of the self-styled Muslim parliament are described. So too are the views of British Muslims who consider his comments ludicrous. Siddiqui, an experienced journalist and publicist, advocated the merits of Islamic law, including the amputation of the hands of thieves, death by stoning for extra-marital sexual relationships and eighty lashes for drinking alcohol. Provided he does not transgress the requirement of the Race Relations Act by, for example, inciting racial hatred, Siddiqui is perfectly entitled to express his views and to persuade others of their value here. This is possible because our democratic society values freedom of speech highly. Members of other faith communities would be unlikely to find reciprocal tolerance of their advocacy of somewhat contrasting Christian principles in, for example, Iran, Iraq, Libya and other fundamentalist Islamic states.

Overt and covert power struggles are ongoing in all nations or communities, including their educational systems. The primary-school classroom provides the daily setting for many such struggles. The ethos of the classroom and the school reflects the means whereby such pupil–pupil and teacher–pupil tensions are addressed. (The example of a school-based 'peace-education' programme will be described in the 'Responses' section of this paper.)

At a national level, where a country has sufficient space and resources such that its citizens are not forced into overtly stressful competition for the necessities of life, the tensions of such power struggles are less evident. When opportunities for education, housing and work are readily available, inter-individual and group tensions within a society are reduced. This is not to say that competition disappears. The struggle for valued resources continues. Education is seen by parents and society as one important avenue to many opportunities. It is a field in which cooperation and competition coexist, even when the State provides, via taxation, 'free' education for all children. However, when opportunities for particular educational, housing and employment opportunities become increasingly limited by virtue of economic and social pressures, competition for resources rises. Intolerance between groups also tends to rise, scapegoats are sought and racism is often manifest in its most violent forms. The evils of extreme nationalism and xenophobia flourish in such conditions.

Sadly, prominent members of political parties frequently set powerfully damaging examples of intolerance. The gap between words and deeds is exemplified when, for example, political debates are broadcast from the Houses of Parliament. Politicians are not alone. The same can be said of individuals representing any pressure group. In all societies, material resources are finite;

demand infinite. The determination of priorities and the allocation of community resources to these priorities is undoubtedly a power struggle.

Primary schools in England and Wales are no exception, as the recently published *League Tables* of pupils' attainments in the core subjects at Key Stage 1 demonstrate (DES, 1991; DFE 1992). At the local level, do you consider that your school satisfactorily addresses the two cross-curricular dimensions discussed earlier? Would you as a parent or guardian send your child to the school? Will the 'consumer-led' (parents) market-economy forces, on which the government pins so much faith, result in an educational system characterized by a judicious balance between competition and cooperation? Does such a philosophy promote the acceptance that all children and their parents are equal members of one society? Is it a recipe for social cohesion or social disintegration? Can polarization be avoided?

The *raison d'être* of the present series is that it can, and that there are promising policies and practices showing how this can be done.

Minority Ethnic Groups: Demographic Data

In June 1993, at Bolton, Winston Churchill, Member of Parliament for Davyhulme warned of racial violence unless immigration was stopped. In the *Manchester Metro News*, dated 23 July 1993, he is reported as calling on the government to end immigration in an address to a meeting of Jewish ex-servicemen at the House of Commons on 19 July 'The unhappiness — indeed bitterness — of the indigenous population runs very deep in those areas of our inner cities where the native English find that they have become the ethnic minority in their own land . . . The relentless flow of tens of thousands of immigrants to this country each year risks breaching the limits of toleration. If we are to curb the scourge of racism in our society we must first and foremost stop adding to the problem . . . I'm strongly opposed, and always have been, to racism in all its forms, and that is why I said what I said, because I want to see a nation at ease with itself.' As would be expected, such pronouncements produced many polarized reactions.

Many misconceptions exist concerning the size, growth and composition of the minority ethnic groups living in the UK. Both teachers in training and qualified teachers in the UK have been shown to lack correct information in this field (Cohen, 1989; Pumfrey, 1990). Few citizens could rank by size the minority ethnic groups resident in the UK. Almost half our ethnic-minority population was born in Britain and nearly three-quarters are British citizens. Primary immigration is relatively low; secondary immigration is somewhat higher. The distinction between these two groups of immigrants is relevant to this issue.

A study of interethnic relations in schools was recently carried out in the Greater Manchester area (Verma, 1992). Schools containing considerable numbers of pupils from minority ethnic groups were much more advanced in

Peter D. Pumfrey

Table 2.3: Estimated Size of Total Ethnic-minority Population in Great Britain, 1951–1991

	1951	1961	1971	1981	1991
N (thousands)	200	500	1,200	2,100	3,006
%age of total population	0.4	1.0	2.3	3.9	5.5

Source: Shaw, 1988, Table 2; Haskey, 1990, Table 1; OPCS, 1992; Owen, 1992.

developing school policies on race relations than schools with few such pupils. Gaps between policy and practice were evident: 'few teachers were at all knowledgeable about the religions, cultures, values and customs of the ethnic minority groups of their pupils. Often this was attributed to the fact that, with very few exceptions, issues of ethnicity and culture formed no part of their initial training. There was some evidence that this lack had been compensated for by INSET, but the take-up had been patchy and, in the opinions of the teachers, its quality had varied significantly.' (Verma, ibid.). Ignorance provides a ready breeding ground for prejudice and racism.

The issue is an extremely sensitive one. Emigration from the country in which one is born is a tremendous step, not lightly undertaken. Understandably, the vast majority of individuals and families wish to migrate to countries where their life chances are perceived as being greater than if they remain in the land of their birth. The tremendously strong magnetism of materialism in this and other industrially developed countries is reinforced by the visual and verbal messages of materially rich lifestyles conveyed so rapidly by the mass media across the world.

The increased mobility, symbolized by the aeroplane, and the availability of credit to pay for the expenses of moving, helps to convert an aspiration into an actuality. Getting away from civil wars and the associated threats to life and limb, from the destruction, disease, starvation, and anguish that such conflicts represent in many countries are also an important causes of migration. The issue of asylum is but one aspect. The Home Secretary is reported as saying 'we turn away people who might otherwise come in excessive numbers, imposing a burden on our public services when in reality they have no legal or other basis for doing so'. In 1992, some 24,500 new asylum applications were received. It is claimed that only one in twenty asylum seekers to Britain qualified to stay.

The increasing ethnic diversity of the population of Great Britain over the period 1941 to 1991 shows that currently minority ethnic groups comprise approximately 5.5 per cent of the total population.

A question on ethnic-group membership was considered for use in the 1981 Census, but was abandoned because of public opposition. Despite this, a similar question was used in two of the government's major social surveys in the early 1980s: the *Labour Force Survey* and the *General Household Survey*. (The nine major reasons for requiring such information are summarized in

Table 2.4: The 1991 Census of Population: Ethnic Classification

4-fold classification	10-fold classification	Full listing
White	White	White Irish Greek/Greek Cypriot Turkish/Turkish Cypriot Mixed White
Black groups	Black — Caribbean	Black — Caribbean Caribbean Island West Indies Guyana
	Black — African	Black — African Africa south of the Sahara
	Black — other	Black — other Black — British Black — Mixed Black/White Black — Mixed Other
Indian/Pakistani/Bangladeshi	Indian Pakistani Bangladeshi	Indian Pakistani Bangladeshi
Chinese and others	Chinese Other — Asian	Chinese East-African Asian Indo-Caribbean Black-Indian subcontinent Black-other Asian
	Other — other	North Africa/Arab/Iranian Mixed Asian/White British ethnic minority (other) British (no indication) Other Mixed Black/White Other Mixed Asian/White Other Mixed — other

Volume 3, Chapter 3.) By 1989, following earlier preparatory discussions concerning the 1991 Census, opposition to the use of a question based on ethnic-group membership had markedly reduced to the point where its inclusion was seen as not significantly harming the 1991 Census response rate.

The Office of Population Censuses and Surveys for England and Wales (OPCS) and the General Register Office in Scotland devised thirty-five ethnic-group descriptions based on extensive pilot work. The thirty-five descriptions were organized into a fourfold and tenfold classificatory system. These classifications are shown above.

The Census Offices use the three levels of classification for differing purposes. The most detailed classificatory systems are used in the tables that are published in the *Country/Region Reports* and the *Local Base Statistics*. The fourfold classification is used in the *Small Area Statistics*. This is a computerized data set containing details of the population characteristics for the 145,000 enumeration districts and output areas in Great Britain. These areas represent the smallest units for which Census data are released. Each of these areas comprises an average of around 200 households (Owen, 1992).

Peter D. Pumfrey

Table 2.5:   Population of Great Britain by Ethnic Group in 1991

	N	%age	Rank size order based on N
White	51,843	94.5	1
All ethnic minorities	3,006	5.5	
South Asian	1,477	2.7	
Indian	841	1.5	2
Pakistani	476	0.9	4
Bangladeshi	160	0.3	9
Black	885	1.6	
Caribbean	499	0.9	3
African	207	0.4	6
Other	179	0.3	8
Chinese and others	644	1.2	
Chinese	157	0.3	9
Other Asian	197	0.4	7
Other minority groups	290	0.5	5

Source: 1991 Census
Note: Figures in thousands

Table 2.5 presents data based on the 1991 Census tenfold classification for Great Britain.

For the fifty-five major Census areas in England and Wales, the numbers and percentages of the ethnic-group composition are presented in Table 2.6. The Census Microdata Unit at the University of Manchester has recently published an analysis of the ethnic dimensions of the 1991 Census (Ballard and Kalra, 1994).

The Wider Context

No country can ignore the fact that all countries are, in varying respects and degrees, interdependent. The wider European and world communities of which we and our pupils are members, cannot be ignored. The apparent worldwide rise of nationalism, of racism and of religious fundamentalism, their manifestations across Europe and their existence within the UK have to be acknowledged. Measures must be taken to deal constructively with these potentially destructive phenomena at all levels. It is within this global perspective that we turn to the domestic educational context in England and Wales and to the challenges presented by cultural diversity and the curriculum.

Challenges

Provided that readers can accept the anachronism of gender bias within it, the following statement encapsulates an important truth concerning the varied ethnocentricisms to which we are all prey. 'No person knows his own culture who knows only his own culture' (Allport, 1954).

In the 1960s and early 1970s, some readers may recall that educational policies were considered aimed at restricting the proportion of minority ethnic-group pupils in individual schools. The purposes included assisting acculturalization, providing equality of educational opportunities and encouraging social cohesion. The policies were never developed. In the 1990s, the issue re-emerges in a different form.

The big worry today is that parents may choose schools for racial reasons. A London Weekend Television poll found that 40 per cent of white parents preferred a school for their own race. Only 15 per cent of Afro-Caribbean parents and 19 per cent of Asians wanted this' (BBC and Commission for Racial Equality, 1992). Even when one (rightly) questions the validity of a TV-conducted survey and the subsequent interpretation of the data it yields, neither can be lightly dismissed. What kind of society do we wish to live in and our children's children to inherit?

A related concern arises where the selection of schools allows parents virtually no choice, resulting in schools in which the proportion of pupils from minority ethnic groups exceeds 90 per cent. Ethnic minorities become majorities in the given context. In practice, this is frequently a consequence of members of minority ethnic groups tending to live in communities because of the support and security that geographical propinquity affords them. They know that they live in a larger society in which racial discrimination and intimidation are common, despite the law.

In Cleveland, a mother wanted to move her daughter from one primary school to another. She said she thought the school was 'very good, but . . . I just want her to go to a school where there will be a majority of white children, not Pakistani'. Her daughter's school was 40 per cent Asian and 60 per cent white. The school her mother wanted was 98 per cent white. As the education law says parents have a choice, and as there was a place at the school, she got her request. The courts are now looking at the problem of which law comes first, the law against racial discrimination or the education law' (BBC and the Commission for Racial Equality, 1992).

Six years ago, the mothers of two pupils attending a primary school in Manchester took their children away from the school. The mothers had complained that the multifaith assemblies failed to meet the requirements of the Education Reform Act 1988 that collective worship must be 'wholly or mainly of a Christian character'. Their claim that multifaith teaching and worship in state-school assemblies was unlawful under the Education Reform Act, 1988, was rejected in February 1993. Mr Justice McCullough ruled that no grounds existed for the parents' claim that the Secretary of State for Education had acted unreasonably in refusing to take up their complaints. The mothers have pursued the case on a point of principle. They are reported as considering making an appeal against the judgment. Moving from the individual to the group, analogous issues exist.

Social cohesion and national unity within the UK is counterbalanced by the aspirations of its regions for greater autonomy. Scottish, Welsh and Irish

Table 2.6(a): Estimated Distributions of Minority Ethnic Groups in Areas of England and Wales: Percentages

County	Usual residents	Total (should = 100)	White	Black Caribbean	Black African	Black other	Indian	Pakistani	Bangladeshi	Chinese	Other Asian	Groups other
1 Inner London	2,504,451	100.1	74.4	7.1	4.4	2.0	3.0	1.2	2.8	1.1	1.8	2.3
2 Outer London	4,175,248	99.9	83.1	2.7	1.3	.7	6.5	1.4	.4	.7	1.6	1.5
3 Greater Manchester	2,499,441	100.1	94.1	.7	.2	.4	1.2	2.0	.5	.3	.2	.5
4 Merseyside	1,403,642	100.2	98.2	.2	.2	.3	.2	.1	.1	.4	.1	.4
5 South Yorkshire	1,262,630	100.0	97.1	.5	.1	.2	.3	1.0	.1	.2	.1	.4
6 Tyne and Wear	1,095,150	100.0	98.2	.0	.1	.1	.4	.3	.3	.3	.1	.2
7 West Midlands	2,551,671	99.9	85.4	2.8	.2	.6	5.5	3.5	.7	.2	.3	.7
8 West Yorkshire	2,013,693	99.8	91.8	.7	.1	.3	1.7	4.0	.3	.2	.2	.5
9 Avon	932,674	99.9	97.2	.8	.1	.3	.4	.3	.1	.2	.1	.4
10 Bedfordshire	524,105	99.9	90.1	1.8	.2	.5	2.7	2.3	1.1	.3	.3	.6
11 Berkshire	734,246	100.1	92.4	1.0	.3	.4	2.6	1.9	.1	.3	.5	.6
12 Buckinghamshire	632,487	100.0	94.7	1.0	.2	.3	1.0	1.5	.1	.3	.3	.6
13 Cambridgeshire	645,125	99.9	96.5	.3	.1	.3	.7	.8	.1	.3	.3	.5
14 Cheshire	956,616	100.0	99.0	.1	.0	.1	.2	.1	.0	.2	.1	.2
15 Cleveland	550,293	99.9	98.1	.0	.1	.1	.3	.9	.0	.1	.1	.2
16 Cornwall: Isles of Scilly	468,425	99.9	99.5	.0	.0	.1	.0	.0	.0	.1	.0	.2
17 Cumbria	483,163	100.0	99.6	.0	.0	.1	.1	.0	.0	.1	.0	.1
18 Derbyshire	928,636	99.7	97.0	.4	.0	.2	1.1	.6	.0	.1	.1	.2
19 Devon	1,009,950	99.9	99.3	.0	.0	.1	.1	.0	.0	.1	.1	.2
20 Dorset	645,166	100.1	99.1	.1	.0	.1	.1	.0	.0	.1	.1	.3
21 Durham	593,430	99.8	99.3	.0	.0	.0	.2	.0	.0	.1	.1	.1
22 East Sussex	690,447	99.8	98.1	.1	.1	.1	.2	.1	.1	.2	.2	.5
23 Essex	1,528,577	100.1	98.1	.2	.1	.1	.3	.1	.1	.3	.2	.4
24 Gloucestershire	528,370	100.0	98.2	.4	.1	.2	.5	.0	.1	.1	.1	.3
25 Hampshire	1,541,547	100.0	98.1	.2	.1	.2	.5	.1	.1	.2	.1	.3
26 Hereford and Worcester	676,747	100.0	98.7	.2	.0	.1	.5	.3	.1	.1	.1	.2
27 Hertfordshire	975,829	100.0	96.0	.5	.1	.2	1.2	.5	.2	.3	.4	.6
28 Humberside	858,040	100.0	99.0	.0	.1	.1	.2	.1	.1	.1	.1	.2
29 Isle of Wight	124,577	100.0	99.3	.1	.0	.1	.1	.0	.0	.1	.1	.2

Area	Population											
30 Kent	1,508,873	99.9	97.7	.1	.1	.1	1.0	.1	.1	.2	.2	.3
31 Lancashire	1,383,998	100.0	95.6	.1	.1	.1	1.5	1.9	.2	.1	.1	.3
32 Leicestershire	867,534	100.0	88.9	.6	.0	.3	8.4	.3	.2	.2	.4	.6
33 Lincolnshire	584,534	100.0	99.2	.1	.1	.1	.2	.0	.0	.1	.1	.2
34 Norfolk	745,613	99.9	99.1	.1	.1	.1	.1	.0	.0	.1	.1	.2
35 Northamptonshire	578,807	99.9	96.5	.8	.1	.3	1.1	.1	.2	.2	.2	.4
36 Northumberland	304,694	99.9	99.5	.0	.0	.0	.1	.0	.0	.1	.1	.1
37 North Yorkshire	702,161	100.0	99.3	.0	.0	.1	.1	.1	.0	.1	.1	.2
38 Nottinghamshire	993,872	99.9	96.0	1.1	.1	.4	.8	.8	.0	.2	.2	.4
39 Oxfordshire	547,584	100.0	96.7	.4	.2	.4	.5	.5	.1	.3	.3	.6
40 Shropshire	406,387	100.0	98.4	.2	.0	.1	.5	.2	.0	.2	.2	.2
41 Somerset	460,368	100.0	99.5	.0	.0	.1	.1	.0	.0	.1	.0	.2
42 Staffordshire	1,031,135	100.0	98.2	.2	.2	.1	.3	.7	.1	.1	.1	.2
43 Suffolk	636,266	100.0	97.8	.4	.1	.6	.2	.0	.1	.2	.1	.4
44 Surrey	1,018,003	100.0	97.2	.1	.1	.1	.7	.4	.1	.3	.5	.5
45 Warwickshire	484,247	99.9	96.6	.3	.0	.1	2.2	.1	.0	.2	.1	.3
46 West Sussex	702,290	100.0	88.0	.1	.1	.1	.6	.3	.1	.2	.2	.3
47 Wiltshire	564,471	100.2	98.3	.3	.1	.2	.4	.1	.1	.2	.2	.3
48 Clwyd	408,080	99.8	99.4	.0	.0	.0	.1	.0	.0	.1	.1	.1
49 Dyfed	343,543	99.9	99.3	.0	.0	.1	.1	.0	.0	.1	.1	.2
50 Gwent	442,212	99.9	98.5	.1	.1	.1	.2	.4	.1	.1	.1	.2
51 Gwynedd	235,452	100.1	99.2	.0	.1	.1	.1	.1	.0	.2	.2	.2
52 Mid Glamorgan	534,101	100.0	99.2	.0	.1	.1	.2	.1	.0	.1	.1	.1
53 Powys	117,467	99.9	99.4	.0	.0	.1	.0	.0	.0	.1	.1	.2
54 South Glamorgan	392,780	99.9	95.2	.5	.5	.5	.7	.7	.4	.3	.3	.8
55 West Glamorgan	361,428	100.2	98.8	.1	.0	.1	.2	.1	.3	.2	.1	.3
Total	49,890,276	100.0	94.1	1.0	.4	.4	1.7	.9	.3	.3	.4	.6

Source: 1991 Census: Ethnic group
N.B. There are small rounding up errors associated with the percentages.

29

Peter D. Pumfrey

Table 2.6(b): Estimated Distributions of Minority Ethnic Groups in Areas of England and Wales: Numbers (Thousands)

County	White	Black Caribbean	Black African	Black other	Indian	Pakistani	Bangladeshi	Chinese	Other Asian	Groups other
1 Inner London	1,863	178	110	50	75	30	70	28	45	58
2 Outer London	3,470	113	54	29	271	58	17	29	67	63
3 Greater Manchester	2,352	17	5	10	30	50	12	7	5	12
4 Merseyside	1,378	3	3	4	3	1	1	6	1	6
5 South Yorkshire	1,226	6	1	3	4	13	1	3	1	5
6 Tyne and Wear	1,075	0	1	1	4	3	3	3	1	2
7 West Midlands	2,179	71	5	15	140	89	18	5	8	18
8 West Yorkshire	1,849	14	2	6	34	81	6	4	4	10
9 Avon	907	7	1	3	4	3	1	2	1	4
10 Bedfordshire	472	9	1	3	14	12	6	2	2	3
11 Berkshire	678	7	2	3	19	14	1	2	4	4
12 Buckinghamshire	599	6	1	2	6	9	1	2	2	4
13 Cambridgeshire	623	2	1	2	5	5	1	2	2	3
14 Cheshire	947	1	0	1	2	1	0	2	1	2
15 Cleveland	540	0	1	1	2	5	0	1	1	1
16 Cornwall: Isles of Scilly	466	0	0	0	0	0	0	0	0	1
17 Cumbria	481	0	0	0	0	0	0	0	0	0
18 Derbyshire	901	4	0	2	10	6	0	1	1	2
19 Devon	1,003	0	0	1	1	0	0	1	1	2
20 Dorset	639	1	1	1	1	0	0	1	1	2
21 Durham	589	0	0	0	1	0	0	1	1	1
22 East Sussex	677	1	1	1	2	1	1	1	1	3
23 Essex	1,500	3	2	2	8	2	2	5	3	6
24 Gloucestershire	519	2	1	1	3	0	1	1	1	2
25 Hampshire	1,512	3	2	3	8	2	2	3	3	5
26 Hereford and Worcester	668	1	0	1	1	2	2	1	1	1
27 Hertfordshire	937	5	1	2	12	5	2	3	4	6
28 Humberside	849	0	1	1	2	1	1	1	0	2
29 Isle of Wight	124	0	0	0	0	0	0	0	0	0
30 Kent	1,474	2	2	2	15	2	2	3	3	5

County	Total								
31 Lancashire	1,323	1	1	1	21	26	3	1	1	4
32 Leicestershire	771	5	1	3	73	3	2	2	3	5
33 Lincolnshire	580	1	0	1	1	0	0	1	1	1
34 Norfolk	739		1		1	0	0	1	1	1
35 Northamptonshire	559	5	0	2	6	1	1	0	0	2
36 Northumberland	303	0	0	0	0	0	0	1	1	0
37 North Yorkshire	697	0	1	1	1	1	0	2	2	4
38 Nottinghamshire	954	11	1	4	8	8	0	2	1	3
39 Oxfordshire	530	2	0	2	3	3	1	1	0	1
40 Shropshire	400	1	0	0	2	1	0	0	1	1
41 Somerset	458	0	0	0	0	0	0	1	1	2
42 Staffordshire	1,013	2	0	4	3	7	1	3	5	3
43 Suffolk	622	3	1	1	1	0	1	1	0	5
44 Surrey	989	1	1	0	8	4	0	1	1	1
45 Warwickshire	468	1	0	1	11	0	1	0	0	2
46 West Sussex	688	0	1	1	4	2	0	0	0	2
47 Wiltshire	555	2	0	0	2	0	0	0	0	0
48 Clwyd	406	0	0	0	0	0	0	1	0	1
49 Dyfed	341	0	0	0	0	0	0	0	0	1
50 Gwent	436	0	0	0	1	2	0	1	1	0
51 Gwynedd	234	0	0	0	0	0	0	1	0	1
52 Mid Glamorgan	530	0	0	2	1	0	0		1	0
53 Powys	117	0	0	0	0	3	2			3
54 South Glamorgan	374	2	2	2	3	0	1			1
55 West Glamorgan	357	0	0	0	1					
Total	46,940	496	209	175	828	455	161	143	189	280

Source: 1991 Census: Ethnic groups

Note: Provisional estimates (derived from percentages). Because of rounding errors, the estimated column totals differ slightly from the arithmetic sums of the column entries.

nationalism represent such forces. Myriad inter and intra-religious and cultural group rivalries exist in all countries. The effects of these rivalries are easily exported across the world.

Nationalism and religious fundamentalism are extremely powerful forces in any society. Both can be used to constructive and/or destructive ends. In combination, their influences are considerably amplified. Divisions between groups are easily exacerbated. For example, the effects of the Irish Republican Army's terrorist activities associated with Irish nationalism, (to most members of the public, a movement loosely associated with Roman Catholicism) and of the opposing Ulster Freedom Fighters movement (equally popularly and tenuously linked to Protestantism) in Northern Ireland, are exported to mainland Britain and the USA.

Religious tensions between Hindus and Muslims have frequently led to bloody confrontations. In 1992, the destruction of the early Mughal mosque at Ayodhya by Hindus is reported as having resulted in about 400 deaths in the first two days of rioting. The Bharatiya Janata Party (BJP) was alleged to have encouraged this act for what its leaders and sympathizers considered entirely valid historical and religious reasons.

The firebombing of Hindu temples in Bolton, Bradford, Coventry, Derby, Forest Gate, Sheffield, Wembley and West Bromwich are examples of actions destructive of social cohesion (Roy, 1992). Coexistence of cultures inevitably contains the potential for both collaboration and confrontation. There is always a dynamic equilibrium between cooperation and competition between individuals and groups within any society. A society, and its schools, have to encourage an acceptable balance between cooperation and competition. The philosophy of the school, its 'mission statement', its policies and practices, will derive from that balance and determine its ethos.

Even the remote prospect of the ethnic and/or religious Balkanization of Britain must focus our attention on the development of social cohesion in our communities. Education can provide a means whereby the adults and children in a community can learn to respect cultural, ethnic and religious differences. This will be achieved by actions, rather than words. Within the context of a national educational policy, the leadership provided by the headteacher, governors and the staff of primary schools are central to addressing this challenge.

National Policy

Section 1 of the Education Reform Act 1988 requires that all maintained schools provide

a balanced and broadly based curriculum which:

- promotes the spiritual, moral, cultural, mental and physical development of pupils at the school and of society; and

• prepares such pupils for the opportunities, responsibilities and experiences of adult life.

A central plank of the ERA 1988 is development of a common curricular language across all ages and subjects. Knowing, understanding and using that vocabulary is an important professional challenge to teachers, governors and parents (see Volume 3, chapter 3). Once its use is firmly established, communication between those working in state schools anywhere in England and Wales will be facilitated (NCC 1989b, 1992a, 1992b). Here the concepts central to the cross-curricular elements listed earlier are considered more fully.

Dimensions

The commitment to providing equal opportunities for all pupils is one major cross-curricular dimension of the curriculum. Another is preparation for life in a multicultural society. Both of these 'should permeate every aspect of the curriculum' (NCC, 1990a, p. 2). Enabling all pupils to fulfil their potential, irrespective of disability, sex, social, cultural or linguistic background represents the spirit of the ERA. The National Curriculum is an entitlement curriculum. By creating a common curriculum for all pupils, premature restriction of subjects to students is avoided thereby increasing access to the curriculum for all pupils.

Pupils from certain minority ethnic groups may require language support. For example, Section 11 of the Local Government Act 1966 empowered the Home Office to reimburse local-authority expenditure on various measures that would assist ethnic-minority communities to enter fully and benefit from the mainstream of national life. 'To this end, the grant has provided and will continue to provide support in the teaching of English, in strategies aimed at improving educational performance, and in tackling particular needs which arise where economic, social or cultural differences impede access to opportunities or services . . . The Government fully recognises the benefits that derive from the maintenance of religious, artistic, cultural and linguistic traditions among ethnic minority communities. It does *NOT*, however, consider Section 11 grant to be an appropriate use for initiative aimed at such purposes'. (Details of this ongoing battle for resources are given in Appendix 3.)

In *A Curriculum for All* (NCC, 1989c), the identification of pupils with special educational needs, and with making arrangements to address these needs, are discussed. These concerns demand 'whole-school' policies in which all staff subscribe to the value of, and aim to develop, positive attitudes towards 'gender equality, cultural diversity and special needs of all kinds (ibid., p. 3). Whilst not denying the importance of the other issues, our concern with cultural diversity leads to a focus on the second of these, and to a key challenge (see section below on 'prejudice, racism and racialism').

Skills

The intricate interplay of developing skills, so vividly seen throughout all the aspects of work in primary schools, underpins the importance of a pedagogy that acknowledges and uses such interactions. Put simply, topic work provides an excellent motivational, integrative and creative educational vehicle. When the concept of skills is operationally defined, as in Table 2.2, the six skills presented are clearly seen as neither mutually exclusive of each other nor of the dimensions. The National Curriculum Council requires that these skills are systematically and conscientiously fostered across the whole curriculum.

Themes

National Curriculum Council Circular No. 6 defines cross-curricular themes as 'elements that enrich the educational experience of pupils . . . [They] are more structured and pervasive than any other cross-curricular provision. They include a strong component of knowledge and understanding in addition to skills. Most can be taught through other subjects as well as through themes and topics (NCC, 1989a).

In March 1990, the NCC published *Curriculum Guidance No. 3: The Whole Curriculum* (NCC, 1990a). This document comprised two major sections. The first described whole-curriculum policy in terms of the materials that schools are required to teach (see Table 2.1). Five cross-curricular themes were identified. These are shown in Table 2.2. Developing educational approaches that use the opportunities these five themes provide, is a challenge that primary-school teachers are well placed to meet by virtue of their long experience with topic work.

Each of these five themes is addressed by specialists in the field of primary education in the present volume (Chapters 3–7). For each cross-curricular theme, the context within which ethnic diversity can be utilized in achieving the objectives of the Education Reform Act 1988, is set out. Challenges are identified by the respective authors and responses suggested. It is important to appreciate that other cross-curricular themes exist. A selected number of these are included in this volume (Chapters 8–15).

Prejudice, Racism and Racialism

In a multicultural society, enabling pupils to obtain the benefits of the curriculum to which all pupils attending state schools are entitled, involves considerable efforts by all parties to the endeavour (Centre for Ethnic Studies in Education, 1992, 1993). Equality of opportunity requires that teachers, governors, parents and pupils have an awareness of the nature of prejudice, racism, racialism, their interrelationships and their corrosive effects on individuals and groups. They also need to know how these dangers can be countered.

Prejudice refers to either unfavourable or favourable attitudes, feelings and beliefs that have been constructed without prior knowledge, understanding or reason. The prime attribute of prejudice is its irrationality. It is characterized by a mind closed to evidence supporting the validity of conflicting views. All of us acquire a range of prejudices through the socialization processes of the family, peer group, school, neighbourhood and society. When individuals and groups are competing for power and influence, the potential for prejudice to flourish is high. That propensity is exacerbated when resources, for example, employment, housing, health care and educational opportunities, are insufficient to meet the expectations that the population has developed. Recessions are prime times for the emergence of prejudice. Positive prejudices are largely focused on whichever groups hold views and a set of values that commands the individual's allegiance; unfavourable prejudices are directed at those who do not conform.

Racism involves the combination of prejudice with the ability or power to subordinate other individuals or groups, either consciously or otherwise. It is often argued that minority ethnic groups in the UK are relatively powerless. From this, it follows that minority ethnic-group members may be prejudiced, but they cannot be racist. Not all would agree that all minority ethnic groups are either individually or collectively powerless. It does not follow that all members of all minority ethnic groups are necessarily non-racist. Despite this, even if some members of minority ethnic groups do manifest racism, they are less likely to be in positions whereby they can significantly affect the life chances of members of the majority group.

The term 'racism' does not appear in statute law in either England, Wales or Scotland. The law is restricted to addressing particular manifestations of racism. The provisions of the Race Relations Act 1976 makes it unlawful to discriminate either *directly* or *indirectly* on grounds of colour, race, nationality or ethnic or national origins. Incitement to racial hatred is illegal. Thus anyone who 'publishes or distributes written matter which is threatening, abusive or insulting' has committed such incitement. In this country, to be charged with racism is a serious matter. Libel cases have been brought where the use of the term has been challenged as defamatory (Kloss, 1990).

The Race Relations Act 1976 lays upon local authorities two major responsibilities concerning the services they provide. The first of these responsibilities is that unlawful racial discrimination must be eliminated. The second is that they must provide equality of opportunity and encourage good relations between members of the various ethnic groups comprising the community. According to a House of Lords judgment, the term 'ethnic' is to be construed broadly to include groups with a long shared history and separate cultural tradition of their own. Thus in the case of 'Mandla versus Lee', it was decided that a private school in the West Midlands which excluded boys wearing turbans, because turbans were not part of the school uniform, had acted unlawfully in discriminating against Sikhs because they comprised a separate ethnic group, as well as being members of a particular religious tradition. It is arguable that the same applies to Jews, but not to Hindus or Muslims, who, like Christians, are drawn from a variety of differing societies and sects (Kloss, ibid.). An Asian teacher with perfect English was refused a post as a teacher of English because the students, who were mostly Italian, preferred 'an English person'. The judgment in the case of 'Hafeev versus Richmond School' was that the school had acted unlawfully (Palmer and Poulter, 1987). *Racial Discrimination* is a helpful guide to the provisions of the Race Relations Act 1976 and is available from the Home Office (Home Office, 1987). Every school should have a copy.

> In education, there is evidence of significant underachievement among some ethnic-minority groups. It is more difficult in this area to identify and measure the nature and extent of discrimination, but the commission's investigation in Birmingham showed different levels of suspensions which could not be explained by factors other than race; research published in the Swann report revealed discriminatory patterns of behaviour in the classroom; and the Eggleston report in 1986 pointed to discrimination of pupils to sets, streams, etc. It is also disturbing that ethnic minorities are underrepresented amongst those who hold power in the education system, whether as governors, administrators, inspectors or teachers. (Commission for Racial Equality, 1991)

Equally important is the fact that ethnic-minority groups are significantly underrepresented among teachers. Role models matter in the development of self-esteem. Whereas some 5.5 per cent of pupils come from ethnic-minority groups, only 3.3 per cent of teachers do so. A number of universities and colleges run courses specifically designed to attract black and Asian trainees. Problems of recruitment are exacerbated when Moeen Yaseen, the education adviser to the Islamia Schools Trust is reported as saying that teaching is 'a second-class profession' and that even Muslim schools do not have enough Muslim teachers.

'Only connect' is a maxim with much to commend it. The NCC foundation subjects and religious education represent but a part of the whole curriculum (see Table 2.1 above). Important as these foundation subjects and religious education are, by themselves they cannot provide the variety of experiences whereby primary-school pupils will be able to acquire the knowledge, understandings, skills and attitudes required to live and function effectively in a culturally diverse community such as the United Kingdom.

The challenges of, and responses to, cultural diversity and the delivery of the National Curriculum in relation to:

- institutional and individual racism;
- tensions between ethnic groups in the UK; and
- religious sensitivities

have been discussed earlier in Chapter 3 of Volume 3.

There is a danger that dealing constructively with ethnic diversity through the cross-curricular elements (dimensions, skills and themes) may lose out to demands for the delivery of the subject-specific aspects of the National Curriculum. If this possibility is to be avoided, a clearly articulated school policy is a key requirement. In this, the roles of the governors and the headteacher are crucial. All too easily, a professional responsibility readily accepted 'in principle' as the collective responsibility of all staff can become, 'in practice', the responsibility of no one. Specific responsibilities in relation to the cross-curricular elements must be collectively identified and accepted by the staff. The effects of the practices that flow from the policy must be monitored.

In 1981, the then Inner London Education Authority (ILEA) published a document entitled *Education in a multiethnic society: an aide-memoire for the Inspectorate* (Cocking, Craig and Mahon, 1981). The document is in two sections. The first is entitled *Aspects for Review*. It identifies thirteen key aspects of school policy and poses general questions bearing on the appropriateness of the school's policies and practices in providing the educational opportunities required in a multiethnic society. These are:

- school policy;
- equality of opportunity;
- racism;
- curriculum;
- classroom strategies;
- resources;
- language;
- ethos and atmosphere;
- support and care of pupils;
- staff development;
- parents and their communities;
- school to work; and
- pupils.

The second section is entitled *Specific Questions* and, within each of the thirteen areas identified in section 1, provides an extended list of points to be considered when reviewing the school's work in this field. The document is mentioned because it makes the point that excellent work was being developed in our schools long before the ERA arrived.

Harmony
By Derek Curtis (aged 10)

I get on with my mates
at school and at home.
I get on with a lot of people
at school and my family, including
my grandad and nan.

It's best not to fight or you
will lose your friends.
We must share the world or it
will lead to destruction.
If there is no harmony in the
world we would always be fighting.

Names can cause a fight. You
might say, you stupid wally-bean,
at least I haven't got saw-dust in my head!
Harmony is great.

In summary, within the existing educational and legal contexts, major challenges identified include the following.

- To capitalize on community resources that can be utilized by schools, as represented by the cultural, ethnic and religious diversity in the community the school serves.
- To demonstrate, through the daily life and work of the school, respect for cultural, ethnic and religious differences.
- To use creatively the opportunities incorporated within the framework of the Education Reform Act 1988.

Responses

Membership of School-governing Bodies

In 1992, in England alone, there were 26,956 schools. Of these, 19,486 were nursery and primary schools. Each has a governing body (DFE, 1993). Readers are asked to reflect on the ethnic composition of their primary school and the ethnic composition of their school's governing body. If a culturally diverse community is to see its local primary school as an organization appreciative of, and responsive to, cultural, ethnic and religious diversity, the composition of the governing body sends out very loud and clear signals to the community served by the school. What signals do you think that your school is sending to all its parents and pupils? The presence on such governing bodies of members of ethnic-minority groups would help ensure that the two major dimensions of the cross-curricular elements are not inadvertently overlooked.

The representation of members of minority ethnic groups on the governing bodies of schools is an important issue. In 1992, the Commission for Racial Equality, in collaboration with Racial Equality Councils, carried out a survey involving thirty-six Local Education Authorities in the North of England. The survey looked at the following six broad areas:

- number of governors;
- ethnic monitoring;
- recruitment;
- training;
- school governor support; and
- clerks to governing bodies.

Thirty-two LEAs (89 per cent) responded. Thirty-one of these knew the number of governors that were serving. Across the LEAs there was a total of 80,280 places. Only fourteen of the LEAs (44 per cent) could identify governors from minority ethnic groups serving on governing bodies. The total of such individuals was 290. 'In every one of these LEAs the proportion of ethnic-minority governors serving is disproportionately lower than the percentage of the population from ethnic minorities living in the community' (Commission for Racial Equality, 1993). It is estimated that a total of 29,699 vacancies would exist in twenty-nine of the LEAs in 1992/3.

Only seven out of thirty-two LEAs monitored the ethnic origins of governors. These LEAs were Cleveland, Doncaster, Leeds, Newcastle, Sheffield, Sunderland and Tameside. Of the twenty-five LEAs not carrying out such monitoring, only six indicated that they had plans so to do in the future. Even if all six did so, this would still mean that in only thirteen out of thirty-two LEAs would such monitoring occur.

Sixteen out of thirty-two (50 per cent) of the LEAs had recruitment drives to encourage individuals from minority ethnic groups to apply for election to membership of schools' governing bodies. This sixteen included six of the LEAs that did monitor the ethnic origins of governing bodies. Two other LEAs plan to implement proposals to encourage ethnic-minority group membership (South Tyneside and Sunderland).

Thirty out of thirty-two (94 per cent) of the LEAs incorporate training for governors that includes particular attention to equal opportunity and antiracism training. The two LEAs reported as providing no such training are Bolton and North Yorkshire LEAs. Seven out of thirty-two (20 per cent) used trainers from ethnic-minority groups as part of the equal-opportunities training. These LEAs were: Bradford, Durham, Kirklees, Manchester, Rotherham, Sheffield and Tameside LEA.

School Governor Advice/Support Units were available in thirty-one out of thirty-two LEAs (97 per cent). Of these, twelve out of thirty-two (38 per cent) provide support to meet the special needs of school governors from minority ethnic groups. Typically, these LEAs were in areas where there was a considerable ethnic-minority population. The support that was provided included:

- language support interpreters;
- leaflets in various languages;

- the use of experienced governors to support new governors; and
- provision of details of race-relations organizations.

The ethnic origins of the clerks to governing bodies was monitored in six out of thirty-two (19 per cent) of the LEAs. Of these six, two did not monitor the ethnic origins of governors. These were Sheffield and North Tyneside. One LEA, Bury, had plans to monitor the ethnic origins of clerks to governing bodies in the future. The remaining twenty-five LEAs had no such plans.

The overall picture underlines the failure of LEAs to be proactive in encouraging and supporting the involvement of members of minority ethnic groups on the governing bodies of schools. Despite this, the report identified examples of 'good practice'. For example, as part of its equal-opportunities policy, Leeds LEA has developed a system whereby the ethnic monitoring of school governors is carried out. The monitoring is to continue throughout the year and the information is to be returned to the Governor Support Unit.

In 1992 Leeds LEA also produced a report on 'governor recruitment and retention campaign 1992'. One section was devoted to the representation of minority ethnic groups. In order to address the problem of underrepresentation of certain minority ethnic groups, work with community groups on this issue has been set in train. The City of Manchester has a full-time 'governor recruitment officer'. The officer's brief includes increasing the participation of parents in schools and on the governing bodies of schools.

An optional workshop for governors on 'equality and the school governor,' developed by Wirral LEA, has been offered on three occasions. Feedback from participants was obtained to ensure that the workshop was meeting its objectives.

The Leeds LEA is quoted as providing school-governor support that meets the needs of ethnic-minority group members. This is done by providing:

- information in six community languages;
- interpreters for governors' meetings;
- interpreters for governors' training sessions;
- training sessions within ethnic-community areas; and
- financial support and assistance for the Black Governors' Information Network (BGIN).

Sheffield LEA has its own multicultural education unit with which the Governor Support Unit collaborates in order to address the needs of school governors from minority ethnic groups.

The ethnic monitoring of governors is seen by the Commission for Racial Equality as essential. Without it, it is impossible to determine whether or not the governing bodies of schools reflect the ethnic composition of their communities. From the information presented above, it is also clear that the issues of recruitment, training and support for members of minority ethnic groups becoming school governors is also far from satisfactory.

The CRE initiative in mounting this type of survey is a welcome attempt to develop policy and practice. The information provided can help LEAs and schools develop governing bodies that will demonstrate the cooperation and collaboration that is required if the cross-curricular theme of 'Education for Citizenship' is to mean anything.

The second challenge identified involved demonstrating, through the daily life and work of the school, respect for cultural, ethnic and religious differences. Within the primary school, cross-curricular dimensions and themes can be systematically addressed through the project work that is extensively used in primary schools. A consideration of the ideas developed in Volume 3 underlines this point.

Cross-curricular Developments

The NCC has provided some general advice concerning ways in which the opportunities inherent in cross-curricular work can be realized (NCC, 1990a). More specific curricular guidance was published later in 1990 bearing on each of the five cross-curricular themes (see Table 2.7).

Table 2.7: Cross-curricular Materials Produced by the National Curriculum Council

Curriculum Guidance Series

NCC (1990c)	*Curriculum Guidance No. 4: Education for Economic and Industrial Understanding*
NCC (1990d)	*Curriculum Guidance No. 5: Health Education*
NCC (1990e)	*Curriculum Guidance No. 6: Careers Education and Guidance*
NCC (1990f)	*Curriculum Guidance No. 7: Environmental Education*
NCC (1990g)	*Curriculum Guidance No. 8: Education for Citizenship*

The elaboration of this work owes much to the efforts of teams of advisers and teachers in a number of LEAs. Manchester is one of these. The city is a multicultural community. Before the Education Reform Act had received the 'Royal Assent', the Education Department of the City of Manchester had established a collaborative strategy to ensure that the cross-curricular elements were suitably addressed at all stages. Those involved included advisers, inspectors, teachers, support service members and members of organizations having links with industry.

The project was led by Diane King of the City of Manchester Inspection and Advisory Service. Teams worked on the five major themes to produce suggestions on the curricular management of these. In November 1991, a pack of six loose-leaf folders was published. The first of these presents an overview of the project. It provides an analysis of the nature and interrelationships between cross-curricular themes, skills and dimensions as essential components of the whole curriculum. Strategies for implementing cross-curricular themes are suggested, models of delivery identified, exemplars and case-studies provided and examples given of planning guides for cross-curricular activities

(King, 1991). The other five handbooks provide cross-curricular theme-specific advice and guidance (see Table 2.8).

Table 2.8: Cross-curricular Materials Produced by the City of Manchester LEA Inspection and Advisory Service

Overview

Cross-Curricular Themes, Skills and Dimensions: implementing the Whole Curriculum (King, 1991)

Cross-Curricular Themes

- Economic and Industrial Awareness (Ramsay, M., Savori, A. and Fuller, S., 1991)
- Health Education (Ramsay, M. and Savori, A., 1991)
- Careers Education (Rogers, R. and Wickham, D., 1991)
- Environmental Education (Greehnough, P. Hyde, M., Kirby, B. and Murray, P., 1991)
- Education for Citizenship (Cooke, D., King, D., Rushforth, C. and Steiner, M., 1991)

Seven major models for the delivery of cross-curricular developments were identified and their applications discussed. Planning sheets for primary schools, assessment sheets and a topic planner are provided (see Table 2.9).

Table 2.9: Cross-curricular Theme-delivery Models (Manchester, LEA)

- Permeating the whole curriculum
- As part of a separately timetabled personal and social-education programme
- As a separately timetabled space
- As part of pastoral/tutorial programme
- Long-block timetabling
- Through opportunities arising from after-school initiatives/activities
- Through using resources within the LEA

Examples and case-studies based on work in primary schools and illustrating various of the seven models include the following accounts. The links with the NC subjects are specified.

- planning the cross-curricular delivery of the theme 'Change' in an infant school;
- the whole-school environment: greening the school;
- a cross-curricular model using 'cooperative group work': primary school;
- school-based business project: special school and primary-school examples; and
- city museum and art-gallery services resource-based topics undertaken by various primary schools:
  'Slums, bugs and diseases'
  'Brass roots'
  'Myths, magic and mystery'

'Celebrations'
'British mammals'.

A further section provides an 'issue-based' approach to cross-curricular themes, skills and dimensions. Suggestions at KS1 include development through a citizenship-based model using 'Teaching about the Gulf War'. The strategy suggested can equally well be applied to any other war. Sadly, there are plenty to choose from. Wars are often widely reported and raise important issues that can be addressed at all stages of the NC. An example of how INSET can be used to develop 'cooperative learning through the expressive arts' is also presented.

The Centre for Cross-Curricular Initiatives, based at Goldsmiths' College, Lewisham Way, New Cross, London, SE14 6NW, has produced a publication entitled *Curriculum Guidance No. 1. Whole School Provision for Personal and Social Development: The Role of the Cross-Curricular Elements* (Buck and Inman, 1992). A model of personal and social development is presented. There is also a framework provided describing a coherent and integrated approach to delivering cross-curricular themes at all stages of the NC. The same authors have also published illustrative case studies of work implementing cross-curricular elements in the curriculum (Buck and Inman, 1993).

In 1987 the then Prime Minister Margaret Thatcher asserted that 'There is no such thing as society . . .' Not all citizens or politicians agreed with her on that or on other issues. Earlier recognition of the importance of 'Education for Citizenship' and its achievement through the subject fields has been discussed in Volumes 1 and 2 of this series. Its roots in state education probably lie within the Reform Bill 1886 which created a mass male electorate. 'The earliest known text was *The Citizenship Reader*, which underwent twenty-four reprints between 1886 and 1904' (Abrams, 1993).

The importance of education in preparing youngsters to play a full part in a democratic society led to the establishment in 1989 of the House of Commons Speaker's Commission on Citizenship. Guidance on the principles was published in November 1990 and the topic was identified as one of the five cross-curricular themes within the NC. A survey carried out in 1990 revealed that 43 per cent of schools had agreed policies on citizenship. The Centre for Citizenship Studies in Education was established in 1991, in response to the Speaker's Commission. It has produced a pack whereby schools are shown how to carry out an audit of existing citizenship activities that are already being carried out within existing NC activities.

The following three organizations are active in developing and researching in this area:

- Centre for Citizenship Studies in Education,
  Queens Building,
  University of Leicester,
  Barrack Road,
  Northampton.

- The Institute for Citizenship Studies,
  20 St James's Square,
  London, SW1.
- The Citizenship Foundation,
  63 Charterhouse Street,
  London, EC1.

The Institute for Citizenship Studies was established in 1990 and in 1993 is hosting a series of events in celebration of the 2,500th anniversary of the birth of democracy in ancient Greece. **The Citizenship Foundation** developed from the earlier School Curriculum Development Committee's 'Law in Education Project'. The foundation is involved in a two-year primary-citizenship project intended to help pupils become aware of, and consider, social and moral issues and to appreciate the effects which their behaviours have on others (Abrams, ibid.).

Conflict Resolution

The aim of helping people understand and reduce both the causes and consequences of conflict is an essential ingredient of any programme of education for citizenship in a democratic society. Programmes that help individuals and groups better to understand and adopt alternatives to aggression and violence, whether verbal or physical, have much to commend them '. . . to look for underlying unity in cultural and religious diversity and attempt to break the cycle of violence in both human and international affairs', are objectives clearly related to those of the ERA.

The Education Advisory Programme of Quaker Peace and Service provides training workshops in conflict resolution under the umbrella of the European Network for Conflict Resolution in Education (ENCORE) and MEDIATION UK (Bentley and Leimdorfer, 1992). MEDIATION UK is 'a network of projects and organisations interested in mediation and other alternative forms of conflict resolution' (ibid.). The addresses of these two organizations are listed below.

Education Advisory Service,
Friends House,
173–177 Euston Road,
LONDON, NW1 2BJ.

MEDIATION (UK),
82a Gloucester Road,
BRISTOL, BS7 8BN.

The Friends' Book Centre produces a helpful six-page (A4) publications list on 'Co-operative Games and Peace Education'. Many of the materials listed are well-suited to cross-curricular work in the primary school.

Education for Peace in Manchester has been developed over a ten-year period as part of a wider programme of personal and social education. Two publications entitled *Education for Peace in Manchester: Guidelines* and *Education for Peace in Manchester: Case Studies* describe the development of this work (Manchester City Council Education Committee, nd,a; nd,b). The origin of the work predates the Education Reform Act, but anticipates certain of its constructive aspects. 'All the fields of activity . . . are likely to be primarily concerned with multidisciplinary cross-curricular or whole-school initiatives and policies, rather than with the development of new subject areas, either individually or in combination, but there should be the opportunity at some time for unique extended or special experiences through particular projects or events' (nd,a, p. 2). The twenty-page list of organizations and resources included in this publication is particularly helpful.

Shakespeare Nursery School: Peace Education and Discipline

The encouragement of social cohesion and the establishment and maintenance of a happy, safe and orderly environment in a multiethnic school provides the ethos within which desirable learning and development can take place. Such aspirations are easily stated but require considerable and continuing efforts if they are to be attained in practice. Within an LEA with well-developed equal opportunities and antiracism policies and practices, schools can address related cross-curricular themes. The following example is indicative of the largely unsung professionalism of schools, school staff and parents in such work.

Shakespeare Nursery School is a Manchester LEA inner-city school. It is situated in a socio-economically deprived area where the incidence of unemployment and crime is high. A considerable number of single-parent families live in the area. The school's pupils are drawn from many different ethnic and religious groups. As part of its school-development plan, through discussions involving all the staff and governors, a document was prepared in which a policy for Peace Education and Discipline was produced. In it, rules for the behaviour of *all children and adults* on the school premises were specified. Actions to be taken in cases of inappropriate behaviour by children were agreed. Means of constructively addressing temper tantrums, conflicts between children, defiance and parent–staff conflict were spelled out and a staff code of behaviour specified. All of this was summarized in a succinct, simply expressed, eight-page document.

In June 1993, the school was visited by an LEA inspector to discuss, observe in action and make recommendations on the school's approach to Peace Education and Discipline. The following extract from the draft report indicates the merits of the policy.

Overall, the school functions as a safe, orderly, corporate community.
The atmosphere both indoors and outside is peaceful and purposeful.

Adults apply the discipline policy consistently and a number of children, although very young, are able to articulate some understanding of what is expected as appropriate behaviour.

Children are given the opportunity to work and play co-operatively, learning to take their turn. They are generally polite to one another: in an imaginative play situation — at the travel agents — one girl asked another, 'Please don't do that, I'm working'. Staff, equally, requested children politely but firmly to refrain from inappropriate behaviour on the rare occasions when this was necessary. Generally, a reason was given for a request: 'Please don't go on the grass, as its wet and you'll get all muddy.'

Examples were noted of affirmation of pupils by teachers both verbally and in the form of the good-behaviour lists on the wall. The latter are helpful, when read out daily, in explaining to children when the behaviour is good: 'X helped Y to feel better when she was sad', for example. There were instances during the inspection when adults were clearly trying to help pupils to articulate their feelings and those of others.

Although outdoor play perhaps offers more scope for minor squabbles, no real conflict occurred in the course of the observation. Children are able to share the space, and play harmoniously. One temper tantrum was dealt with calmly by the adult concerned, according to the guidelines in the discipline policy. In the case of one other child exhibiting much more extreme behaviour, the situation was handled calmly and consistently by a number of different adults.

In their interactions with each other, staff are calm and polite, demonstrating to children that adults can get on well with each other.

At lunchtime, children enter the hall, accompanied by adults, in a smooth manner. The atmosphere over the meal is calm and harmonious, with good interactions between adults and pupils.

Both direct and indirect evidence gathered during the course of the inspection indicate a high level of success. Amongst notable achievements are:

- the provision of appropriate INSET for the staff concerned and the degree of staff participation in the development of the policy;
- the dimension of parental involvement;
- the actual production of the policy document.

Main action points: Within the context of this well-founded success, the school should:

- continue to monitor the implementation of its policy and review it periodically as necessary;

- consider making some cross-references in its *Attitudes and skills checklist for assessment* to those attitudes, skills and behaviours promoted in children specifically through the peace-education and discipline-policy document.

Shakespeare Nursery School provides an example whereby cultural, ethnic and religious diversity can be constructively accommodated within the curriculum. As such, through its Peace Education and Discipline initiative it probably demonstrates one effective way of simultaneously providing that equality of opportunity, antiracist education and 'Education for Citizenship' towards which the whole curriculum aims.

The key lesson is that teachers and other adults must model the behaviours and attitudes that are consonant with social cohesion. What has been demonstrated at Shakespeare Nursery School is not an isolated example of good practice. It presents a well-developed cross-curricular initiative, within the context of its school-development plan, on which the latter stages of education can build.

Conclusion

I believe deeply that all men and women should be able to go as far as talent, ambition and effort can take them. There should be no barriers of background, no barriers of religion, no barriers of race. I want . . . a society that encourages each and every one to fulfil his or her potential to the utmost . . . let me say here and now that I regard any barrier built on race to be pernicious. (Prime Minister John Major, September 1991)

In 1990, the National Curriculum Council appeared to put the cross-curricular elements firmly on the educational map. The two dimensions and five themes received particular attention from LEAs, as is indicated above. A major problem that was never fully addressed was how such cross-curricular concerns could be integrated with a National Curriculum that was strongly subject-based. At the Key Stage 3 and 4 levels, a questionnaire survey of 25 per cent of the secondary schools in England and Wales, coupled with a detailed study of a sample of eight schools, indicates that the cross-curricular themes are assessed mainly though the Attainment Targets for particular subjects. Only 37 per cent of schools intended to assess themes separately from subjects, and the majority of these were using Records of Achievement. If the themes are to meet the aims of Section 1 of the Education Reform Act 1988, it has been argued that the assessment of themes should be based on the pupils' ability to integrate knowledge and relate it to their own lives' (Rowe and Whitty, 1993).

Whatever curriculum audits showed, the themes had a rather shadowy presence in most of the schools that we visited. It is difficult to see how they will recover from their present position when so much emphasis is placed on the subject Orders. Few people would probably support the idea of legislation to give themes more of a real presence in the classroom. But the six themes in the Northern Ireland curriculum are actually written into the Education Reform Order. The Inspectorate also makes it clear that curriculum organisation will not be considered good where 'although there has been discussion about the introduction of the educational themes . . . the themes make little impact at classroom level'. (ibid., p. 8)

In relation to organization and pedagogy, primary schools are currently less overtly subject-dominated than secondary schools. How long this will continue remains to be seen. Impending changes in the initial teacher training of primary-school teachers with an increased emphasis on subject specialization at the older age levels in the primary school could impede the development of cross-curricular activities (See Chapter 14). If this were to happen, an essential means of enriching the educational programme of primary-school pupils could be put at risk.

Table 2.10: *Sources of Information, Advice and Materials*

Access to Information on Multicultural Education Resources (AIMER), Faculty of Education and Community Studies, The University of Reading, Bulmershe Court, Earley, Reading, RG6 1HV.	**Bilingual Support Service,** Crosby Primary School, Frodingham Road, Scunthorpe, Humberside, DN15 7NL.
Acorn (Percussion) Ltd, Unit 34, Abbey Business Centre, Ingate Place, London, SW8 3NS.	**Board of Deputies of British Jews,** Woburn House, Tavistock Square, London, WC1H 0EP.
African Video Centre, 7 Balls Pond Road, London, N1 4AX.	**Centre for Ethnic Studies in Education,** School of Education, University of Manchester, Manchester, M13 9PL.
Afro-Caribbean Education Resource (ACER), Wyvil School, Wyvil Road, London, SW8 2TJ.	**Centre for Multicultural Education,** Rushey Mead Centre, Harrison Road, Leicester, LE4 6BR.
Avon Section 11 Education Team, Education Development Service, Horfield, Bristol, BS7 0PU.	**Centre for Multicultural Education,** University of London Institute of Education, 20 Bedford Way, London, WC1 0AL.
	Centre for Research in Ethnic Relations, Resources Centre Librarian, University of Warwick, Coventry, CV4 7AL.
BBC Educational Development, P.O. Box 50, Wetherby, West Yorkshire, LS23 7EZ.	**Centre for World Development Education,** 1 Catton Street, London, WC1R 4AB.

Table 2.10: (Cont.)

Childsplay,
112 Tooting High Street,
London, SW17 ORR.

Christian Education Movement,
Royal Buildings,
Victoria Street,
Derby, DE1 1GW.

Close Links,
c/o Grimwade Street,
Ipswich, IP4 1LS.

Commission for Racial Equality,
Elliot House,
10–12 Allington Street,
London, SW1E 5EH.

**Commonwealth Institute Resource
Centre,**
Kensington High Street,
London, W8 6NQ.

**Council for Education in World
Citizenship,**
Seymour Mews House,
London, W1H 9PE.

Development Education Centre,
Selly Oak Colleges,
Bristol Road,
Birmingham,
B29 6LE.

**Development Education in Dorset
(DEED),**
Lowther Road,
Bournemouth, BH8 8NR.

**Early Years Trainers Anti-Racist
Network,**
The Lyndens,
51 Granville Road,
London, N12 0JH.

**Education Development Centre (EMSS/
MPU),**
Popes Lane,
Oldbury,
Warley,
Sandwell, B69 4PJ.

Education Development Centre, EO Unit,
Room 14,
Field Road,
Bloxwich,
Walsall,
West Midlands, W53 3JF.

Education Materials,
OXFAM,
274 Banbury Road,
Oxford, OX2 7DZ.

Elm Bank Teachers Centre,
Mile Lane,
Coventry,
CV1 2LQ.

Ethnic Minority Project,
103 Preston New Road,
Blackburn, BB2 6BJ.

Faculty of Multicultural Education,
Martineau Education Centre,
Balden Road,
Harbourne,
Birmingham, B32 2EH.

Folens Publishers,
Albert House,
Apex Business Centre,
Boscombe Road,
Dunstable, LU5 4RN.

Heights Culture Shop,
13 Middle Row,
Stevenage Old Town,
Herts.

Hounslow Primary Language Service,
Civic Centre,
Lampton Road,
Hounslow,
Middlesex, TW3 4DN.

Humming Bird Book and Toy Services,
136 Grosvenor Road,
St. Pauls,
Bristol, BS28 1YA.

Institute of Race Relations,
2–6 Leeke Street,
King's Cross Road,
London, WC1X 9HS.

Islamic Cultural Centre,
146 Park Road,
London, NW8 7RG.

**Joint Council for the Welfare of
Immigrants,**
115 Old Street,
London, EC1V 9JR.

**Kemet Educational Materials
Consultancy,**
111 Lakenheath,
London, N14 4RY.

Kirklees Supplementary Schools Project,
Multicultural Education Unit,
Huddersfield Technical College,
New North Road,
Huddersfield, HD1 5NN.

Table 2.10: *(Cont.)*

Leeds Development Education Centre,
153 Cardigan Road,
Leeds,
LS6 1LJ.

Letterbox Library,
Leroy House,
436 Essex Road,
London, N1 3BR.

Manchester City Council Education Committee,
Peace Education Project,
North Manchester Resources Centre,
Harpurhey,
Manchester, M10 7NS.

Marigold Bentley and Tom Leimdorfer,
Education Advisory Programme,
Friends House,
Euston Road,
London, NW1 2BJ.

Minority Group Support Service,
Southfields Old School,
South Street,
Coventry, CV1 5EJ.

Minority Rights Group,
379 Brixton Road,
London, SW9 7DE.

Multicultural Education Centre,
Stirling School,
Prospect Place,
Doncaster, DN1 3QP.

Multicultural Education and Language Service,
Broadbent Road,
Oldham, OL1 4HU.

Multicultural Education Resources Centre,
66 Cedar Road,
Bedford, MK42 0JE.

Multicultural Education Service,
Spencer Centre,
Lewis Road,
Northampton, NN5 7BJ.

Multicultural Resource Centre,
Holne Chase Centre,
Bletchley,
Milton Keynes, MK3 5HP.

Multicultural Support Team,
Jennie Lee Community and Professional Centre,
Lichfield Road,
Wednesfield,
Wolverhampton,
Staffordshire, WV1 1PC.

National Association of Racial Equality Councils,
8–16 Coronet Street,
London, N1 6HD.

National Council for Civil Liberties,
21 Tabard Street,
London, SE1 4LA.

National Educational Resources Information Service,
Maryland College,
Leighton Street,
Woburn,
Milton Keynes, MK17 9JD.

National Union of Teachers,
Education and Equal Opportunities Department,
Hamilton House,
Mabledon Place,
London, WC1H 9BD.

Peterborough Centre for Multicultural Education,
165a Cromwell Road,
Peterborough, PE1 2EL.

Publications Unit,
Jordanhill College of Education,
Southbrae Drive,
Glasgow, G13 1PP.

Resources for Learning Development Unit,
Sheridan Road,
Horfield,
Bristol, BS7 0PU.

The Refugee Council,
Bondway House,
3–9 Bondway,
London, SW8 1SJ.

The Runnymede Trust,
11 Princelet Street,
London, E1 6QH.

Standing Conference on Racial Equality in Europe,
Unit 303,
Brixton Enterprise Centre,
444 Brixton Road,
London, SW1 8EJ.

Star Apple Blossom,
13 Inman Road,
London, SW18 3BB.

Table 2.10: (Cont.)

Working Group Against Racism in Children's Resources, 406 Wandsworth Road, London, SW8 3LX.	Zuma Art Services, Kings Place, 16 Stony Street, Nottingham, NG1 1LH.

References

ABRAMS, F. (1993) 'Rights, duties and the greater scheme', *Times Educational Supplement*, No. 4020, 16 July.

ALLPORT, G.W. (1954) *The Nature of Prejudice*, Reading, Mass., Addison-Wesley.

BALLARD, R. and KALRA, V.S. (1994) The Ethnic Dimensions of the 1991 Census — A Preliminary Report, Manchester, University of Manchester Census Microdata Unit.

BENTLEY, M. and LEIMDORFER, T. (1992) *Once upon a conflict. A fairytale manual of conflict resolution for all ages*, London, Religious Society of Friends Communications Services Department.

BIBBY, C. (1959) *Race, Prejudice and Education*, London, Heinemann.

BRITISH BROADCASTING CORPORATION AND THE COMMISSION FOR RACIAL EQUALITY (1992) *Race through the 90s*, London, BBC and CRE.

BUCK, M. and INMAN, S. (1992) *Curriculum Guidance No. 1. Whole School Provision for Personal and Social Development*, London, Goldsmiths' College, University of London.

BUCK, M. and INMAN, S. (1993) *Curriculum Guidance. No. 2. Re-affirming Values: Practical Case-studies in implementing cross-curricular dimensions, themes and skills*, London, Goldsmiths College, University of London.

CENTRE FOR ETHNIC STUDIES IN EDUCATION (1992) *The Education Reform Act and Equal Opportunities: Emerging Patterns*, Centre for Ethnic Studies in Education, School of Education, University of Manchester.

CENTRE FOR ETHNIC STUDIES IN EDUCATION (1993) *Curriculum Entitlement for All? Myth or Reality for Black Children in the 1990s*, Centre for Ethnic Studies in Education, School of Education, University of Manchester.

COCKING, L., CRAIG, D. and MAHON, S. (Eds) (1981) *Education in a multiethnic society*, London, Inner London Education Authority Learning Materials Service.

COHEN, L. (1989) 'Ignorance, not Hostility: Student Teachers' Perceptions of Ethnic Minorities in Britain', in VERMA, G.K. (Ed) *Education for All: A Landmark in Pluralism*, London, The Falmer Press.

COMMISSION FOR RACIAL EQUALITY (1991) *Second Review of the Race Relations Act 1976*, London, CRE.

COMMISSION FOR RACIAL EQUALITY (1993) *School Governors Evaluation: Survey carried out in the North of England 1992*, London, CRE (in conjunction with Racial Equality Councils).

COOKE, D., KING, D., RUSHFORTH, C. and STEINER, M. (1991) *Education for Citizenship*, Manchester, Manchester LEA Education Committee.

DEPARTMENT FOR EDUCATION (1992) *Your Child and the National Curriculum. A parent's guide to what is taught in schools*, 2nd edition, London, DFE.

DEPARTMENT FOR EDUCATION (1992) *Testing 7 year olds in 1992: results of the National Curriculum assessments in England*, London, HMSO.

DEPARTMENT FOR EDUCATION (1993) 'Statistics of Schools in England: January, 1992', *Statistical Bulletin 18/93*, London, DEF.

DEPARTMENT OF EDUCATION AND SCIENCE (1991) *The Parent's Charter. You and Your Child's Education*, London, DES.

GREEHNOUGH, P., HYDE, M., KIRBY, B and MURRAY, P. (1991) *Environmental Education*, Manchester, Manchester LEA Education Committee.

HASKEY, J. (1990) 'The ethnic minority populations of Great Britain: estimates by ethnic group and country of birth', *Population Trends*, 60, pp. 35–8.

HASNIE, N.S. (1993) *A report of an audit of the ethnic minority voluntary supplementary schools in Kirklees*, Kirklees, Kirklees LEA.

HOME OFFICE (1987) *Racial Discrimination: A Guide to the Race Relations Act 1976, Circular 7/87*, London, HMSO.

KING, D. (Ed) (1991) *Cross-Curricular Themes, Skills and Dimensions: implementing the Whole Curriculum*, Manchester, Manchester Education Committee.

KING, M. and REISS, M.J. (Ed) (1993) *The Multicultural Dimension of the National Curriculum*, London, The Falmer Press.

KLOSS, D.M. (1990) 'The legal context of race-relations in England and Wales', in PUMFREY, P.D. and VERMA, G.K. (Eds) *Race Relations and Urban Education*, London, The Falmer Press, pp. 23–35.

LEICESTER, M. and TAYLOR, M. (Eds) (1992) *Ethics, Ethnicity and Education*, London, Kogan Page.

LYNCH, J. (1991) *Education for Citizenship in a Multi-Cultural Society*, London, Cassell.

LYNCH, J., MODGIL, C. and MODGIL, S. (Eds) (1992a) *Cultural Diversity and the Schools, Volume 1, Education for Cultural Diversity: Convergence and Divergence*, London, The Falmer Press.

LYNCH, J., MODGIL, C. and MODGIL, S. (Eds) (1992b) *Cultural Diversity and the Schools, Volume 2, Prejudice, Polemic or Progress?*, London, The Falmer Press.

LYNCH, J., MODGIL, C. and MODGIL, S. (Eds) (1992c) *Cultural Diversity and the Schools, Volume 3, Equity or Excellence? Education and Cultural Reproduction*, London, The Falmer Press.

LYNCH, J., MODGIL, C. and MODGIL, S. (Eds) (1992d) *Cultural Diversity and the Schools, Volume 4, Human Rights, Education and Global Responsibilities*, London, The Falmer Press.

MACDONOGH, S. (1993) *The Rushdie Letters: the Freedom to Speak, Freedom to Write*, London, Brandon.

MANCHESTER CITY COUNCIL EDUCATION COMMITTEE (nd(a)) *Education for Peace in Manchester: Guidelines*, Manchester, Manchester Education Committee.

MANCHESTER CITY COUNCIL EDUCATION COMMITTEE (nd(b)) *Education for Peace in Manchester: Case Studies*, Manchester, Manchester Education Committee.

NATIONAL CURRICULUM COUNCIL (1989a) *An Introduction to the National Curriculum*, York, NCC.

NATIONAL CURRICULUM COUNCIL (1989b) *Curriculum Guidance No. 1. A Framework for the National Curriculum*, York, NCC.

NATIONAL CURRICULUM COUNCIL (1989c) *Curriculum Guidance No. 2. A Curriculum for All: Special Educational Needs in the National Curriculum*, York, NCC.

NATIONAL CURRICULUM COUNCIL (1990a) *Curriculum Guidance No. 3. The Whole Curriculum*, York, NCC.

NATIONAL CURRICULUM COUNCIL (1990b) *The National Curriculum: A guide for parents of primary children*, York, NCC.

NATIONAL CURRICULUM COUNCIL (1990c) *Curriculum Guidance No. 4. Education for Economic and Industrial Understanding*, York, NCC.

NATIONAL CURRICULUM COUNCIL (1990d) *Curriculum Guidance No. 5. Health Education*, York, NCC.

NATIONAL CURRICULUM COUNCIL (1990e) *Curriculum Guidance No. 6. Careers Education and Guidance*, York, NCC.

NATIONAL CURRICULUM COUNCIL (1990f) *Curriculum Guidance No. 7. Environmental Education*, York, NCC.

NATIONAL CURRICULUM COUNCIL (1990g) *Curriculum Guidance No. 8. Education for Citizenship*, York, NCC.

NATIONAL CURRICULUM COUNCIL (1992a) *Why a National Curriculum?* (leaflet), York, NCC.

NATIONAL CURRICULUM COUNCIL (1992b) *Starting Out with the National Curriculum — An introduction to the National Curriculum and Religious Education*, York, NCC.

OFFICE OF POPULATION CENSUSES AND SURVEYS (OPCS) (1992) *Census Newsletter*, 19 March.

OWEN, D. (1992) *Ethnic Minorities in Great Britain: Settlement Patterns*, 1991 Census Statistical Paper No. 1, National Ethnic Minority Data Archive, Centre for Research in Ethnic Relations, University of Warwick.

PALMER, C. and POULTER, K. (1987) *Sex and Race Discrimination in Employment*, London, Legal Action Group.

PUMFREY, P.D. (1990) 'Improving race-relations in urban education', in PUMFREY, P.D. and VERMA, G.K. (Eds) *Race Relations and Urban Education: Contexts and Promising Practices*, London, The Falmer Press, pp. 309–30.

PUMFREY, P.D. and VERMA, G.K. (Eds) (1993) *Cultural Diversity and the Curriculum, Vol. 3, The Foundation Subjects and Religious Education in Primary Schools*, London, The Falmer Press.

RAMSAY, M. and SIVORI, A. (1991) *Health Education*, Manchester, Manchester LEA Education Committee.

RAMSAY, M., SIVORI, A. and FULLER, S. (1991) *Economic and Industrial Awareness*, Manchester, Manchester LEA Education Committee.

ROGERS, R. and WICKHAM, D. (1991) *Careers Education*, Manchester, Manchester LEA Education Committee.

ROWE, G. and WHITTY, G. (1993) 'Five themes remain in the shadows', *Times Educational Supplement*, No. 4006, 9 April, p. 8.

ROY, A. (1992) 'Where cultures co-exist . . . and collide', *The Sunday Telegraph*, 13 December, p. 15.

SHAW, C. (1988) 'Latest estimates of ethnic minority populations', *Population Trends*, 51, London, Office of Population Censuses and Surveys.

Peter D. Pumfrey

SWEETMAN, J. (1992) The Complete Guide to the National Curriculum: Curriculum Confidential Three, Tamworth, Bracken Press.
VERMA, G.K. (1992) 'Inter-ethnic relationships in Schools', Unpublished Report based on a study of schools in Greater Manchester, Centre for Ethnic Studies in Education, School of Education, University of Manchester.

54

Part 2

National Curriculum Cross-curricular Themes

Chapter 3

Economic and Industrial Understanding

Mike Harrison and Diana Rainey

Context

Writers in this series have explored various means by which teachers can begin to tackle issues of racism, disadvantage and oppression with their classes. It is no easy task. In the current political climate, exacerbated by the media, the rights and needs of individuals and family are championed at the expense of those of community and society. In an atmosphere which blames individuals for their own disadvantage rather than remedy contributory societal and political causes, it is difficult for primary schools to underpin their curriculum with ideals of social justice or even to set a tone in which work of this nature can begin. The ERA, as is argued by Hardy and Vieler-Porter (1992) is only the latest in a long line of recent legislation with the ideological thrust toward a shift from public service to private practice. After-all, you scarcely need public service in a land where 'There is no such thing as society. There are individual men and women and there are families' (Margaret Thatcher, February 1989). Thus 'education is no longer seen as representing any collective, community or social interest — but rather as an institution through which to pursue self interest' (Hardy and Vieler-Porter, 1992). What the ERA gave us was a centralized curriculum, spurious parental choice, short-sighted governing bodies able to give vent to their prejudices and a long silence on matters of race and culture.

> despite the presence in the education system of over half a million children and young people perceived as racially or ethnically different to a white norm, there was no mention in the Act of race, ethnicity or even multicultural education. (Tomlinson, 1989, p. 461)

As racism is embedded in our culture and practices in school and we are without an adequate policy on race-related matters, it has been the initiative and enterprise of individual LEAs which have supported and developed such work. Now that LEAs have been sidelined and destabilized as a deliberate policy to exclude the fostering of 'anti-family, anti-police and anti-competitive values in schools' (Baker, 1987), there is a vacuum which can only be filled by teachers who appreciate the need for action to confront this issue. As has been argued by Troyna and Carrington (1990)

> Curricular initiatives to combat racism should form part of a wider programme of political education which seeks first to develop peoples' understanding of fundamental issues relating to human rights, social justice and the exercise of power and to equip them to be decent, fair minded, responsible and informed citizens. (Troyna and Carrington, 1990, p. 97)

Verma (1989) demonstrates that, before the National Curriculum, race-equality issues had begun to be addressed in the school curriculum, although progress was patchy. With so much of the primary timetable now dedicated to an externally imposed curriculum, it is only by seeking sympathetic threads within that curriculum which can serve to expose attitudes and explore issues, that teachers will be able to continue with such work.

The study of 'Economic and Industrial Understanding' seems to be uniquely suited to such a purpose. It is 'people centred'; can be used to introduce concepts of human causation; describes community and cumulative effort; studies the choices which have to be made between different courses of action and, integral to the area, is the opportunity to tackle head-on the aspect of racism and racial prejudice most commonly found, that of employment practices. What is more, it appears to be a respectable area of study, supported by all political parties. Indeed it has been recent Conservative governments that have encouraged a considerable growth in close links between education and industry. This evolved from the lead provided by the Labour Prime Minister, James Callaghan, who, in his Ruskin College speech in 1976, suggested that there was a need for a closer relationship between school and the world of work. Shirley Williams in the first Priestley lecture (September 1977) appealed for closer consultation between industry and science teachers. In order to make education more applicable to the 'needs' of the economy then young people would have to acquire more 'realistic' and 'responsible' attitudes to the world of work (Sarup, 1982). Whatever the political party in power the requirement to provide a workforce for the twenty-first century able to tackle problems, take initiatives, persevere, be flexible and be able to work as part of a team, is paramount. Government sees that through 'Economic and Industrial Understanding' (EIU) pupils can be helped to gain these important qualities. So EIU is officially encouraged and teachers tackling this cross-curricular dimension are working within the National Curriculum. Looking at issues in this area however, also forces children to face economic dilemmas such as the deployment of scarce resources, globally as well as within Britain, the structure of the labour market and racial and social justice in employment. In fact, helping children come to terms with ideas in the area of EIU probably has a closer identity with teaching for racial equality and social justice than many other areas of the curriculum.

Key concepts common to both include justice (who gets what out of any economic situation), equality (in employment, in opportunity to benefit from enterprise), freedom (do market forces operate giving everyone freedom of choice?) and use of resources (are scarce resources used efficiently and what are the short and longer term consequences?).

Over the last fifteen years there has been a profusion of school and industry links. These have not been confined to links between industry and secondary schools (though sometimes industrialists need to be persuaded of the importance of working with primary-school children). EIU is much more than a partnership between school and industry. It is also concerned with persons being aware of the economic factors in their lives which shape their communities and how these factors affect the decisions they and their friends may make and the choices available. Primary schools have always been involved with instilling an 'economic awareness' in children as part of the curriculum, even if it was not always labelled as such, e.g., when such issues as 'pocket money' were discussed, and all primary-school children have been familiar with the need to raise money for the school through 'sponsored activities', 'school fairs', 'jumble sales' and 'car boot sales'. It then needed to be decided how the money raised should be spent. Many children are also used to working on topics which can provoke issues of interdependence and human rights such as 'What's in a cup of coffee?' (Greer, 1991). Economic awareness and the idea of 'opportunity cost' can start at a very early age. A recent example was observed by one of us which involved a two-year old child at a swimming pool who bit through her inflatable ring — 'mummy buy a new one' was met with the reply 'we will try to mend it'.

The School Curriculum Development Committee (1986) identified a continuum which consisted of economic awareness, economic understanding and finally economic competency. Teachers can build upon the economic awareness that children have when they come to school to develop economic understanding with the view to creating economic competence.

That EIU can become a potent vehicle for the political education referred to earlier can be seen from the HMI Curriculum Matters series 'Economic and Industrial Understanding'. EIU is:

> concerned with helping pupils at all stages in their lives to make sense
> of the world in which they live and to participate fully in society as
> far as they are able or have the desire to do so. (DES, 1985)

In order to do this children need to be able to make informed choices about the economic and social issues surrounding the world of work. According to the National Curriculum Guidance document, in developing an EIU curriculum:

Schools should consider how and when to help pupils, between the ages of 5 and 16, to develop . . . knowledge and understanding . . . analytical, personal and social skills . . . attitudes . . . (NCC, 1990)

It is particularly with the attitudes underpinning EIU that primary teachers must concern themselves if they are to provide an EIU curriculum which gives equal opportunity to all pupils regardless of their cultural or ethnic background. These attitudes as listed in the NCC guidance document are similar to any list of good practice in getting children to think critically about the ways of the world in which they live. Children should develop:

an interest in economic and industrial affairs;
respect for evidence and rational argument in economic contexts;
concern for the use of scarce resources;
a sense of responsibility for the consequences of their own economic actions, as individuals and members of groups;
respect for alternative economic viewpoints and a willingness to reflect critically on their own economic views and values;
sensitivity to the effects of economic choices on the environment; and concern for human rights, as these are affected by economic decisions. (NCC, 1990)

It is through attempting to develop these attitudes that primary teachers must help children challenge stereotypes and ensure that they consider the needs of the different cultural groups comprising our society. In order that all cultural groups are valued, the development of the 'attitudes' component of EIU must do more than deal sensitively with the children and families of ethnic-minority groups. True multicultural education as suggested by the Swann Committee Report (DES, 1985) is that which: 'is considered appropriate for all children if they are to be adequately prepared for life in a pluralist society.'

Burgess-Macey (1992) goes further:

We will have to look at the experience of discrimination, not just celebrate cultural diversity; look at experience of being an oppressed group, not just the identity of being a black girl. (Burgess-Macey, 1992, p. 282)

This means therefore, that the kind of educational experience of EIU that might be promoted in primary schools will be similar for all children.It is important that primary teachers are aware that the values that are implicit in the planned work must be shared values, appropriate for all pupils and value pupils' religious / cultural perspectives, not just describe them. For example, several world religions condemn charging interest. In the Koran gaining money from lending money is described as to 'reap what you have not sown'. It has been suggested by Pike and Pointon (1991) that the Islamic banking system is moving toward sharing in the profits (and losses) of businesses in which they invest rather than charging a premium on the money lent. Teaching children about setting up a mini-enterprise needs to take account of these matters, otherwise a proportion of children will be alienated form the exercise from the very start.

Attitudes and beliefs are formed at an early age and the older the pupils become the less likely they are to change any beliefs or attitudes that they hold. At the same time, the responsibility that the primary teacher, together with the family, has during the time these young people are forming attitudes cannot be overemphasized. In today's society, where media coverage is extensive and its impact on young people is continually becoming more influential, it is very important that teachers examine very carefully the values they hold and the ways in which these values influence the children they teach. This is the case in all areas of the curriculum, including EIU.

The NCC Curriculum Guidance Document on EIU stresses the importance of equality of access to the curriculum:

> All pupils, regardless of culture, gender or social background, should have equal access to a curriculum which promotes EIU. Schools should be aware of pupils' attitudes and assumptions which relate to this component of the curriculum. (NCC, 1990)

From these beginnings Manchester teachers (Ramsay and Sivori, 1992) suggest that 'Economic and Industrial Understanding' is about the empowerment, relationships, rights and responsibilities, systems, structures and forces of change listed below.

Empowerment:
This involves teachers helping pupils become increasingly able:

- to make choices about the uses and allocation of resources;
- to be able to evaluate critically alternative decisions;
- to participate in democratic decision-making processes at work and in the economy and society generally;
- to understand and use economic terminology; and
- to prepare pupils for their future roles as producers, consumers and citizens.

Relationships between:

- individual, group and community, national and international interests;
- the economy and society in different economic systems;
- government and citizens;
- economic, political and social issues; and
- education, work and industry.

Rights and responsibilities:

- personal and human;
- social, political and economic;
- government and citizens;
- producers and consumers; and
- employers and employees.

Systems, structures and forces of change:

- local, regional, national and international;
- the organization of production, consumption and distribution;
- industry and industrial relations;
- the impact of economic, social, political and environmental forces; and
- the structural constraints on the dynamics of change.

In considering how to plan for EIU in the primary-school curriculum, teachers will not be concerned with attitudes alone but also with knowledge, understanding and analytical, personal and social skills. In considering the challenges facing the teacher in developing EIU in the primary school the authors will consider EIU in its entirety but with special emphasis upon those attitudes which are most relevant to multicultural issues.

Challenges

During the last ten years in schools and in the *era of the ERA* the teaching profession has undergone trial by media. This has been without specific charge and therefore hard to defend, but its consequence is that there has been a rush for measures of accountability. In response to this, schools have produced a proliferation of policy documents. Some teachers might want to argue that they are spending more time 'talking about what to do' than getting on with the job of teaching the children. The examination of why and how the curriculum should be 'delivered' is, however, extremely important. It is during the discussion with colleagues that issues are raised, debated and decisions about school policy are made. For many schools it has been a huge task to produce policy documents for the core and foundation subjects of the National Curriculum and the themes and dimensions have had to take second place. Of all the themes and dimensions EIU has perhaps received more attention because of agencies and initiatives that were set up during the 1980s.

The School Curriculum Industry Partnership (SCIP) is an agency which has been successful in disseminating ideas to teachers about ways in which EIU can be taught. For any teaching strategy to be successful it is important that the teachers, and through them the children, become motivated and filled with enthusiasm. Many initatives set up through SCIP have helped in this respect. In order for school–industry links to be most effective it is important that not only the teachers understand about what is involved in teaching EIU but that those in industry also appreciate the value of this aspect of school work. Any teaching programme must start from the question — what do children usefully need to know about industry? — rather than informing children about industry.

There is a danger in the use of the term 'industry' in that although the word is defined in the Oxford Dictionary as 'habitual employment in useful work' it is also defined as 'branch of trade or manufacture'. For many people the term 'industry' conjures up the latter definition and as Roberts and Dolan (1989) argue children's perceptions of 'work' are very sophisticated and any teaching strategies developed need to build upon the ideas that children already have about the nature of 'work' and the accompanying economic and social issues. There is scope here to discuss the value of work done and the relative difference in wages received. Work can be paid and unpaid. Often unpaid work can be considered more valuable than work that receives remuneration. Day care, meals on wheels, rehabilitation therapy, all add to our quality of life and very 'low-status' jobs like cleaning and cooking are essential to our very existence, yet these jobs are either unpaid or very poorly paid and often delegated to ethnic-minority groups or women.

Children also have preconceptions about industry as Sheila Burleton found when questioning a class of primary children at Freshfield Primary School, Formby (Smith, 1988). To the children, industry meant factories which were noisy and dirty and in which they would not like to work. By becoming involved with the textile industry through a school–industry link the children had the opportunity for first-hand experience of an industry that they had studied historically and thus the opportunity to question the people working in this industry.

In a very crowded National Curriculum one of the greatest challenges for the primary-school teacher is that of *time*. Any school–industry link that is set up cannot stand on its own; it will be necessary to relate it to other areas of the curriculum and this can often prove challenging. However, if the link is well planned and is made exciting and fascinating for the children then they will learn at a faster pace and the time will have been well spent.

Whilst teaching EIU through the school–industry partnership it will be important for industrialists and teachers alike to appreciate the importance of allowing children to maintain open minds so that issues concerning equal opportunity can be dealt with through children asking questions. Education is concerned with the raising of self-esteem in all pupils and in looking at EIU and the world of work, teachers will be encouraging children to consider questions concerning economic success both in the UK and the wider world and the value of the contribution that an individual makes to society as a whole through the work he or she is involved in. These challenges are summarized in Table 3.1

Table 3.1: Challenges for the Primary-school Teacher in Developing Economic and Industrial Understanding in the Primary School

1. How to use the platform provided by issues in EIU to teach for racial equality and social justice.
2. Getting colleagues to understand what is involved in EIU and how it can enrich the education of children.
3. Creating links with both industry and the local economic community and making the link a two-way process by getting both industry and the local economic community to understand what is involved in primary education.
4. Finding the time to fit EIU into a crowded curriculum.
5. Ensuring that children receive positive images of 'workers' regardless of their ethnicity or social class and that they develop a critical awareness of cultural difference and stereotyping.

Responses

Many teachers have very little experience of building a career in indusry. Yet a report on a recent national survey shows that student teachers come to the profession with a range of economic understandings (Harrison, 1992). 'Students have a . . . extensive and varied work experience . . . many have a substantial full-time work record. A third have belonged to a trade union, had done regular voluntary work and 41 per cent have, at some time, been registered as unemployed'. Most will have spent some time involved in casual work, a 'Saturday job' whilst at school or vacation work whilst a student. The current government moves toward reducing student grants and increasing student debt makes the point. They have plenty of experience of economics as part of the economic unit of the family. This they have in common with their pupils and it is possible to use this first-hand experience in order to develop economic understanding in the classroom. The geography curriculum at Key Stages 1 and 2 includes the study of the local area, which in turn includes field work. A visit which is frequently included in infant and indeed nursery schools is a visit to the local shop or shops. This is accompanied by the development of a classroom shop where children are encouraged to engage in economic activity for themselves. Other visits might include the local health centre, garden centre, garage, to name but a few. Teachers do not have to be persuaded of the importance of using the local community and environment to enrich the children's education. All these agencies are those with which they are already involved. They may need persuasion and help, however, to become more involved in the sort of environment with which they are less familiar, that of the factory floor.

Smith (1988) gives us many examples of the increase in interest in industry education and the world of work. Blyth (1984) talks of 'education for industry' and the 'perceived need' for a means of changing attitudes towards industry through making children more aware of industrial matters. Through its funding of Education Business Partnerships (EBPs) and such agencies as SCIP,

Table 3.2: *Responses to the Challenges for the Primary-school Teacher in Developing Economic and Industrial Understanding in the Primary School*

1. Invite visitors from a variety of ethnic backgrounds into the classroom to talk about their jobs and how they help society in what they do. Brief the speakers beforehand on the aspects you wish to highlight (creating wider horizons for all children, communal enterprises where all have a valued role to play)

   include workers from the emergency services, retired and unemployed workers, trainees, unpaid workers.

2. Set up a mini-enterprise to provide a service, produce, distribute or exchange something.

   sell greetings cards in various languages, sweets from different culinary traditions, set up car-washing scheme or a school newsletter, distribute snacks, stationery, barter with other schools, swap seeds from wild gardens, organize a social event

3. Survey reactions to a service or product.
   Is it value for money, can it be modified to fit in with all cultural heritages, does it offend some?

   school dinners, local bus services, facilities in local parks

4. Role-play workplace situations, simulating production-line workers doing different tasks, running a group meeting taking all views into account, health and safety matters.

   acting out an interview where one person does not get a job because she is pregnant, wears a turban, is a catholic, is disabled, help children empathize with the situation of others

5. Visit local workplaces such as supermarkets, local parks, a building site or examine the school itself as a workplace.

   take photographs, tape-record interviews, find out about trade unions, explore equal-opportunites practices in the work situation

primary teachers are being encouraged to become more actively involved in industry education and teaching EIU through the medium of industry. Those involved in encouraging primary teachers to become active in establishing school–industry links will stress the importance of giving teachers first-hand experience by getting teachers out into industry before embarking upon such a link. By taking children out into the world of work they become highly motivated and enthusiastic. Learning becomes relevant and they can relate economic concepts with which they are already aware e.g., how to plan the spending of their own pocket money, with the decisions made by industrialists. Where to play football in the school grounds can then be related to how industrialists make decisions about where to site a new factory. SCIP newsletters are full of examples where teachers, and in turn the children that they teach, have become highly motivated and enthusiastic through school–industry links. By centring on the people involved and the full range of skills factories need they can be shown as common enterprises which call upon the talents of all employees to be successful. This aspect is bought out in Juliet's account of a visit to a supermarket (Greer, 1991).

Jobs in a Supermarket

You may think that there aren't many jobs in a supermarket but there are. When we went to Asda we found that there were over 250 employees, which means there are many jobs and the employees have to work long hours. One job is cleaning but another job is manager, there are lots of jobs in between those two. In a supermarket there are a lot of jobs which need trained people like security, and store detectives.

The personnel manager has the responsibility of the staff like looking after them or firing them. The general store manager has the responsibility of the whole store. Then there are the check-out people who take the money from you after you have bought the goods. The cashiers take money from the till and check that it is all there. The supermarkets also have secretaries who order stock, answer the phones and type. There are also people who prepare fish, meat etc. The supermarket has to have engineers because if anything breaks down like a freezer they have to mend it straight away or they will lose customers and the food will go bad.

Asda employ over 250 people in Derby. Asda sell 80 cases with 24 jars of 100g Nescafé instant coffee each week. If the retailers profit is 9.9 per cent and a 100g costs £1.30 then Asda made £264.20 to pay the wages (13.7p profit per jar). (Greer, 1991)

Which individuals do which jobs, and why, become important issues in a multiculturally sensitive analysis.

Any school–industry link must be a two-way process and industrialists will need to be helped to understand what primary education is all about. This is an opportunity to market the outstanding achievements of primary education and the principles behind primary practices as well as explaining about the National Curriculum and what 'Education for Industrial Understanding' actually means for the primary-school child. Many in industry understand the importance of involving the secondary-school child but not the younger children. There sometimes seems to be a view held by some in society that primary education is less important than secondary or higher education. Take for example the anomaly in funding between the primary and secondary schools. The 1992 primary discussion paper, for example, argued that:

> there is no justification for the fact that Year 6 pupils in primary schools are funded less generously than Year 7 pupils in secondary schools. (DES, 1992)

By helping industrialists and the local economic community to recognize the needs of primary children and to appreciate the importance of equal opportunity in education they may come to see the important role that EIU has to play in building the kind of climate which promotes greater cultural understanding of the diverse nature of society. As has been stated previously, of particular importance will be the development of pupils' attitudes and assumptions which relate to EIU. In considering the development of these attitudes teachers and employers alike will need to examine their own values and attitudes and consider any bias. Through discussions along these lines they will come to appreciate the importance of adding a critical dimension to the primary child's natural curiosity.

Teachers involved in promoting EIU will need to work out what to do about the fact that Curriculum Guidance No. 4 tends to endorse a free market view of the world (Carter, 1991). There are many other factors which may need to be considered: the role of the unpaid worker in society, the importance of the caring industries are but two. It is important that children are permitted to develop a balanced and unbiased view. Teachers and industrialists need to consider how mini-enterprise ventures are handled. Should it always be the aim of a scheme to produce a profit at all costs? Some children will have parents who receive unemployment benefit. It may be valuable for children to link with an appropriate government department but this will require sensitive handling. In the same way some of the ethnic-minority children may have parents who are unemployed or alternatively in full employment in an area where many of indigenous white population are unemployed. They could then be labelled 'lazy' or, alternatively, in direct competition for the few jobs available.

Breaking down the barriers which arise through job stereotyping must be one of our main aims in this area. Forbes (1993) summarizes this as 'the Chinese are good at running take-aways; Pakistanis 'run corner shops and work all hours; Afro-Carribeans are good at sports and music; Asians all want to be dentists and lawyers, the Irish are all road-diggers and so on.' and goes on to quote the Swann report in that racial groups are said to have unrealistic expectations if they aspire outside their racial stereotypical jobs.

'Education for Economic and Industrial Understanding' needs therefore to include appropriate aspects of multicultural education. One of these aspects is the importance of raising the self-esteem of all pupils. Trips to successful industries can also include, where possible, visits to ethnic-minority businesses. Through involvement with local businesses and by asking appropriate questions children will come to appreciate that economic success can be achieved through ability and hard work but only if this is accompanied by opportunity. Children also need to see examples of people from ethnic-minority groups who are economically successful. This can be through inviting someone in to talk to the children or as part of the children's topic work. For example, a topic such as 'Textiles' could easily include all areas of the National Curriculum, core, foundation, themes and dimensions. Retail outlets studied could include silks and saris in addition to mail-order companies selling clothing; the latter will undoubtedly include workers from all cultural groups.

Brown *et al.* (1990) describe how work with some Cumbrian school children suggested that many had developed stereotypical images of Africans, believing them to be helpless, starving and waiting for western aid to 'save' them. A visitor who had lived for some time in Kenya was able to show pictures of rural houses built of local material and multistory buildings in Nairobi. They saw shambas (small cultivated plots) where people were using hand tools, and they saw large industrial concerns. This challenged the stereotypes held by many of the children. EIU and teaching for equality and justice were brought together in this session. Brown goes on to describe:

> Some of the slides showed the creativity of different communities: the beautifully polished carvings of the Kimba people; the brightly patterned sisal baskets and mats of the Kikuyu; the highly decorative bead and leather work of the Masai; and they were full of admiration for the way school children modelled human and animal figures out of banana fibre, sticks and thorns. (Brown, *et al.* 1990)

West (1991) takes this concept further with older children, who are encouraged to discuss and represent differing viewpoints and economic interests in a simulation, which involves decisions to be reached by a multinational company considering buying tobacco from Brazil. Children can easily simulate the interests of consumer and producer but what of the other parties involved: the current producers, the shipping companies, the workers on the plantations, the end users? The topic is ripe for discussion of colonial exploitation and the movement of people from one place to another in search of employment, covering a number of matters of concern to those wishing to raise pupils' awareness of and to teach for equality and justice. Materials of this sort are available from the Development Education Centre.

EIU is a cross-curricular dimension and it is unlikely to be taught as a specific element on the timetable in the primary school. Research by Webb (1993) into the implementation of Key Stage 2 of the National Curriculum confirms that there is considerable curriculum overload. Lack of time is one of the greatest challenges for the busy primary teacher and it will be necessary for the teacher to decide how to fit EIU into a crowded timetable. Webb found that in order to maintain quality of work teachers were having to make conscious decisions about what to leave out. In planning, teachers will therefore need to decide how to incorporate EIU either into a thematic or single-subject approach. Whichever way this is done, it should still be possible to use links with the local economic community as a vehicle for planning so that the other areas of the curriculum can be incorporated.

The nature of the topics chosen will be crucial to the success of the initiative as Wright (1992) shows 'topics . . . associated with ethnic minority values and cultures appear exotic, novel, unimportant, esoteric or difficult.' 'In living memory' was a topic which built upon previous work on 'the second world war' by Short and Carrington (1992) with children in a school in the north-east of England. One of its aims was to expose the myth of immigration as a cause of unemployment. 'The children were informed, with the aid of archive photographs, of London Transport's recruitment drive in the West Indies. The children were then asked to design a "Welcome to Britain" poster themselves.'

Further examples of how EIU can provide a vehicle for planning can be seen in the Wigan LEA 'Language at Work Project' and other SCIP initiatives. Some of these industrial visits have led to children setting up their own mini-enterprise schemes where the children are involved in planning, market research, raising capital, organizing production, advertising and selling a product. Some teachers do not feel happy with such a scheme because it focuses on the need to make a profit and oversimplifies some of the issues: but it can provide experience to develop EIU. An excellent outline of how Birchen Coppice Middle School in Kidderminster devoted a whole week to EIU describes a strategy that any primary school could readily adapt to suit its own circumstances (O'Connor, 1993).

Every school will have access through the Education Business Partnership scheme to an officer who can help them to set up an appropriate link between the school and the economic community. Many LEAs have advisory teachers who have considerable experience of helping teachers to incorporate EIU into the curriculum.

Sometimes links can be established through a parent or a school governor and this can lead to a partnership. To ensure progression and continuity, the school will need to consider the production of a policy document for EIU and how assessment can be addressed. If a class is to make a visit once a year, which is to contribute to the children's EIU, then this needs to be recorded and there may be the need to re-visit at a later stage in order to build upon previous experience. Included in the school's policy document should be a reference to the relationship between multicultural education and EIU. Such a policy may not be in place at the moment because of the demands made through the introduction of the core and foundation subjects but it could be considered as part of the school's development plan. Like all policy documents it will need to be produced with full consultation of all the staff in the school so that many of the issues surrounding EIU discussed in this chapter may be considered.

One of the most important aspects of children's development of EIU in children is the importance of allowing them to question openly those in the economic community. EIU is concerned with developing the kind of critical awareness which enables children to consider what is fair and unfair in business. Although teachers will be involved with encouraging children to ask appropriate questions, it is important that the questions come from the children themselves. Young children will ask very searching questions and it is important that they be given the opportunity so to do.

Through studying economic activity at home and abroad children can begin to understand how often interests are in conflict when decisions are made. The relationship between EIU and development education is an important one. Pike and Pointon (1991) reiterate that 'Economic awareness can only be partial, . . . unless it is clearly understood that all of us are part of a global economic system.' The impact of development education on society as a whole is beginning to take effect. Children's television programmes are much more conscious of the need to focus on the successful development of the poorer countries rather than portraying the Third World countries in a patronizing way. Through studying developing countries and the economic activity that takes place in them, children, through questioning, will come to understand why people move and migration occurs. They can also become aware of the difficulties involved and the opportunities presented by such movement to both the host and immigrant communities.

Although it is possible to make visits into the local economic community this obviously becomes impossible for practical reasons when studying economies abroad. Here the use of photographs and videos becomes invaluable in taking children beyond the range of their own lives and experiences, their commonly held attitudes and understandings but these photographs and videos must be used with discretion. Although the camera cannot lie in that it accurately records the image it cannot accurately record the context in which it was taken. Children must be encouraged to ask 'Why was this photograph taken?' and in this way they themselves will learn to challenge stereotypes. It is important to provide positive images of 'workers' but even more important to provide children with the skills needed to be critically aware of how issues of race and culture affect those issues surrounding economics and the world of work.

Throughout this chapter we have attempted to highlight ways in which EIU can be used to enrich the whole education and the lives of children. It can be seen that, through the EIU curriculum, there are opportunities for children to ask questions and develop a critical awareness of such issues as race, culture and social justice. Teachers and student teachers need to be made aware of ways in which this may be achieved. It is very important that these issues are addressed in order that the adults of the future will have the means of dealing critically and constructively with the problems and issues of to-morrow's world.

References

ALEXANDER, R., ROSE, J. and WOODHEAD, C. (1992) *Curriculum Organisation and Classroom Practice in Primary schools*, London, HMSO.

BAKER, K. (1987) 'Speech to the Annual Conservative Party Conference', Blackpool, 7 October.

BLYTH, A. (1984) 'Industry Education: Case Studies from the North West; in JAMIESON, I.M. (1984) *We make Kettles: Studying Industry in the Primary School*, London, Longman.

BLYTH, A. (1990) 'Social Demands and Schools' Responses' in PROCTOR, N. (Ed) (1990) *The Aims of Primary Education and the National Curriculum*, London, The Falmer Press.

BROWN, C., BARNFIELD, J. and STONE, M. (1990) *Spanner in the Works*, Stoke, Trentham Books.

BURGESS-MACEY, C. (1992) 'Tackling racism and sexism in the primary classroom', in GILL, D., MAYOR, B. and BLAIR, M. (Eds) *Racism and Education — Structures and Strategies*, London, Sage, pp. 269–84.

CARTER, R. (1991) 'A Matter of Values; A review of Curriculum Guidance 4: Education for Economic and Industrial Understanding', in NCC (1990) *Teaching Geography*, January 1991.

DEPARTMENT OF EDUCATION AND SCIENCE (1985) *Report on Economic Understanding*, London, HMSO.

DEPARTMENT OF EDUCATION AND SCIENCE (1985) *Report of the National Committee of Inquiry into the Education of Children from Ethnic Minority Groups* (The Swann Report), London, HMSO.

FORBES, A. (1993) 'Economic and Industrial Understanding', in VERMA, G.K. and PUMFREY, P.D. (Eds) *Cultural Diversity and the Curriculum, Vol. 2, Cross Curricular Contexts, Themes and Dimensions in Secondary Schools*, London, The Falmer Press.

GREER, J. (1991) 'What's in a cup of coffee?' *Economic Awareness*, 3, 3 May, pp. 20–3.

HARRISON, M. (1992) 'Review of EATE investigation into the EIU and background of primary student teachers in training', *Economic Awareness*, 5, 1 September, pp. 30–1.

HARDY, J. and VIELER-PORTER, C. (1992) 'Race, schooling and the 1988 Education Reform Act', in GILL, D., MAYOR, B. and BLAIR, M. (Eds) *Racism and Education — Structures and Strategies*, London, Sage publications, pp. 101–14.

MERCER, D. (1988) 'Economic Awareness in the Primary School', *Education*, 3, 13 March.

NATIONAL CURRICULUM COUNCIL (1990) *Curriculum Guidance No. 4*, York, NCC.

O'CONNOR, M. (1993) 'A buzzing hive of Industry, *Times Educational Supplement*, 29 October, p. 4.

PIKE, G. and POINTON, P. (1991) 'A global approach to economic awareness: Curriculum Guidance Reinterpreted', *Economic Awareness*, September.

RAMSAY, M. and SIVORI, A. (1992) 'Economic and Industrial Understanding: A Cross Curricular Theme', Manchester, Manchester LEA.

ROBERTS, R.J. and DOLAN, J. (1989) 'Children's Perceptions of "Work" — an exploratory study', *Educational Review*, 41, 1, pp. 19–28.

SARUP, M. (1982) *Education, State and Crisis*, London, Routledge and Keegan Paul.

SCHOOL CURRICULUM DEVELOPMENT COMMITTEE (1986) *Consultative Conference on Economic Awareness*, July.

SHORT, G. and CARRINGTON, B. (1992) 'Towards an antiracist initiative in the all white primary school: a case study', in GILL, D., MAYOR, B. and BLAIR, M. (Eds) *Racism and Education — Structures and strategies*, London, Sage publications. pp. 253–69.

SMITH, D. (Ed) (1988) *Industry in the Primary School Curriculum*, London, The Falmer Press.

TOMLINSON, S. (1989) 'Education and Training', *New Community*, 15, 3, pp. 461–9.

TROYNA, B. and CARRINGTON, B. (1990) *Education, Racism and Reform*, London, Routledge.

VERMA, G. (1989) *Education for All: A landmark in pluralism*, London, The Falmer Press.

WEBB, R. (1993) *Eating the Elephant Bit by Bit: The National Curriculum at Key Stage 2*, London, ATL.

WEST, N. (1991) 'Economics for Change: A development Education Perspective on Economic Awareness', in *Economic Awareness*, May.

WRIGHT, C. (1992) 'Early Education: multicultural primary school classrooms', in GILL, D., MAYOR, B. and BLAIR, M. (Eds) *Racism and Education — Structures and Strategies*, London, Sage publications.

Resources

Images of Africa Development Education Project, c/o Manchester Metropolitan University, 801 Wilmslow Road, M20 8RG.

SCIP/MESP, School Curriculum Industry Partnership, /Mini Enterprise in School, Centre for Education and Industry, University of Warwick, Westwood Site, Coventry CV47AL.

EcATT (Economic Awareness Teacher Training Programme), University of Manchester, Oxford Road, Manchester, M13 9PL.

Chapter 4

Careers Education and Guidance: Pastoral Care and Career Needs

Jo Jolliffe and Pushpa Jhingan

Context

Not many would disagree that the process and quality of nurturing has a great influence upon the building of a child's character and its future. Section 1 of the Education Reform Act 1988 (ERA) places a statutory responsibility upon schools to provide a balanced and broadly based curriculum which:

- promotes the spiritual, moral, cultural, mental and physical development of pupils at the school and of society, and
- prepares such pupils for the opportunities, responsibilities and experiences of adult life. (DES, 1988)

The integration of the knowledge, skills and attitudes in the foundation subjects and the cross-curricular aspects of the National Curriculum clearly demonstrate the importance placed upon the development of the whole child. If the aim of the school is to prepare the child for adult life, pastoral care and careers guidance must remain a central concern of the whole-school curriculum. It is essential to remember that a school is a community in which children live, learn and grow into individuals who can achieve and participate in a pluralist democracy.

Careers Education and Guidance is described by the National Curriculum Council (1990) as one of the five cross-curricular themes, the other four being:

- economic and industrial understanding;
- education for citizenship;
- health education; and
- environmental education.

Careers education and guidance is a vital part of the individual pupil's curriculum entitlement which should help pupils to:

- know themselves better;
- be aware of education, training and career opportunities;
- make choices about their own continuing education and training, and about career paths; and
- manage transitions to new roles and situations.

At Key Stages 1 and 2, these aims should promote the development of four 'strands': 'self', 'roles', 'work', 'transition' (The fifth strand, 'career', is developed in Key Stages 3 and 4). At Key Stage 1 when children are becoming aware of work through the family, media and their environment, 'Careers Education and Guidance' should help pupils to:

- begin to form impressions about themselves (self);
- develop and describe ideas about roles at work (roles);
- develop and describe ideas about work (work); and
- begin to appreciate the nature of change (transition).

At Key Stage 2 when children's awareness of adults and their work is expanding, 'Careers Education and Guidance' should focus on:

- increasing self-awareness and forming ideas about personal preferences (self);
- extending understanding about the variety of work roles and their interrelationships (roles);
- exploring various kinds of work, identifying feelings about work, carrying out simple classifications of categories of work (work);
- preparing pupils for changes brought about by moving to a new school (transition).

The DES/DoE report 'Working together for a better future' (1987) required Local Education Authorities to produce policy statements, and schools to develop their own policy statements in response. These should be based on the NCC stated aims and should: 'Challenge stereotyped attitudes to education, training and career opportunities.' (NCC, 1990).

The NCC guidance (1990) sees the planning process as a key feature in ensuring that appropriate careers education and guidance is provided, within the subjects of the National Curriculum and whole-school curriculum. It also advises that this:

Will mean giving consideration, on an individual basis, to pupils with ethnic minority backgrounds and to those who are bilingual. Careers education and guidance should promote equal opportunities and help pupils to overcome both the overt and subtle barriers which may be encountered as they progress through school and into adult working life. (NCC, 1990)

It is worth recalling that, much earlier, the Rampton report had signalled that appropriate, quality pastoral and careers guidance is most important in combating these inequalities *at an early stage.*

> Careers education begins when a child enters school through the mes-
> sages given consciously and subconsciously by teachers and others
> and the materials used. Primary and secondary schools in their early
> years have an important contribution to make in arousing interest in
> and awareness of occupations. (DES, 1981)

The cross-curricular approach to pastoral care (a dimension) and career guidance (a theme) can be used by teachers to enhance the school curriculum and make it more sensitive to the needs of all children. Yet Marland (1989) and McIntyre (1990) found that there was widespread neglect in schools of issues concerning pastoral care and ethnic-minority children.

In an analysis of ethnic groups by age and population, a report by the Policy Studies Institute shows a growing young ethnic-minority population (Jones, 1993). Whilst 34 per cent of ethnic minorities are aged under 15 years, only 19 per cent of the white population are in the same age group. The report shows that the rate of unemployment amongst the ethnic-minority population is much higher than that of the white population and 'it is a salient feature in many societies that as unemployment increases, ethnic minorities suffer disproportionately' (Mallick, 1993). In the present economic recession when ethnic-minority children are witnessing the effects of unemployment and low paid jobs, they are inadvertently receiving stereotyped images projected by the media and are suffering from a lack of positive role models.

Jones (1993) argues that 'it is likely that a part of the disadvantage faced by racial minorities in Britain is related to their education.' His report also found that 'within the ethnic minority population, there is an increasing disparity between the circumstances of specific groups.' The statistical evidence based on the 1991 census evidence that the Asian population contains both the most and least successful of the ethnic-minority groups studied.

In order to participate in the learning process and benefit from the whole-school curriculum, children need to be in a relaxed, stress-free and supportive environment within which they can achieve educationally and develop their full potential. Effective pastoral care and careers guidance needs to take into account all that happens to the child both in and out of the primary school. The local community and the ethnic-minority community to which the child belongs give messages about job roles and potential success (or lack of success) with which he/she can identify.

The issue is then not merely one of recognition of the needs of ethnic-minority children, but the understanding, willingness and ability to meet them along with the needs of other children. Yet, ethnic-minority children brought up and living in a linguistic and cultural environment different from that of their home, in an atmosphere of overt and covert discrimination, have very specific additional needs which are not always understood by schools that do not share either their language, culture or traditions (DES, 1985; Duncan, 1988). The many linkages between EIU and this chapter underlines the importance of project work in relation to cross-curricular elements (see Chapter 3).

Challenges

Ethnic-minority pupils not only have the same pastoral and career needs as all children in British schools, they require care which takes into account the racist nature of the society in which they live and must succeed.

> Careers education and guidance should promote equal opportunities and help pupils to overcome both overt and subtle barriers which may be encountered as they progress through school and into adult life. (NCC, 1990).

In the primary school, unlike the secondary school where personal and social education and careers guidance may be more structured, it is essential to integrate fully pastoral and careers education into the curriculum.

> Schools in the 3–11 phase are increasingly developing excellent education and industry and world of work based projects — usually linked to class or whole school themes, their own general school's objectives and the National Curriculum. How they relate to appropriate Careers Education and its relevance to their pupils is less clear. (Rogers and Wickham, 1991)

Rogers and Wickham (1991) point out that guidance on Careers Education and Guidance from HMI (1988) and the National Curriculum Council (1990) fails to provide teachers with details on issues of major importance such as policy, methodology, structures and equal opportunities.

If schools are to adopt a whole-school approach to pastoral and careers education, then it is important that the whole-school curriculum, including the 'hidden curriculum', values each child and his/her cultural and linguistic heritage. Yet, there is a commonly held view that the school curriculum does not always represent all cultures positively or equally. 'A major concern about curriculum practice, at present, is that it presents people, places and things of white European stock as superior to all else' (Duncan, 1988). If this Eurocentric curriculum does exist, then the pastoral and careers guidance offered to ethnic-minority pupils in schools in the context of the whole-school curriculum cannot adequately prepare them for their active participation in the social and economic future of this country.

The Swann report (DES, 1985) found that many schools failed their pupils in preparing them for their future in a multiracial society. If a major function of education is to induct children into society, through the whole-school curriculum and in particular through the National Curriculum, then a largely Eurocentric curriculum will not provide all pupils with the necessary positive images and sense of belongings. Internalization of negative stereotypes of black and ethnic-minority people in books and other resources is not conducive to good pastoral care and careers guidance. As a consequence, many black and ethnic-minority pupils will be prevented from accessing higher education and career opportunities which give greater economic power and social mobility.

The Swann Report (DES, 1985) as well as the Macdonald Report (1989) produced evidence of the deep-seated prejudices encountered by black and ethnic-minority pupils both in and out of school. Discrimination operates at many levels both consciously and unconsciously and is instigated by adults and other children alike. Indeed, 'by the time they are of nursery school age, children know many ways in which they can hurt others' (Tattum and Lane, 1989). Kelly's study of racism in schools (1989) found that it is not just in the classroom that children can feel vulnerable, but also in the corridors, the playground and outside of the school gates, where they experience bullying, threats and racism. Tattum and Lane (1989) argue strongly that 'children have a basic right to freedom from pain, humiliation and fear, whether caused by adults or other children.' This is a challenge which schools must deal with. A recent study of racism in mainly white primary schools has demonstrated the various and damaging ways in which racist name calling takes place (Troyna and Hatcher, 1992). The effects on the self-image of the victims, including any nascent notions of what a child is likely to do 'when I'm bigger' are more likely to be restricted than expanded by such experiences.

In view of this and a wealth of other evidence demonstrating that even very young ethnic-minority children must overcome barriers in order to succeed, one might have expected the National Curriculum to take more positive action in ensuring the delivery of a more culturally and linguistically appropriate curriculum. However, there is little evidence currently to suggest that the plural nature of our society is adequately reflected in the National Curriculum. 'Contained therein is a Eurocentric concept of a static Anglo-Saxon culture which no longer exists. It does not merely disseminate the dominant ideologies but projects and legitimizes white superiority' (Verma, 1990). Verma argues that the concept of identity is 'crucial in one's life'. It is therefore a responsibility of the school to present black and ethnic-minority people in a positive way. The ethos and practices of a school are therefore central if the child is to be presented with positive reinforcement through role models as well as the whole-school curriculum. In reality there is an under-representation of black and ethnic-minority teachers and other black professionals (Jones, 1993). The absence of positive role models in a child's formative years can be particularly damaging and may lead to low self-expectation, restricting personal and career ambition.

The role models seen by primary-school pupils in their experiences both at school and in the wider society are potent forces that can either inhibit or promote occupational awareness and aspirations, even at the earliest stage of education. Many primary schools arrange visits to enable pupils to observe, meet and talk with workers engaged in a range of occupations. Demographically, many occupations are dominated by the numerically larger non-immigrant group. This is even more marked in high-status occupation groups.

What subconscious messages do such scenarios convey? Put crudely, if black people are only seen in unskilled semi-labelled occupations, what messages does this give to all pupils? The primary-school teacher needs to be sensitive to such issues and to ensure that pupils appreciate that occupations are not necessarily the preserve of any particular ethnic or cultural group.

It is of vital importance to the well-being of young children that their school experience is one which is not totally alien from their home background. Many ethnic-minority children are confronted by an unfamiliar environment, a language foreign to their own, teachers who generally come from a different culture, and a curriculum which may not take account of their experiences. All young children on first entering school can encounter difficult experiences. For ethnic-minority children these experiences can be even more traumatic since they will face additional transition problems. For instance, a child who is a competent user of the mother tongue may be faced with the need to use English not just for general communication but also for conceptual development, participating in the learning of core and foundation subjects and being assessed in the language he/she is in the process of acquiring often a language in which he/she cannot fully demonstrate his/her capabilities and intelligence.

Some ethnic-minority children from refugee groups will have encountered emotional stress before arriving in Britain from countries with civil unrest, wars or other natural calamities. Their need to build confidence in themselves and trust in other humans will be different from those of children whose parents and grandparents have lived in this country for a long period of time but who nevertheless are still suffering from the effects of racism.

Any parent or carer would rightly expect schools to provide a stress-free and nurturing environment for their child. Although the ERA (1988) has increased parental power it has not in reality encouraged greater participation of ethnic-minority parents, who are still reluctant to become involved in the life of the school (Ranger, 1988). This prevents them from working as full partners in the education and welfare of their child.

That minority ethnic-group primary-school pupils, their parents and teachers should see members of such groups as active in all occupations and activities is essential if stereotyped occupational and career aspirations and expectations are not to be reinforced. The example of encouraging members of minority ethnic groups to take active roles in the governing bodies of schools is but one promising practice that can be extended (see Chapter 2 for details). The same principle applies to membership of the teaching profession where members of minority ethnic groups are underrepresented.

Section 11 of the 1966 Local Government Act acknowledged the cultural and linguistic differences of black and ethnic-minority communities and became a mechanism for directing additional support at ethnic-minority children of New Commonwealth heritage. Many local authorities and schools failed until recently to properly use funding to address specific needs (Bagley, 1992). Whilst English as a Second Language was an obvious area of support through Section 11 funding, the needs of ethnic-minority pupils beyond that of language were not tackled (Duncan, 1988). As mentioned earlier, the school-age ethnic-minority population is increasing yet the government intends reducing Section 11 staff, reducing specialist support to ethnic-minority children. This will inevitably place greater demands on mainstream staff. The National Curriculum's 'acknowledgment' of the needs of ethnic-minority children assumes an expertise amongst all teachers for dealing with children from a wide variety of cultural and linguistic backgrounds. If teachers are to guide children towards extending and fulfilling their potential as valued and useful members of society then they must be suitably prepared. Many teachers are, in fact, ill-prepared for catering for the pastoral and career needs of ethnic-minority children (Committee of Inquiry, 1985; Duncan, 1988). It is too often only due to personal commitment or the presence of ethnic-minority staff that some schools come close to understanding and responding to the specific needs of ethnic-minority pupils. Teacher education must take fully into account the needs of a changing population (see Chapter 14).

If the pastoral and career needs of young ethnic-minority pupils are to be met, it is important that schools give careful thought to the planning of the whole-school curriculum, to the values and behaviours fostered and to the caring practices. The school, its practices, structures and procedures must all be free of racism in order to establish a secure and happy environment in which ethnic-minority pupils and their peers from the white majority group can develop. Assessment procedures, teaching methods, home–school relationships, classroom organization, staffing and materials are all important factors which need consideration. Should we fail to meet the pastoral as well as academic needs of children in our schools, we shall have also ensured that there is unequal access to career opportunities and economic power, thus maintaining rather than removing the existing racial inequalities in our so-called plural society.

Responses

As already argued, the pastoral care and career needs of primary-age children must permeate the whole-school curriculum and its practices. A school which cares for *all* its children cares for *each one*, taking into account all he/she brings to the school, thereby enriching its racial, cultural and linguistic make up. It is vital that school managers, together with support from governing bodies, provide the necessary leadership, ensuring that equal value is placed on each child, and that the school is a welcoming place, not just for the first visit, but for every day of the child's life in school. The vision is needed if the reality of practice is to improve.

If 'Pastoral Care and Careers Education and Guidance' are to be integral to the whole-school curriculum an agreed school policy should be the starting point. Rogers and Wickham (1991) include a Manchester policy statement on careers education and guidance. Governors, headteacher, teaching staff, support staff, parents/carers and children should be involved in the negotiation of the policy. School policies on pastoral care and careers education and guidance should include issues relating to language, profiling, equal opportunity, bullying, resources, staffing, school environment, home–school partnership and community links. Clear procedures should be included and communicated to all concerned.

In the USA many school systems equivalent to our LEAs have specially developed careers programmes that are designated as 'K-12'; they cover the age range from kindergarten to 18 years. These curricula accept the continuities and discontinuities in the development of pupils' awareness, knowledge and understanding of the occupational opportunities available in a community and society. The programmes are designed on the basis of well-developed theories of career development and consequently are not narrowly concentrated on occupations alone. The issues of cultural diversity are not neglected in such schemes. This area of the curriculum is less well-developed in the UK, but has been given a considerable boost by the inclusion in the National Curriculum of the cross-curricular theme of 'Careers Education and Guidance'.

During the pre-school and early years, children are learning from all that is around them; their home, family, neighbourhood, wider environment and media, especially television. Their knowledge and ideas of the world of work are developing through their immediate contacts and experiences. By Key Stage 2 their awareness of work is expanding. They become aware that work can be paid or voluntary, have some appreciation of job roles and their usefulness to the community. They may also classify work such as jobs involving people or machines and have some ideas of what they would like to do.

Carefully selected multicultural books, posters and other teaching materials should represent people from all races and cultures in roles which make an important contribution to society. Since there is a dearth of resources appropriate for careers education in a multicultural society at Key Stages 1 and 2, teachers will need to adopt a multicultural approach to topic-based career work. See Hessari and Hill (1989) for some practical ideas into which careers education might be integrated. Rogers and Wickham (1991) make numerous valuable and tested suggestions for developing 'Careers Education and Guidance' with an equal-opportunities perspective which can readily be integrated into the primary-school curriculum.

The work by the City of Manchester in developing cross-curricular materials and methods in careers education, as part of implementing the whole curriculum, has been mentioned above (Rogers and Wickham, ibid.). A few details of its genesis and content underlines its value as a K-12 programme. The development team comprised a core of seven workers and involved a further forty-five professionals. It involved thirty-three educational institutions including infant schools, special schools and high schools. The Manchester Careers Service, the Education Development Service and the City's Inspection and Advisory Service also collaborated in the project. The provision of examples of work done in schools of all types is particularly helpful. These include the following:

- a whole-school primary project — Miles Platting at work;
- a whole-school infant project — Music and the world of work;
- Manchester City Football Club — A world of work; and
- Metrolink Manchester: A junior-school project.

The localized context of three of these reflect the reality of primary schools capitalizing on community resources in a multicultural city.

The primary-school teacher needs to be aware of, and exploit, opportunities in the National Curriculum for encouraging positive self-identity in all children, particularly those from ethnic minorities. Visits, stories, songs, poems and role-play can all be used to develop language, extend ideas and promote equal opportunities in a pluralist society. Through carefully guided role-play, interaction in school with positive role models and a sense of belonging in an environment which recognizes that black and ethnic-minority people can and do play important roles in the socio-economic life of the country, they will be better able to recognize their own skills, strengths and abilities.

It is not possible for any one person fully to understand and appreciate the values, attitudes, beliefs and patterns of behaviour of all cultural and religious backgrounds in depth. Teachers need to be *aware* that within each group of people there is individuality and that no culture is static. The daily experience of the primary-school teacher is a continuing contact with a vast range of inter and intra-individual differences between pupils and groups. Recognizing such differences is a first step in using them constructively in all aspects of the curriculum including the early stages of careers education. Although knowledge of the cultural backgrounds of children is important, it is the consciousness of the dangers of cultural and religious stereotyping which is crucial. It is a responsibility of schools to combat negative stereotyping and combat low expectation, and to promote instead a healthy self-esteem amongst black and ethnic-minority pupils. Appropriate teaching and other resources, classroom organization and management, as well as continued curriculum and staff development, all need consideration if black and ethnic-minority children are to succeed academically and 'make choices about their own continuing education and training, and about their career paths' (NCC, 1990).

Commitment to being involved in a caring, multiracial school in which the children are participating as fully as possible in the whole life of the school includes a willingness to confront issues such as racist bullying preferably before it becomes an established source of conflict or of discomfort. A planned and well-managed whole-school response can be made. It is important that all staff in the school, including lunchtime supervisors, secretaries and other support staff understand and are involved in implementing school policies concerning the welfare of all children. Children, parents and community all need to have confidence in the school's ability and willingness to respond effectively. Strategies and case-studies are given in Tattum (1993). An effective communication system needs to be established and reviewed and information relevant to the school's policy and practice should be easily accessible to all participants in the life and activities of the school.

If the child is to feel comfortable in the school environment, a positive home–school relationship can help secure this sense of belonging. The onus is now on schools to develop stronger links with the home and encourage parental participation. (see Chapter 2 concerning governing bodies of schools). Some schools already operate systems to ensure the involvement of parents and other community members and value their special contribution to the children's education. The employment of bilingual and other ethnic-minority staff to whom parents and children can easily relate is a positive measure and can facilitate communication. The proposed cuts to Section 11 funding will inevitably have an impact on the level of specialist and bilingual support in schools (see Appendix 3). The headteacher, governors and staff will therefore need to review staffing and other policies in order to make mainstream more responsive to the needs of ethnic minorities. The Scarman report (1981) found there was a need for teacher training which meets the cultural needs and expectations of children and parents from black and ethnic minorities. This need continues in the 1990s (see Chapters 2 and 15). However, through ongoing staff development and a genuine partnership with all parents, teachers may move closer towards dealing with the pastoral and career needs of a range of pupils from a variety of backgrounds (Rogers and Wickham, 1991).

In order to begin understanding the individual differences and specific needs of the child, schools need to maintain records which help build a positive pupil profile with full parental involvement. Important information in the profile might include the child's personal name and its pronunciation (not all children have 'Christian names'); religion (possibly including degree of observance); special dietary needs; the child's first language; the parents' first language; languages spoken at home; attendance at supplementary school etc. This record should form the basis of an unbiased, unprejudiced profile of the child and his/her achievements. The child and the parents'/carers' participating in the process will increase self-awareness, encourage decision-making and help manage transition.

Teachers or instructors from the same cultural and linguistic backgrounds as the children can provide other staff with additional information and different perceptions of the child which contribute to the overall pastoral care, and careers guidance. Their presence and skills also enable more holistic observation and assessment of the child. Initial and ongoing assessment of the child's progress can be seriously hampered by insufficient knowledge of a child's cultural, religious or linguistic background. Good bilingual assessment helps differentiate between learning difficulty and linguistic need.

> A child is not to be taken as having a learning difficulty solely because of the language (or form of the language) in which he is, or will be taught is different from a language (or form of a language) which has at any time been spoken in his home. (DES, 1981).

Given the crucial role that testing and assessment now plays in the National Curriculum both in terms of academic achievement and ultimately in career opportunity and success, it is surprising, particularly since the majority of teachers are white, European and monolingual, that any degree of accuracy can be assumed through existing tests and testing procedures. This can only serve to create further disadvantage unless the limitations of such procedures are born in mind when they are used.

Children should be positively encouraged to use their first language. This not only makes them feel valued and stress-free but the use of first language for conceptual development, problem-solving and assessment enhances achievement and consequential motivation. Age-related dual-language texts and other resources which reflect the language and culture of the child can make an important contribution towards the development of self-identity, since separation of language from culture can in itself be problematic. An excellent source of materials and considerations enabling teachers help bilingual pupils overcome difficulties in relation to the National Curriculum has been developed by a team involved in this work (see Appendix 2 for details of Access to Information on Multicultural Educational Resources AIMER).

Ethnic-minority parents, like any other parents, are interested in the welfare, education, achievement and careers education of their children. Schools need to understand their aspirations, views and frustrations on the one hand and value their skills, expertise and contributions on the other, in order to work with them as partners for the benefit of the children and as valued members of the community. If there is reluctance on the part of parents to visit school and fully participate in their children's education and welfare, the reasons need to be investigated and addressed. Parents and other community members can act as positive role models and can make a useful contribution through reading or telling stories, participating in classroom and other school activities and sharing experiences. Inviting parents to talk about their work requires careful negotiations and preparation by all involved, but can increase pupils' awareness of occupations in society. Communications between home and school, both verbal and written are most effective if carried out in the home language. Schools need to be aware that some parents or carers may not be literate in their first language in which case other strategies for communication with parents need to be considered. If bilingual staff are not available then the school needs to consider other ways of obtaining translations of letters to parents or enabling verbal communication with the school through

Table 4.1: Careers Education and Guidance: Pastoral Care and Career Needs in the Primary School

Challenges	Responses
Integrating pastoral and careers education for a plural society into the whole-school curriculum	• Leadership from headteacher, governors • Whole-school policy evolved through consultation process • Partnership with S11 staff
Valuing the cultural and linguistic heritage of all pupils	• Review staffing policy • Bilingual/multilingual staff • Welcoming environment • Dual language books • Multicultural books, posters and other resources • Communications with parents in home language where appropriate • Partnership with S11 staff
Tackling overt and covert racism and other prejudices	• School policy on racism and bullying jointly agreed and including clear procedures communicated to all staff, parents/carers and pupils alike • Willingness to deal effectively with racism, other prejudices and bullying
Creating a caring and responsive ethos and practices	• Consulting and involving everyone caring for the child • Staff development • Awareness raising (languages, culture, religion) • Partnership with S11 staff • Multicultural and Multilingual resources
Facilitating transition from home to school	• Awareness of cultural and linguistic difficulties encountered by children from minority groups • Use of mother tongue • Partnership with parents • Role models • Creating an environment which is friendly to pupils from all backgrounds • Presence of staff from some linguistic and cultural backgrounds as pupils • Partnership with S11 staff
Establishing and developing home–school partnership	• Review staffing policy • Request specific S11 support to help develop home–school links • Role models • Mainstream S11 practices • Community links • Communication with parents/carers where appropriate in mother tongue
Adapting initial teacher training and continued professional development in a plural society	• Raise awareness of all staff • Review school staffing policy • Take account of plural nature of society (including population changes) in planning staff development programme • Use community resources including making contact with supplementary school staff

the presence of a skilled translator. In the absence of bilingual staff, schools often resort to using bilingual children or friends to help communicate between home and school whilst a few local authorities have central professional translation and interpretation services.

Many ethnic-minority communities have supplementary or alternative schools staffed by volunteers from the community. They determine their own curriculum, often in response to perceived inadequacies of mainstream schooling such as lack of provision of mother-tongue teaching. These schools typically provide a valuable service to their communities helping its cohesion and continuity. They are also concerned, as are mainstream schools, with the achievement and welfare of children from their respective communities. Sadly, many mainstream schools do not know which of their pupils attend supplementary schools and often fail to make what might be valuable and productive links. For instance, supplementary-school staff can be a valuable community resource, who can support the children's learning, help liaise with the home and provide cultural information and advice (DES, 1985).

It is interesting to note that, under the new Home Office Section 11 guidelines (1990), bids which fell within the stated policy area of pastoral care, careers guidance and other applications to provide special support to ethnic-minority pupils in school were invited. LARRIE (1992) reported in its survey of Section 11 funded projects that nineteen LEA bids for careers guidance were accepted. This indicates that Section 11 provision is no longer seen simply in the narrower context of English as a Second Language and is now being used to respond to the pastoral and careers needs of ethnic-minority children. Rogers and Wickham (1991) make some useful suggestions for cross-curricular development of pastoral and careers development which can be used by mainstream and Section 11 staff alike.

In conclusion, pastoral, and careers education in the primary school needs to permeate the whole-school curriculum, adjusting to respond to the social and economic reality of life in a plural society. There needs to be greater sensitivity and awareness in every aspect of school policy and practice and in developing responses which specifically and adequately address the needs of all children. The delivery of the cross-curricular aspects of the National Curriculum, should be met with due regard to the cultural and linguistic needs of individual children and with the full participation of parents. Only then can primary-age children begin the long path towards extending and achieving their potential and ultimately becoming participants in a truly plural and democratic society.

References

BAGLEY, C.A. (1992) *Back to the Future-Section 11 of the Local Government Act 1966: LEAs and multicultural/anti-racist education*, Slough, NFER.

BAKER, C. (1993) *Foundations of Bilingual Education and Bilingualism*, Avon, Multilingual Matters.

CENTRAL ADVISORY COUNCIL FOR EDUCATION (1967) *Children and Their Primary Schools*, Vol. 1 (The Plowden Report), London, HMSO.

CLINE, A. and FREDERICKSON, N. (1991) *Learning Resource Materials — Bilingual Pupils and the National Curriculum: Overcoming Difficulties in Teaching and Learning*, London, University College.

COMMITTEE OF INQUIRY (1985) *Education for All: The Report of the Committee of Inquiry into the Education of Children from Ethnic Minority Groups*, London, HMSO.

CRAFT, C. (1993) 'Teacher Education in a Multicultural Society', in VERMA, G.K. (Ed) *Education for All: A Landmark for Pluralism*, London, The Falmer Press.

DEPARTMENT OF EDUCATION AND SCIENCE (1981) *Education Act 1981*, London, HMSO.

DEPARTMENT OF EDUCATION AND SCIENCE (1981) *West Indian Children in our Schools: Interim Report of the Committee of Inquiry into the Education of Children from Ethnic Minority Groups* (The Rampton Report), London, HMSO.

DEPARTMENT OF EDUCATION AND SCIENCE (1985) *Education for All: Report of the Committee of Inquiry into the Education of Children From Ethnic Minority Groups (The Swann Report)*, Cmnd. 9453, London, HMSO.

DEPARTMENT OF EDUCATION AND SCIENCE (1988) *Education Reform Act 1988*, London, HMSO.

DEPARTMENT OF EDUCATION AND SCIENCE (1989) *National Curriculum Council, Curriculum Circular Number 6*, London, HMSO.

DEPARTMENT OF EDUCATION AND SCIENCE (1989) *National Curriculum: From Policy to Practice*, London, DES.

DEPARTMENT OF EDUCATION AND SCIENCE (1990) *National Curriculum Guidance Council, The Whole Curriculum Number 3*, London, HMSO.

DEPARTMENT OF EDUCATION AND SCIENCE AND DEPARTMENT OF EMPLOYMENT (1987) *Working Together for a Better Future*, London, HMSO.

DUNCAN, C. (1988) *Pastoral Care: An Anti-Racist / Multi-Cultural Perspective*, London, Blackwell.

EGGLESTON, J. (1993) 'Educating Teachers to combat Inequality', in VERMA, G.K. (Ed) *Inequality and Teacher Education-an International Perspective*, London, The Falmer Press.

FIGUEROA, P. (1991) *Education and the Social Construction of Race*, London, Routledge.

HER MAJESTY'S INSPECTORATE (1988) *Curriculum Matters 10: Education and Guidance 5–16*, HMSO.

HESSARI, R. and HILL, D. (1989) *Practical Ideas for Multi-cultural Learning and Teaching in the Primary Classroom*, Routledge.

HOME OFFICE (1989) *A Scrutiny of Grants under Section 11 of the Local Government Act. Final Report*, December 1988, London, Home Office.

HOME OFFICE (1990) *Section 11 Ethnic Minority Grants. Grant Administration: Policy and Guidelines*, London, Home Office.

JONES, T. (1993) *Britain's Ethnic Minorities*, London, Policy Studies Institute.

KELLY, E. (1988) *Racism in Schools: New Research Evidence*, London, Trentham.

LOCAL AUTHORITIES RACE RELATIONS INFORMATION EXCHANGE (LARRIE) (1992) *Guide to Section 11 funding, the 1992/93 Section 11 Allocation*, LARRIE Research Report Number 3, London.

MacDonald, I. (1989) *Murder in the Playground (The Burnage Report): a report into the Macdonald Inquiry into Racism and Racial Violence in Manchester Schools*, London, Longsight Press.

Mallick, K. (1993) 'Careers Education and Guidance', in Verma, G.K. and Pumfrey, P.D. (Eds) *Cultural Diversity and the Curriculum, Vol. 2 — Cross Curricular Contexts: Themes and Dimensions in Secondary Schools*, London, The Falmer Press.

Manchester City Council Education Department (1991) *5–16 Curriculum for Manchester Schools*, Careers and Occupational Information Centre.

Marland, M. (1989) 'Shaping and Delivering Pastoral Care: The New Opportunities', *Journal of Pastoral Care*, December, pp. 14–21.

McIntyre, K. (1990) 'The Pastoral Needs of Black Pupils: An Evaluation of Current Trends and Practices', Unpublished PhD Thesis, University of Manchester.

McIntyre, K. (1993) 'Personal and Social Education: a Black Perspective', in Verma, G.K. and Pumfrey, P.D. (Eds) *Cultural Diversity and the Curriculum — Cross Curricular Contexts, Themes and Dimensions in Secondary Schools, Vol. 3*, London, The Falmer Press.

National Curriculum Council (1990) *Careers Education and Guidance*, York, NCC.

National Curriculum Council (1991) *Linguistic diversity and the National Curriculum, Circular Number 11*, York, NCC.

Ranger, C. (1988) *Ethnic Minority School Teachers*, London, CRE.

Rogers, W. and Wickham, D. (1991) *Implementing the Whole Curriculum: Careers Education*, Manchester, City of Manchester Education Department.

Ross, C. and Ryan, A. (1990) *'Can I Stay in today Miss?': Improving the School Playground*, London, Trentham.

Scarman, Lord (1981) *The Brixton Disorders*, 10 to 12 April, London, HMSO.

Singh Brar, H. 'Teaching, Professionalism and Home School Links', in *Multicultural Teaching*, 9, 3, Summer.

Stone, S. and Pumfrey, P.D. (1990) 'The Child using English as a Second Language (ESL) and the National Curriculum 5–11', in Pumfrey, P.D. and Verma, G.K. (Eds) *Race Relations and Urban Education*, London, The Falmer Press, pp. 259–77.

Tattum, D.P. (Ed.)(1993) *Understanding and Managing Bullying*, London, Heinemann.

Tattum, D.P. and Herbert, G. (1993) *Countering Bullying*, London, Trentham.

Tattum, D.P. and Lane, D.A. (1989) *Bullying in Schools*, London, Trentham.

Troyna, B. and Hatcher, R. (1992) *Racism in Children's Lives: A Study of Mainly White Primary Schools*, London, Routledge.

Verma, G.K. (1990) 'Identity, Education and Black Learners: Are Things Improving?', in *Multicultural Teaching*, London, Trentham.

Verma, G.K. and Ashworth, B. (1986) *Ethnicity and Educational Achievement in British Schools*, London, Macmillan.

Chapter 5

Health Education

John Bennett and Peter Pumfrey

Context

Health education has always been an integral element of state education in this country, from Victorian times schools subscribed to the philosophy of a 'healthy mind in a healthy body' and there was great emphasis on personal hygiene and physical training. School reflected society's concerns about public health and the rising power of a working class which believed that access to education, adequate housing, public facilities and medical services contributed to the health of the nation. Subsequent legislation and social changes have meant that different concerns and issues have become health-education priorities but the school is still seen by many as a key place where the problems facing the health of the nation should be addressed. This has led to the growth in the numbers of professionals who are in some way concerned with the health of young people and their families, from school nurses whose priorities are too often dismissed as 'teeth, nits and naughty bits' to directors of public health who believe that schools' main aim should be to address health education at the expense of all else in the curriculum. Somewhere in the middle lies the school and the individual primary-school teacher who may have to deliver all of the National Curriculum, which includes elements of health education, as well as addressing many of society's concerns about issues ranging from HIV/AIDS to poor diet. All this must be done often without any initial training, little appropriate in-service training or ongoing support. In respect of the latter, the work of the Health Education Authority in general and its Primary School Project in particular merit commendation (Williams, Wetton and Moon, 1989a; 1989b).

In the past it has been tempting to view issues such as health as being value-free. Surely all parents and teachers would want children to enjoy good health and would not act in a way that might be damaging? The reality is that health issues are as complex as many others facing society and the answers are not as simple or as clear-cut as they might first appear. Cultural diversity is one of the factors that might influence health choices made by groups, families or individuals and simply giving information so that they have the appropriate knowledge does not always influence behaviour towards a healthy lifestyle. For example, the vast majority of adults know that smoking is bad for them and organizations such as the Health Education Authority spend millions of pounds reinforcing this message but still a significant minority chooses to smoke.

Cultural factors that may affect health choices are many and varied from religious beliefs that influence diet to social conventions that might limit access to exercise opportunities. For teachers and schools the challenge is to offer health education that is about empowering individuals to make informed health decisions while at the same time respecting the cultural values of the pupils and their families. It is important to remember that, if we define cultural diversity as embracing the ethnic, cultural, social and religious heritages brought by children to education, teachers should be aware of the implications of preconceptions related to children's home and family environment. It is often tempting to address the issues of cultural diversity in terms of problems that need solving instead of involving recognition of different needs. Teachers can benefit from an enhanced awareness of the relationships between ethnicity and health. This aspect of the demographic context within which health education likes places has recently been published by the Department of Health (Barlarjan and Raleigh, 1993).

Health education has been included in the curriculum often as a reaction to changes in society, for example, the post-war increase of illegitimate births saw the development of sex education in schools. The identification of links between cancer and smoking meant that education about the effects of tobacco became an issue that was tackled in schools. It was the newer drug scares of the mid-1980s, however, that lead to health education becoming a more formal part of the curriculum rather than something that was in primary schools at least, left to the whim of the individual teacher. The mid-1980s was a period of high youth unemployment and there were media reports of young people turning to illegal drugs, particularly heroin, as a means of escape. Associated with this use of drugs were antisocial behaviours to finance their purchase, most usually petty crime such as stealing from cars, burglary and prostitution but also more serious acts of violence. The first response to this public concern about drug misuse was the advertising campaign 'heroin screws you up'. It failed mainly because it emphasized the dangers of heroin, therefore implying that other drugs were acceptable. This was followed by another advertising campaign 'just say "no" to drugs' that failed because, for many young people, it was the lack of adult acceptance that made drugs so attractive and besides most adults do not 'just say no' to things they know are bad for them. The next stage of the anti-drugs strategy was to offer LEAs 'Education Support Grants' (ESG) to appoint drug-education coordinators to work in schools with teachers. This funding was initially for one year but was extended as the work of these coordinators grew to meet the needs of the schools and it became apparent that a one-off lecture on drugs just before the pupils left school was of little or no value. To be effective, drug education had to have a curriculum context: one should not just be teaching about illegal drugs in isolation but also about legal drugs and other health issues. It was also apparent that drug education in particular and health education in general should not be the domain of the secondary school but should start in the primary school beginning from Key Stage 1.

Challenges

The place of health education in the National Curriculum was established early on as a cross-curricular theme, one of five that formed the basis for Personal and Social Education (PSE). These themes could be taught through the Programmes of Study for the core and foundation subjects or they may require their own distinct slot in the timetable. The place of PSE was further formalized in 'Curriculum Guidance 3 — the Whole Curriculum' which stated that a school teaching only the core and foundation subjects would not be fulfilling 'a broad and balanced curriculum' (NCC, 1990a). The publication in 1990 of 'Curriculum Guidance 5 — Health Education' (NCC, 1990b) established health education as nine overlapping components that should all be taught across the four Key Stages. These components are:-

- substance use and misuse;
- sex education;
- family life education;
- safety;
- health-related exercise;
- food and nutrition;
- personal hygiene;
- environmental aspects of health education; and
- psychological aspects of health education.

Each of these components raises issues related to cultural diversity and presents challenges to educationists if they are to offer health education that meets the needs of young people, their parents and of society in general.

Responses

Substance Use and Misuse

The fact that this component is called 'substance use and misuse', rather than simply drugs, indicates that this issue is far more complex than it might first appear. There is a general assumption that all the drug-taking is 'bad' and should be discouraged. This fails to recognize that we live in a drug-taking

Table 5.1: Health Education: Challenges

Component of Health Education	Possible Challenges
Use and misuse of substances	• Recognizing acceptability or not of different legal and illegal substances
Sex education	• Recognizing different cultural responses to issues of sexual health
Family life	• Recognizing different patterns of family life and not presenting one as being acceptable and others as 'not'
Safety	• Recognizing that the need to keep safe may require certain precautions that may appear to be unrealistic or over-protective to some but are necessary to certain cultures
Health-related exercise	• Recognizing that access to exercise may be linked to cultural values
Food and nutrition	• Recognizing that diet is an integral aspect of any culture and that it may be influenced by religion and/or social requirements
Personal hygiene	• Recognizing that different cultures have specific requirements relating to personal hygiene and the need to accommodate these requirements
Environmental aspects of health education	• Recognizing the different cultures represented within any environment
Psychological aspects of health education	• Recognizing that psychological health is as important as physical health and that cultural influences will affect this, including pressures from different cultures e.g., racism

society and a whole range of drugs is readily available such as alcohol, tobacco, caffeine and beneficial drugs such as medicines. Illegal drugs are also easily available and in certain groups there is an acceptance of certain substances such as cannabis.

The issue of substance use and misuse is value-ridden and teachers must be aware that even drugs that are legal and generally accepted may not be tolerated by certain religious groups. The requirements of Curriculum Guidance No. 5 that by Key Stage 2 children should 'know how to make simple choices and exercise some basic techniques for resisting pressure from friends and others' can be very difficult to achieve (NCC, 1990, a and b). The child may be confused between what is socially acceptable and the cultural norms of the family and it is for the teacher to recognize this potential difficulty and devise appropriate strategies. These may include study of the media, use of role-play and drama techniques as well as considering the many different religious and social groupings each of which has its own set of ground rules.

'The World of Drugs' is one of three key topics covered in the second volume of the Health Education Authority's Primary School Project Materials (Williams, Wetton and Moon, 1989b).

Sex Education

This issue causes the most controversy, has the most potential for confusion and yet most parents want it taught in schools. Little wonder that some primary schools opt not to teach sex education and others operate a policy that is 'to answer questions as and when they arise'. The Education Act 1986 requires

> that governing bodies of county, controlled and maintained special schools should consider whether sex education should form part of the secular curriculum for the school and to make and keep up to date a written statement of their policy. Where they conclude that sex education should not form part of the curriculum then that conclusion should be recorded as a written statement. (NCC, 1990a,b)

Curriculum Guidance No. 5 tries to offer progression in that by the end of Key Stage 1 children should be able to name parts of the body including the reproductive system and understand the concept of male and female. By the end of Key Stage 2 they should know the basic biology of human reproduction and understand some of the skills necessary for parenting. Many parents find it difficult to talk about sex with their children and welcome the school taking on this role but many different cultural groups would want the school to pay regard to their religious beliefs in relation to sexual values and behaviours.

Most ethnic groups would want sex education to be taught in the context of family life and that intercourse is for the purpose of procreation within a married relationship. Problems arise as to how this is presented. For example, can illustrations of genitalia be used and how much information should be given about the physical changes that happen to children themselves, for example, about masturbation and menstruation? Some groups have offered schools detailed guidance as to how they would want these issues to be covered. For example The Muslim Educational Trust (Birmingham City Council, 1989) offers the following:-

> Information about changes in the human physical development should be given to the children objectively (with parental consent) after the age of 10 and it should form part of 'health and hygiene' or personal education either in the final year of primary school or in the first year of secondary school. Allah has made natural arrangements for humans to learn about their sexuality as they grew up, but children need factual knowledge to face real-life situations.

On homosexuality:

A society consisting solely of homosexuals will put an end to the human species since reproduction is impossible. This type of sexual relationship militates against family life, responsibility, sacrifices for children, love and care, being based only on physical gratification.

On contraception:

Islam does not allow any extra marital sex and also prohibits free mixing of grown-up boys and girls. It closes all doors to the growth of extra-marital sex. So, contraception becomes almost unnecessary.

Contraception is allowed only on the following grounds:

- danger to the life of the mother on medical grounds;
- fear of resorting to forbidden acts (Haram) to maintain one's family; and
- fear of child's health because of the pregnancy of a nursing mother (Ghilah).

Some Islamic jurists consider the consent of the wife essential for using any contraception.

On abortion:

Muslim jurists are of the unanimous opinion that after the formation of the foetus in the mother's womb and after it has been given a soul by Allah, it is prohibited (Haram) to abort it. Abortion is allowed only on the grounds that the continuation of a pregnancy might endanger a mother's life. Any other abortion is a criminal offence in Islam and the payment of blood money (Diyah) is obligatory if the baby is aborted alive and then dies. A fine is imposed if the aborted baby is dead.

Some of these issues will not arise in a primary-school sex-education programme but in classes that include many different cultural groups it is inevitable that questions will be asked that go beyond basic human reproduction and the teacher must be aware of how far he/she is prepared to go in answering these questions. The answers must be in line with the school's own sex-education policy that has been approved by the governing body and must be phrased in a way that does not imply that one particular viewpoint is right and others are wrong.

There are other issues that may need careful handling. Both the Muslim and Roman Catholic religions forbid masturbation although many sex-education resources used in primary schools describe it as a natural practice. When dealing with menstruation, teachers should be aware that Muslim girls do not use tampons and that many Catholics also discourage their use as they encourage manipulation of the genitals, i.e., masturbation. Many other cultural groups have their own sets of beliefs about this very sensitive component of health education and this is why it is imperative that the school has a written policy that has evolved from wide consultation as well as the need to meet the requirements of the National Curriculum.

The sensitive nature of sex education sometimes leads to parents wanting to exclude their children from these lessons. Previously they were required to apply to the governing body requesting that their child be withdrawn from sex education. The governors were not obliged to grant their request, although in reality most schools would want to avoid confrontation with parents and would allow the child to be withdrawn. The Education Act 1993, Section 241 has, as from August 1994, given parents of both primary and secondary pupils, the automatic right to withdraw pupils from any sex education other than that in any part of the National Curriculum. The act has also reaffirmed the responsibility of governors to decide whether the school will include sex education in the curriculum, to record that decision in writing and to produce a policy outlining the context and organization of the sex education curriculum. If we are to avoid large numbers of children being withdrawn from this important area of the curriculum, schools must devise policies that are sensitive to the needs of the community that they serve and parents should be consulted on a regular basis so that they are aware of when their child will be receiving sex education and feel confident that their wishes are being respected.

Family-life Education

This component encourages the study of cultural diversity as, in Key Stage 1, children should learn that 'there are different types of family and be able to describe the roles of individuals within the family'. They should also 'know about the rituals associated with birth, marriage and death' and that these vary enormously from culture to culture. By Key Stage 2 they should 'understand what is meant by "relationships" within families, between friends and in the community.' (NCC, 1990a). This would give the teacher the opportunity to consider with the pupils the different cultures represented in the community and to encourage the development of positive attitudes to these differences.

This consideration of differences is further highlighted as children should also 'know how children develop from birth to 5+ and be aware that there are different patterns of child-rearing.' Family-life education offers schools the opportunity to study different facets of the core and foundation subjects whilst fully engaging the cross-curricular dimension of multicultural education as well as considering health education.

Safety

This is probably the least contentious components of health education. The work of John Balding (Balding, 1990) looked at the health priorities for children as perceived by parents, teachers and by children themselves. Both parents and teachers put 'keeping safe' as their number one priority, interestingly children put their number one as 'looking after pets'. The main issue is the different perceptions of the word 'safe'. Within some cultures this may mean isolation from all other cultures; it may mean that access to certain activities is denied or it may mean that the school has to offer certain reassurances to parents. These may include single-sex groupings for some lessons, children to be escorted home after trips or extra-curricular activities, or that the child is allowed to miss certain activities or be offered an alternative. Extensive coverage of 'Keeping Myself Safe' is provided in the HEA Primary School Project (Williams, Wetton and Moon, 1989b).

Health-related Exercise

This component has obvious links with PE, as well as science, but is concerned with much more than simply sport and games. The work of Armstrong (1989) has indicated that the majority of children, like their parents, are unfit. Most do not engage in any daily activity that will raise their pulse rate a moderate amount for a sustained period of between ten and twenty minutes. The opportunities to enjoy exercise may be limited for cultural reasons such as the need for boys and girls to be separated, the reluctance of some cultures to allow girls to wear appropriate sports clothing because this is considered to be immodest and certain activities such as dance may not be permitted. These factors should not discourage a school from encouraging health-education-related exercise as the habits developed as children will certainly have benefits in adulthood. Exercise programmes should start with what the children are comfortable culturally. This may well mean negotiation with parents as to what is acceptable and what is not. Many parents who have insisted on the wearing of religious or traditional jewellery have allowed it to be removed for exercise when the safety implications have been pointed out. Also it is not unknown for some children who do not like exercise to use a purported cultural reason as an excuse that is found to have no validity when checked.

Health-related exercise often involves the use of agencies and facilities away from the school and they must be made aware of the needs of the children and be given the opportunity to respond accordingly. They may mean making some swimming sessions single-sex or allowing girls to swim in leotards or tracksuits. It may mean organizing movement to music that does not culminate in any public performance because dance is not permitted.

This whole component is replete with stereotypes. Too often teachers have said 'Asian boys are no good at games, except hockey, because they are too frail', 'Asian girls are not allowed to go swimming', 'all Afro-Caribbean children are good at all sports' as well as a host of other clichés. Health-related exercises should offer schools the opportunity to challenge the stereotypes and engage in a programme of long-term benefit to the children and perhaps even, by example, to parents as well.

Food and Nutrition

This component offers the opportunity in Key Stage 2 to 'know that there is a wide variety of foods to choose from and that choice is based on needs and/ or culture'. Throughout the primary school the sharing and enjoyment of foods from different cultures should be a feature in fostering an ethos that encourages respect for other cultures. The different dietary needs of children should be known and considered by school meals staff when planning for trips and residential experiences and when food is an element of celebration.

Personal Hygiene

Personal hygiene is important to all pupils and basic good practice is set out in the objectives for both Key Stages 1 and 2 so that cleanliness is encouraged and children should take responsibility where possible for their own personal hygiene. In Key Stage 2 they should 'know about different cultural practices in personal hygiene and food handling' and this would range from washing routines required before prayers to the unacceptability of using the left hand when preparing or eating food. For many primary schools the challenge is to accommodate different cultural needs with inadequate facilities: most do not have showers for use after PE or games; most do not have changing rooms so that considerations of modesty cannot be taken into account.

Environmental Aspects of Health Education

This component has links with science, geography and environmental education, which is a cross-curricular theme in its own right. In Key Stage 1 children should 'know that there is a range of environments, e.g., home, school, work, natural, built, urban, rural; know that individuals are part of these environments and have some responsibility for their care; develop an understanding of how and why rules are made concerning the school and other environments.' In Key Stage 2 children should 'know that within any environment there are people with different attitudes, values and beliefs and that these influence people's relationships with each other and with the environment.'

These objectives sit well with any school aiming to teach respect and consideration for different cultures. They offer the opportunity to formalize these ideas and allocate them curriculum time.

Psychological Aspects of Health Education

This final component is in many ways different from the other eight as they have been mainly concerned with physical health. Psychological aspects and are mainly concerned with mental and social health. The objectives in each Key Stage place emphasis on self-health, recognizing emotions and dealing with them, cooperation, respect for others, recognizing that individuals play many different roles and understanding that actions have consequences. In many ways this is the most vital of the components for health. Without these skills physical health can be meaningless and although the skills can be learnt through the other components, e.g., playing a game may be health-related exercise as well as teaching cooperation and team work, they can also be taught in their own right in a variety of ways. Many schools have already recognized that by building skills they will enable children to make, and perhaps more importantly, implement health choices such as whether to take drugs or not, whether to eat a healthy diet or not, whether to exercise or not. The opportunities to make certain health choices will be influenced by cultural factors but the decision-making process and the skills needed for implementation will apply equally to all cultures. 'Me and My Relationships' is the third key topic addressed in the HEA's Primary School Project (ibid.)

This component also offers the teacher the opportunity to consider a more holistic approach to health than simply the physical. Mental and social health are equally important and pressures on children because of cultural differences such as racism and sexism should not be underestimated. It is important that the school has an equal-opportunity policy that is implemented and acted upon rather than worthy statements to which nobody pays any attention. This policy should be for the whole school, including non-teaching staff, and should make the unacceptability of racist and sexist behaviour clear.

The Health Education Authority's Primary School Project is intended to help teachers plan a tailor-made health education programme for any primary school (Williams, Wetton and Moon, 1989a; 1989b). It is the result of a four-year project based at the University of Southampton and undertaken in association with the Schools Health Education Unit at the University of Exeter. 'Health for Life' comes in two spiral-bound volumes. The first is a teacher's planning guide. The second provides a wealth of information and practical examples on three important health issues: 'The World of Drugs'; 'Keeping Myself Safe'; and 'Me and My Relationships'.

The work is based on an holistic approach to health. It starts from the children's perceptions of health and the function of the school as a health promoting agency. The programme is designed to meet the specific needs of pupils, parents and the community. A 'Scope and Sequence Chart' displays

Table 5.2: *Health Education: Responses*

Component of Health Education	Possible Responses
Use and misuse of substances	• Smoking policy for the whole school including parents, teachers and other staff • Policy on possible responses to pupil drug use, both legal and illegal
Sex education	• A clear school policy that is arrived at following detailed consultation; cultural values should be recognized but also the needs of the children
Family life	• Recognition of the different family groupings represented in a school and awareness of the range that a child may relate to
Safety	• Organize events and trips so that pupils arrive home in daylight and if necessary escorted by an appropriate adult
Health-related exercise	• Link with PE coordinator to offer appropriate range of activities; encourage parents as 'instructors' to share skills so that a wide range of activities representing different cultures are available
Food and nutrition	• Develop awareness of school-meals staff • Offer a 'healthy' tuckshop that does not offend dietary requirements
Personal hygiene	• Be aware of the school toilet facilities and allow time for appropriate hygiene routines
Environmental aspects of health education	• Encourage knowledge of the local environment by appropriate use of visitors and by making visits
Psychological aspects of health education	• Develop a skills-based approach to health issues — knowledge is not enough; you have to know how to deal with the situation e.g., racism

children's age-related perceptions of healthy lifestyles linked to suggested content for a programme and the skills involved in these. The materials are extremely 'user friendly' and include a set of photocopiable worksheets (hence the spiral binding) and Action Planners developed for use in discussions between teachers, parents and health professionals. Also included are over 100 age specific illustrated classroom activities that can be used with children aged between four and eleven. The cross-curricular aspect of health education is clearly articulated and linked with skills development in various aspects of the curriculum. Appendix 2 in both volumes contains a wealth of information in a variety of media concerning materials that the teacher can use in developing a Health Education Programme.

The form and contents of the materials can readily be adapted to include the dimension of cultural diversity. The loose-leaf A4 handbook comprises of six sections plus an appendix. Sections I, II and III consist of a twenty page

Introduction (4 pp.), Components of Health Education (10 pp.) and Know-ledge, Skills, Attitudes and Dimensions (6 pp.). Section IV describes and discusses the processes and policy underpinning the delivery of health educa-tion in schools (10 pp.). The planning and implementing of Health Education at Key Stages 1 and 2 uses the six delivery models described in NCC Curric-ulum Guidance 5 (ibid). It is section V, health education in Practice (57 pp.) that will be particularly useful to hard pressed teachers and schools. (This is not to underestimate the considerable amount of time that can be saved by considering the earlier sections.) An index precedes sections on Key Stages 1 and 2 and Key Stages 3 and 4.

The Key Stages 1 and 2 section includes:

- cross-curricular planning checklist;
- ourselves;
- families;
- people we trust; and
- outside.

Consideration is also given to across Key Stage issues. HIV/AIDS Education covering Key Stages 1–4 is described, as is Health, Safety and Welfare: The World of Work.

Key Stages 3 and 4 topics include:

- Healthy eating.

Another extremely well-organized and flexible system of considerable value to schools, merits mention. It addresses the topic of health education as a cross-curricular theme and has been developed within the Manchester LEA by Ramsay and Sivori as one aspect of a project on implementing the whole curriculum (Ramsay and Sivori, 1991) (see also Chapter 2).

Manchester is unquestionably a culturally diverse city and generally proud of this (sadly, with some dishonourable exceptions that have been described elsewhere in this series). The city council, LEA and its staff are working constructively to develop policies and practices that ensure equality of oppor-tunity. This work is permeated with sensitivity to the fact of considerable cultural, ethnic and religious diversity in the city and its schools.

The city's health education cross-curricular programme builds on earlier work within the LEA (MCC, 1989) and on the nine components for a Health Education Curriculum identified in NCC Curriculum Guidance 5 (NCC, 1990). This particular LEA project involved twenty-six schools and a team of twenty-eight teachers and advisers. A great deal of development, trialling and evaluation took place. This is manifest in the 'user-friendly' quality of the materials and methodology described and illustrated.

- pollution;
- drugs;

- rights and responsibilities;
- safety; and
- developing health education through an industrial topic.

Examples of links both with other cross-curricular themes and with the core and foundations subjects, are presented.

The final section of the manual is devoted to special education. The health education needs of pupils with severe and complex learning difficulties can be encompassed within a cross-curricular model. The use of individualised programmes is outlined.

This is followed by a list of thirty-one additional health education curriculum starting points. These can be adapted to virtually any Key Stage.

The folder continues with a suggested action plan for developing a whole school policy on sex education. It concludes with a diagram of the Manchester City Council Health Education Network. Is there such a supportive network in your LEA? There probably is. If so, does it address some of the many health education issues related to cultural diversity and, finally, is your school linked into it?

All schools teach health education to some degree. In responding to the needs of different cultures in devising a programme that also meets the needs of the National Curriculum, the main point that emerges is the need for a whole-school response that makes explicit what may have been implicit and left to chance. Schools need to have policies on many different aspects of the curriculum, including health education, and these policies need to reflect the particular needs of that school and the community it serves. This will mean consultation with the parents, local religious leaders and any other interested parties so that all will understand what the aims and objectives of the programme are and to what degree individual needs can be met and which elements the school has a statutory obligation to teach. This applies to all that is taught in schools but for health education dealing with contentious issues such as sex, drugs and even challenging the family diet it is essential that the school goes through the process of consultation, writes the policy and then applies it equally across the whole school. Only then will a school be able to feel confident about addressing cultural diversity in health education.

Health education requires a holistic approach in that it is a whole-school concern for the whole person and not just physical health. This broad approach means that individual needs should be met as far as possible. It has been tempting to view different cultural groups as homogeneous instead of recognizing that within every group there will be subgroups. For example, within the Christian churches there are many different sets of beliefs and values and similarly within the various other faiths that might be represented in a school there will be a wide range of attitudes. The response to the challenge of health education should be to meet the needs of the individual pupils in a way that does not perceive differences as problems but as opportunities to share a wide range of mutually beneficial experiences.

References

ARMSTRONG, N. (1989) 'Children are fit but not active', *Education and Health*, 7, 2.

BALDING, J. (1990) 'Health Education priorities and the primary school curriculum', University of Exeter.

BARLARJAN, R. and RALEIGH, V.S. (1993) *Ethnicity and Health: A Guide for the NHS*, London, Department of Health.

BIRMINGHAM CITY COUNCIL (1989) *Sex Education Policy Guidance*.

BRET, R. (Ed) (1990) *Health Education. LEA Guidelines 3–16*, Manchester, Manchester City Council Education Committee.

MANCHESTER CITY COUNCIL (1989) *Health Education LEA Guidelines 3–16*, Manchester, Manchester Education Committee.

NATIONAL CURRICULUM COUNCIL (1990a) *Curriculum Guidance No. 3: The Whole Curriculum*, York, NCC.

NATIONAL CURRICULUM COUNCIL (1990b) *Curriculum Guidance No. 5: Health Education*, York, NCC.

RAMSAY, M. and SIVORI, A. (1991) *Health Education — a cross-curricular theme*, (Manchester City Council Education Department), Sheffield, Careers and Occupations Information Centre.

WILLIAMS, T., WETTON, N. and MOON, A. (1989a) *Health for life 1. A Teacher's Planning Guide to Health Education in the Primary School*, (The Health Education Authority's Primary School Project), Walton-on-Thames, Thomas Nelson.

WILLIAMS, T., WETTON, N. and MOON, A. (1989b) *Health for life 2. Health Education in the Primary School. A Teacher's Guide to Three Key Topics: 'The World of Drugs'; 'Keeping Myself Safe' and 'Me and My Relationships'*, Walton-on-Thames, Thomas Nelson.

Chapter 6

Education for Citizenship

Margo Gorman

Context

The Speaker's Commission on Citizenship was launched in 1989 under Sir Bernard Weatherill. It sets out the principle that Citizenship education should enable young people to learn how to play a full part in a society that is increasingly culturally diverse. Guidance published by the NCC in November, 1990, placed 'Education for Citizenship' as one of the five major cross-curricular themes (NCC, 1990a). The Institute for Citizenship Studies was established in the same year with Weatherill as its first president. Evolving from the earlier work of the School Curriculum Development Committee's 'Law in Education Project', came 'The Citizenship Foundation'. Its two year Primary Citizenship Project is designed to help pupils consider social and moral issues.Citizenship education in England and Wales has a long history with it beginning in the state system probably in the 1884 Reform Bill (Abrams, 1993).

The NCC views education for citizenship as aiming to:

- 'establish the importance of positive, participative citizenship and provide the motivation to join in; and
- help pupils to acquire and understand the essential information on which to base the development of their skills, values and attitudes to citizenship' (NCC, 1990a)

The NCC identifies eight essential components in relation to the *content* of Education for Citizenship.

Broad areas

- the nature of community;
- roles and relationships in a pluralist society; and
- the duties, responsibilities and rights of being a citizen.

Five everyday contexts are identified:

- the family;
- democracy in action;
- the citizen and the law;
- work, employment and leisure; and
- public services (NCC, 1990a).

In this endeavour, the cross-curricular skills of communication, numeracy, study skills, problem solving skills, personal and social skills and information technology skills must be fostered and utilised.

In examining the cross-curricular dimensions of citizenship, it is important to look at the ethos of achievement, which the Education Reform Act (1988) was intended to reflect. The promotion of the National Curriculum has been closely linked to criticisms of child-centred approaches to education. There have been explicit or implicit references to post-1960s approaches and teaching methods which are seen to reflect a woolly liberalism, encouraging sloppy teaching methods and low achievement. Kenneth Clarke, a former Secretary of State for Education (1991) described 'so-called child-centred' teaching methods as 'hindering concentration, disguising time-wasting, leading to a lack of real learning'. Child-centred approaches with the emphasis on the achievement of maximum potential for each individual are presented as an inappropriate preparation for a society where achievement is measured in competitive objectives, goals and targets. This emphasis on competition has operated in sharp contrast to the development of respect for individual rights and a sense of mutual responsibility within the wider society. Concepts of rights, responsibilities, equality and cultural diversity which are central to the development of citizenship, have not been central in the presentation of the National Curriculum.

Some of the work on the implementation of the National Curriculum has managed, in spite of this, to draw together curriculum development on cultural diversity, strategies for peace education and an increased awareness of children's rights. Material on the rights of the child developed by a partnership between Save the Children and UNICEF-UK (1990), stresses the connection between 'Education for Citizenship', the United Nations Convention of the Rights of the Child in 1989 and the National Curriculum. The resource books on children's rights provide teaching materials for use in developing courses in education for citizenship. Support for these approaches can be located in the broad principles voiced in the Education Reform Act (1988), which speaks of entitlement to a curriculum which is 'broad, balanced and relevant' to the needs of the child and which 'promotes the spiritual, moral, cultural, mental and physical development of pupils at the school.' This is reinforced by the National Curriculum Council Guidance No. 8 on 'Education for Citizenship' (NCC, 1990a) which proposes that 'the major conventions on human rights' be used as an area of study. In Appendix 2 to the Curriculum Guidance No. 8, helpful examples of ways in which education for citizenship might be developed across the Key Stages are suggested. Considerable work remains to be done, however, in the matching of activities and subject links to the Programmes of Study and Statements of Attainment for the core subjects in particular.

In the Programmes of Study for speaking and listening, the introductory paragraphs are an indication of some of the underlying difficulties that have to be faced and overcome. The initial reference to children who may communicate through new technology or sign language does not acknowledge how individuals who have forms of communication other than speaking or listening can enrich the understanding of non-verbal communication skills among their peers. Children observing and learning sign language, or attempting to lip-read are learning about the range of skills and observation that are involved in listening of which aural and oral abilities are only a part. These observation skills are important in other core subjects such as science. Similarly, such skills are important to the process of learning to present their views to others.

> Through the programme of study, pupils should encounter a range of situations, audiences and activities which are designed to develop their competence, precision and confidence in speaking and listening, irrespective of their initial competence or home language. (NCC, 1990b, p. 23)

There is an inherent contradiction introduced in the final phrase of the above sentence. Speaking in standard English and tuning in to a range of dialects and accents are undoubtedly useful skills which can be learned. Yet it is difficult to identify teaching strategies which develop confidence without taking initial competence into account. An approach to speaking and listening, which is based on cultural diversity, is more likely to achieve better results and is more in tune with an emphasis on measurable individual progress. This means taking the starting point of each individual and ensuring that opportunities are created which develop the potential of that individual — a familiar approach for teachers who use child-centred approaches, which pay close attention to personal and social development.

The task of interpreting and applying the guidance on specific subjects is daunting enough. To then combine this with cross-curricular approaches which promote awareness and understanding of cultural diversity could be seen as an additional burden by overstretched teachers. Adding a demand to incorporate citizenship into cross-curricular themes can seem like a further distraction. As teachers, advisors and inspectors often suffer from a lack of a broad education which would equip them with the knowledge, skills and abilities which incorporate an understanding of cultural diversity, it is tempting to avoid making that extra effort. On the other hand, when it is approached from the perspective of a teacher who has been teaching imaginatively using a range of methods, which capitalize on correlations between children's behaviours and their social context, the demands of the National Curriculum can seem like a strait-jacket which make it more difficult to match curriculum planning to the needs of the children. In spite of these constraints, it is important to identify ways in which the National Curriculum can offer an opportunity to re-examine, clarify and refine teaching strategies which value the individual development of each child and relate that to their development in the school context and beyond. The voice of those who see no contradiction between the National Curriculum and child-centred approaches presents a challenge well worth facing.

> The irony is, that the National Curriculum, introduced in a political climate that is opposed to the child-centred approach, is potentially a far more child-centred curriculum than that which has been practised in many primary schools since the so-called Plowden revolution! (Abbott, 1992)

In the practical exploration of some of the principles of education for citizenship, this chapter has drawn heavily on the experience of teachers and pupils in Windsor Street Primary School in Liverpool. The school is not held up as an example of how the highest Attainment Targets have been combined with achieving excellence in measures to promote equality and cultural diversity. Indeed it is concerned about the reading level of its pupils and is seeking ways of relating the demands of the National Curriculum to their existing strategies to improve the general level of achievement in school. The inner-city environment, with its high unemployment, poor housing and experience of generations of inequality has a major influence on responses to the implementation of the Education Reform Act. Teachers at Windsor Street School in Liverpool were critical of the emphasis in the National Curriculum which in their view 'was not written for the real world' and shows very little awareness of the social pressures that children living in such socially deprived areas are suffering. Teachers, parents and pupils face what seems at times like insurmountable odds against achievement at any level.

Challenges

The major challenge for teachers in Windsor Street school is developing a coherent approach to the curriculum which combines their approach to the welfare of the whole child with the demands of the National Curriculum (NCC, 1989a). There is very little practical guidance available on the development of material which achieves the combination of precision in measuring progress and ensuring that the curriculum motivates children, increases their self-esteem, their morale and engages them as active partners in their own education. The major barriers to the implementation of guidance on citizenship in schools are management support, increased administration and most of all limited material resources. Insufficient attention is paid to the motivation and morale of teachers and children in supporting the implementation of the Education Reform Act: yet such motivation and morale is the key to success in any management of change. In the latter half of the 1980s, many education authorities and schools were in the throes of re-examining their practice as a result of the Swann report (DES, 1985). The Education Reform Act (DES, 1988) missed an opportunity to incorporate and develop some of the recommendations of the Swann report into an approach to cultural diversity in schools, which could combine holistic methods and specific achievements. There is a danger that the educational and social challenges of cultural diversity may continue to be avoided in many schools, especially those in all-white areas.

Teachers can feel undermined by the implied and direct criticisms of teaching strategies and measurements of success they have used in the past. There is resentment at the lack of recognition of the gap between the level of attainment which some children bring to school and the average level required by the National Curriculum. In Windsor Street School, Liverpool, nursery teachers described how the children appeared to have a limited vocabulary for things which they would consider standard domestic items. It was stressed that this was less of a problem with children who had English as a second language, because parents would often make sure that the children learnt English vocabulary. One of the major reasons for what was seen as a limited vocabulary was the poverty of some homes and of the wider environment.

The teachers at Windsor Street were very open in expressing their anxiety and uncertainty. They are caught between an acceptance of certain advantages in a fixed curriculum which can provide a yardstick which ensures that a child does not drift into an unstructured learning situation and the complexity of the task of applying the National Curriculum in a social context that seems increasingly beleaguered. There are fears that too much emphasis on academic achievement means that other areas of development will be neglected. The Attainment Targets are criticized for providing only a very rough and suspect judgment of a child's ability, and neglecting a range of measurable achievements that would give a more comprehensive assessment of progress. In nonverbal skills, for example, the emphasis is on listening skills. Yet the present writer observed a 7-year-old, at a pupil council meeting, engage in the process of catching the eye of the chair of the meeting, an 11-year-old, and ensuring with an almost imperceptible nod that she would be given an opportunity to speak when one rather loquacious member of the council had finished.

As Argyle (1990) points out, research indicates that bodily communication is highly significant in human social behaviour. Facial expression, gaze and bodily posture can have a major impact on the communication of a message. Clearly cultural factors play a large part in the projection and reception of such bodily communication. Children who possess sophisticated intercultural skills in moving between the very different worlds of school and home may show little evidence of those in measurable achievements as currently

Table 6.1: Highlighting Some of the Challenges Faced in Schools

Challenge	Examples of Problems that Need to Be Addressed
Management of change	• Low morale among teachers and pupils
Abuse of power	• Bullying endemic in schools • Racism leading to pain and humiliation of minority group children • Gender used as basis for skill differentiation
Conflict of interests	• Children bring conflicts in home or community into school • Resentment and frustration at inequalities suffered is articulated in aggressive behaviour • Children with limited control over their own behaviour are disruptive to other children
Many different individual starting points	• Teachers are likely to have very different background and experience from that of the families whose children they teach • There is considerable divergence of ability in children of similar age • Teachers have difficulty in identifying Programmes of Study which are relevant to a wide range of abilities and differences in background, culture and language
Cultural and group differences	• Limitations of knowledge among teachers, advisers and inspectors of culturally diverse content and method • Limitations of commercially produced resources • Lack of time to produce relevant resources
Competitive values based on power relationships	• The most vulnerable children need special attention to enable them to enter into a competitive framework • The more able children can suffer from lack of teacher attention as a result
Extremes of poverty in wealthy society	• Poverty and unemployment in the home affect the children's readiness to learn • Children suffer stress and are more prone to poor health which affect performance • Strategies for survival in the street are not compatible with behaviour required in school

defined. Yet these skills can be a resource in developing their ability to communicate effectively. If the challenges presented by the whole and the National Curriculum encourage us to examine more closely the development of the broad range of skills needed to function effectively in a culturally diverse society, some advantage can be gained. Some of the multicultural approaches which have been used in schools to date have been limited to introducing cultural artefacts and customs as exotic and different. There is a need for approaches which offer positive affirmation to minorities and to majorities whilst developing an understanding that everybody can belong to a minority or a majority in certain circumstances. In order to make some of the links between the range of strategies for promoting diversity across the curriculum, the writer has adopted an intercultural framework.

Responses

The development of a wider European dimension on intercultural methods has challenged the focus on minorities that has accompanied some antiracist and multicultural thinking in the UK (see Chapter 3). Broken into its component parts the term 'interculturalism' is easily accessible. 'Inter' is about interaction, exchange, breaking-down barriers, solidarity, give and take. 'Culture' is about ways of surviving and adapting to the environment — values, knowledge, rules, rituals, codes of behaviour. Intercultural approaches combine antiracism and multiculturalism with dimensions which have been more closely associated with peace education or human rights. They demand a recognition of a more dynamic relationship between the different dimensions of power. Recognition of the current abuses perpetuated by racism and sexism, for example, is important to the development of citizenship yet this must also be transformed into positive responses in order to shift the balance of power into a more responsible use of it. Interculturalism describes exchanges between different social groups and their means of surviving and adapting to their environment. It incorporates concepts of culture, ethnic and social identity combined with issues of power and equality, rights and responsibilities.

Many teachers have, of course, been employing intercultural methods in practice but have not articulated their work in those terms. If the National Curriculum prompts more articulation of the methods which incorporate cultural diversity into the broad curriculum, it could also be used to develop such methods and approaches into a more coherent framework. The criteria for interculturalism combine the objectives, content and activities from the NCC 'Guidance on Education for Citizenship' into a cross-curricular programme. These criteria are then matched with resource materials in Table 6.2.

Whole-school approaches to inequalities and power provide an essential foundation for a whole-school approach on education for citizenship which 'is related to school policies on equal opportunities' (NCC, 1990a, p. 15). Many local authorities have made efforts to combine the demands of the Education Reform Act (1988) with policies and practices which promote equality. The publication of *Cross-Curricular Themes, Skills and Dimensions* in six loose-leaf binders produced by Manchester Education Department is an excellent example (MCCED, 1991). The *Cross-Curricular Theme book on Citizenship* states that 'There should be a coherence about the way the core concepts of justice, power and change are addressed within the curriculum.' (p. 7) Taking a whole-school approach means examining the structures and organization of the school and making explicit informal criteria which may already be in use.

Table 6.2: Resourcing the Theory

The Theory	Ideas and Resources to Help Put Theory into Practice
Whole-school approaches to inequalities and power: • School programme for monitoring and challenging all forms of discrimination • Structures for sharing power with parents and children • Involvement of parents and all staff including ancillary staff in school strategies	• Pupil councils • Behaviour monitored by all staff and pupils with an end-of-year review where results are fed back to whole school • Teacher allocated to assist children develop strategies to combat bullying and discrimination • Strategies introduced throughout school using packs such as — *Sticks and Stones*, Community Unit Central Independent Television plc, Birmingham and *Say No to Bullying* Leeds Department of Education 1992
Conflict resolution: • Preventative measures to tackle conflict • Development of skills in articulation of conflict to enable resolution • Development of team concepts to overcome conflictive competition • Development of flexible concepts of majority or minority	• Materials which promote conflict resolution, affirmation and cooperation such as — *Peace and Reconciliation* — a teaching pack, available from Elmbank Teachers Centre, Coventry; *Introductory Manual for Peace Education*, Manchester Peace Education Group 1984; *Coping with Conflict, a resource book for the Middle School years*, Frances Mary Nicholas; pub. Learning Development Aids 1991; *The Friendly Classroom for a Small Planet*, Priscilla Prutzmal *et al.*, New Society publishers 1988; *Ways and Means: An Approach to Problem Solving*, Sue Bowers, pub. Quaker Meeting House, 76 Eden Street, Kingston Upon Thames, KT1 IDJ; *Winners All — Cooperative Games for all Ages*, 1990, Pax Christi, 9 Henry Road, London N4 21H; *Let's Co-operate*, M. Masheder, Peace Education Project, 1991; *Let's Play Together; Over 300 co-operative games for children and adults* M. Masheder, pub. Green Print, 1989; *The Second Co-operative Sports and Games Book*: Terry Orlick, Pantheon Books, 1982
Cooperation: • Identification of common interests and concerns • Identification of common problems across cultural boundaries	
Person-centred approach: • Affirmation of individual identity • Support for group identity of majority • Support for group identity of minority • Drawing on specific personal and specific group skills for benefit of all	
Valuing diversity • Greater understanding of own cultures • Greater understanding of other cultures • Appreciation of differences	• Activities which develop children's sense of individual identity such as 'affirmation notebooks' and cards, to children are contained in many of the activities to encourage cooperation. For more ideas try *Self-esteem a classroom Affair, Vols 1 and 2* for '101 ways and more to help children like themselves'; M. and C. Borba, pub. Harper and Row 1982; *Learning together: Global Education 4–7* pub. Thornes makes links between self-esteem, communication, cooperation and the National Curriculum
Solidarity: • Actively seeking support of other cultural groups in achievement of goal related to own cultural group or in pursuit of common goal • Exchange and interaction of knowledge, skills and values between range of groups • Opportunities for equal interaction between social groups • Development of cross-cultural communication skills	• *Books to Break Barriers: A guide to fiction reflecting a range of cultures* from

Table 6.2: *(Cont.)*

Social and economic context	Worldwise, 72 Cowley Road, Oxford, OX4 IJB, Tel 0865 723 553
• Social justice • Rights • Environment	• For resources on tackling race issues in white schools — *Spanner in the works*, Brown *et al.*, pub. Trentham Books, 1990 and *Where it really matters*, Epstein and Sealey, pub. Birmingham Development Education Centre, 1990 • *Global Teacher, Global Learner*, G. Pike and D. Selby, Hodder and Stoughton 1990 and *Human Rights — an Activity File*, Graham Pike and David Selby pub. Thornes 1988 • SCF/UNICEF-UK four booklets as part of 'A project to introduce the UN Convention on the Rights of the Child to 8–13-year-olds' (1990); Also published by Save the Children *Homes* and *Doorways*: active learning packs which look at homes and housing in the UK and worldwide • *Drama for Justice* — drama for schools and youth clubs pub. Christian Aid • *Making One World*, An education pack on development and the environment: pub. One World, 2 Ferdinand Place, London, NW1 8EE

An example of how the use of informal criteria can result in assessment of quality, which matches more specific criteria was given to this writer by West Midlands Education Service for Travelling Children. A Gypsy parent who was used to transferring her children from school to school as the family moved around, described how she chose the best school. She walked around observing the children in the playgrounds of schools in the area, and chose the school where the children in the playground played well together and looked happy. The judgment of the parent could be translated into the following criteria:

- location within walking distance;
- ethos of respect;
- children valued;
- positive attitudes;
- learning through play;
- conflict resolution;
- cooperation; and
- group-work methods.

Her intuitive judgment was corroborated by assessment of the school used by the education service. Many teachers would endorse the criteria used by the parent and would relate it to whole-school approaches to equality. Racism and discrimination must be actively and energetically countered, so that all children can feel safe, secure and happy in the learning environment. The criteria used by this parent are also echoed in NCC Guidance No. 8 and reflect an inter-cultural approach to the organization and content of the learning process (NCC, 1990a).

A holistic approach to equality should be evident in the organization and ethos of the school and 'relationships with the wider community' (NCC, 1990a, p. 14). In Windsor Street School in Liverpool, their pupil council plays an important role in establishing a whole-school commitment to participation in decision-making, to learning about the use of power, and exercising rights and responsibilities. Pupils learn about the democratic process through the conduction of elections. The council also offers opportunities to understand individual and group accountability and opportunities to develop commun-ication skills. The issues raised and discussed by pupil councillors include racism, bullying, and the school environment. Discussion and action points are recorded in the minutes of the meeting. For example a group takes respons-ibility for the drafting, finalizing, typing and circulation of a letter to neighbour-ing houses to reduce litter thrown into the school playground. Through the feedback of pupil-council members, and the engagement of children with similar discussion and writing on the same issue, this process can be used to fulfil ATs 1, 3, 4 and 5 in English. They are 'writing in different contexts and for a variety of purposes and audiences, including for themselves.' (NCC, 1990b p. 35) The organization of the meeting and reporting-back process presents opportunity for 'a range of situations, audiences and activities which are designed to develop their competence, precision and confidence in speaking and listening.' (ibid., p. 23) Experiencing democracy in action through a pupil council can fulfil one of the essential components of education for citizenship.

The identification of inequalities and power has to be relevant to the school situation. When asked what they liked about being school councillors, some of the children said in laughter that they liked getting off 'work'; an-other disputed this because she had to give up her favourite — English work. After some thought the chair decided that it was because it makes them feel important. There was some discussion, in her presence, of how this sense of importance led to one of the councillors bullying younger children. Given that bullying is a major item of concern on the pupil-council agenda, this behaviour had to be challenged. The presence of the head at pupil-council meetings is an acknowledgment of its importance but also an acknowledgment of its relative power in the scheme of the whole school. This is not to limit its influence. A pupil council in Mosscroft Primary School in Knowsley pro-posed successfully that a teacher be given a special responsibility for following up complaints about bullying. This meant that the school governing body allocated part of its budget to an 'A' allowance for such a teacher.

The ability to 'discuss differences and resolve conflict' is included in the moral codes and values identified in the NCC Guidance No. 8 (p. 4). A nursery school in Manchester provides a model of cross-curricular work on moral codes and values in its attempts to introduce peace education across the school. As one of the measures of the success of their approach to child-behaviour management, they used data on conflict situations at lunch time. There was a dramatic drop. The staff were surprised themselves at the degree of success of the project overall.

> At the beginning of the school year we were all dismayed by the very
> aggressive behaviour of some children. Now, at the end of the year,
> it is not a significant problem, and the school is a much calmer place.
> (*Cross-Curricular Theme Book on Citizenship* MCCED, 1991, p. 30)

Attention paid to the learning environment will also improve the opportunities for individual children to improve their specific skills and abilities. But if children are to be prepared for 'the opportunities, responsibilities and experiences of adult life', this must also include preparation for taking positive action to face and resolve controversy.

> Education for Citizenship involves discussing controversial issues upon
> which there is no clear consensus. This makes it all the more important
> for pupils to have the opportunity to acquire knowledge, to develop
> a respect for evidence, to clarify their own values. (NCC, 1990a,
> p. 14)

Discussion of values and exchanging views on controversial issues is suitable subject matter for cross-curricular work on specific Attainment Targets. The Programme of Study for English specifies this in Section 4 with particular mention of maths and science:

> [All activities should]
> draw on example from across the curriculum, and in particular those
> existing requirements for mathematics and science which refer to the
> use of spoken language and vocabulary, asking questions, working in
> groups, explaining and presenting ideas, giving and understanding
> instructions. (NCC, 1990b, p. 23)

Considerable efforts made by teachers to make the links between education for citizenship and issues of equality and cultural diversity have extended to a deepening awareness of issues of children's rights. Material on the implications of the United Nations Convention on the Right of the Child and on Human Rights in general reflects the connections between initiatives on peace education, development education and the National Curriculum.

> The school curriculum for all pupils, should therefore include rights,
> duties and obligations as these affect them personally in relation to
> others, and the importance of respecting the dignity and individuality
> of others, refraining from provocative, racist, sexist and offensive

Table 6.3: How Issues of Identity can Be Incorporated into Core Subjects at Level 1

Subject	Statement of Attainment	Sample Activities
English	• Participate as speakers and listeners in group activities, including imaginative play	• Self-awareness through self-portraits • Matching skin tones
	• Use pictures, symbols or isolated letters, words or phrases to communicate meaning	• Naming parts of body linked to social awareness of self and of others colouring, likes and dislikes
Maths	• Talk about own work and ask questions	• Imaginative role-play through first letter association with animals or plants chosen by each child
	• Create simple mapping diagrams showing relationships, read and interpret them	• Issues of personal survival and safety: observe traffic at school gate in pairs at beginning, during and end of school day and report findings; make recommendations for improvements
Science	• Describe and communicate their observations, ideally through talking in groups, or by other means within their class	• Identify message behind basic road-safety symbols or movement symbols such as arrows • Written language as symbol — different scripts
	• Be able to name or label the external parts of the human body and plants . . .	• Different forms of transport, drawing on range of experiences e.g., rural, city, different countries

comments and bullying behaviour. There would clearly be advantage in children being aware of rights and duties in the organisation and management of their school. (Law and Rendel, 1992)

Interculturalism depends on a person-centred approach. A greater understanding of one's own personal identity is an important part to learning to understand and value others. The teacher and other adults are identified as part of the process not as outside of it. The table demonstrates how existing practices can be incorporated into a cross-curricular work on SoAs, with a focus on positive attitudes to self.

The diversity of individual experience can enhance the experience of the school and improve the acquisition of knowledge, skills and abilities. It is important to extend this into valuing diversity in other individuals and other groups. Some multicultural approaches which emphasize the difference and diversity of ethnic minorities and fail to relate that to the experience of the ethnic majority are in danger of perpetuating discrimination rather than challenging it. An understanding of diversity does mean a collection of stereotypes of people or cultures. In order to avoid this, an understanding of diversity should incorporate an understanding of cultures from an historical perspective which demonstrates how cultures change and interact with each other. This will include how individuals can identify themselves as belonging to a range of cultural groups: their ethnic group may or may not be a significant factor in their self-identification. Whether it is or not, other factors are likely also to be significant, for example city experience, rural experience, background, religion, gender, class, skin colour.

The development of an understanding of the concept of solidarity is necessary to the fulfilment of the essential components of community and a pluralist society. Many of the materials selected are suitable for studying a pluralist democratic society with 'interdependence in individuals, groups and communities' (NCC 1989a, p. 6). In a school setting, children can be encouraged to find common denominators between themselves and others which encourage forms of solidarity which cross the boundaries of gender, race, or religion. Story, role-play and drama can also be used to extend the children's own experience and increase their capacity to identify with a wide range of others.

An awareness of the social and economic context is an important foundation for understanding the interaction between the individual and laws, services, work, employment and leisure. The concept development required can be translated into the micro level of the school and home as society. The establishment of a behaviour-management policy, for example, provides important lessons on adherence to social sanctions. Windsor Street School involved their pupil council in consultation over the development of such a policy. This can be linked to an understanding of the operation of law-making in a democratic society. It also helps children see that laws can be modified and changed and that even those who are elected to uphold the law may fail. The establishment of links between home and school help children to see that the various institutions in society have different roles and have varying degrees of success in delivering on goals.

'Citizenship' is the buzz word of the 1990s but it is stretched thin across widening chasms between the 'haves' and the 'have nots'. The schools in areas of high unemployment reflect the poverty around them with leaky roofs, poor heating and cramped conditions. A truly holistic approach to tackling the cross-curricular issues of citizenship in school would make material resources available to invest in the whole-school environment. However, the human resources — children and their teachers — are the crucial ingredients in the translation of theory into practice. The communication of curriculum objectives to children is emphasized in the guidance to the National Curriculum and this is consistent with the approach suggested here. Hard-pressed teachers need research which directs them towards practical methods and resources. For this reason the table 6.2 matches the theory of interculturalism with ready-to-use resources. It is the responsibility of all citizens to ensure that children and their teachers are respected and supported if we expect them to take on the responsibility of shaping citizenship for the next century (Runnymede Trust, 1993).

References

ABBOTT, L. (1992) *A Quality Curriculum for the Under Fives: A Consideration of some of the issues*, The Report of a Conference organized by Manchester Polytechnic, p. 12.

ABRAMS, F. (1993) 'Rights, duties and the greater scheme', *Times Educational Supplement*, 16 July, p. 10.

ARGYLE, M. (1990) *Bodily Communication Introduction*, London, Routledge.

CLARKE, K. (Secretary of State for Education) (1991) 'Primary Education — a Statement', December.

DEPARTMENT OF EDUCATION AND SCIENCE (1985) *Education for All: Report of the Committee of Inquiry into the Education of Children from Ethnic Minority Groups*, Cmnd. 9453 (The Swann Report), London, HMSO.

DEPARTMENT OF EDUCATION AND SCIENCE (1988) *Education Reform Act*, London, HMSO.

DEPARTMENT OF EDUCATION AND SCIENCE (1989) English in the National Curriculum, London, HMSO.

LAW, C. and RENDEL, M. (1992) *Human Rights materials in British Schools*, Council of Europe, Strasbourg Council for Cultural Cooperation.

MANCHESTER CITY COUNCIL EDUCATION DEPARTMENT (1991) *Cross-Curricular Themes, Skills and Dimensions: Implementing the whole Curriculum*, Manchester, MED.

NATIONAL CURRICULUM COUNCIL (1989a) *Curriculum Guidance No. 1: A Framework for the Primary Curriculum*, York, NCC.

NATIONAL CURRICULUM COUNCIL (1989b) *An Introduction to the National Curriculum: Subject Leaflets*, York, NCC.

NATIONAL CURRICULUM COUNCIL (1989c) *Inset Guide 3 and Guide 4*, York, NCC.

NATIONAL CURRICULUM COUNCIL (1990a) *Curriculum Guidance No. 8: Education for Citizenship*, York, NCC.

NATIONAL CURRICULUM COUNCIL (1990b) *Curriculum Guidance No. 2: English in the National Curriculum*, York, NCC.

RUNNYMEDE TRUST (1993) *Equality Assurance*, London, Runnymede Trust.

NB Most of these resource materials and more are available on order from the Development Education Project, 801 Wilmslow Road, Didsbury Manchester M20 8RG

Leeds DEC, 151–3 Cardigan Road, Leeds, LS6 11J

Birmingham DEC, Gillett Centre, Selly Oak College, Birmingham B29 6LE

and the Scottish DEC, Old Playhouse Close, Moray House College of Education, Holyrood Road, Edinburgh, EH8 8RQ.

Chapter 7

Environmental Education

Ian Smith

Context

Two events took place in 1988 which, although they occurred independently of each other, were to have a profound impact on the place of environmental education in the curriculum. One was the publication of the Education Reform Act and its legislation creating a National Curriculum. The other was a meeting, in May 1988, of the Council of Education Ministers of the European Community who agreed 'on the need to take concrete steps for the promotion of environmental education . . . throughout the Community'. The resolution they adopted is one of many international approaches to the importance of education for the environment in recent years, all forming part of the pressure on ordinary citizens and world leaders to consider the implications of their decisions and actions on the world. A culmination of this was the Rio conference of 1992.

Although both events contributed to the current provision of environmental education their impact took different lines, reflecting the motives leading to their development. On the one hand a National Curriculum was created which laid considerable emphasis on the organization of knowledge into discrete subjects; on the other, concern was expressed about the importance of developing skills, attitudes and knowledge to have an informed concern for, and ability to do something about, the environment.

The purpose of environmental education has not changed as a result of 1988; nor would it be fair to say that the National Curriculum militates against its principles. However, the real price of a National Curriculum is the curriculum it replaces, and the time cost is the space left for doing other things. The key issue is the way the two paths of 1988 can be made to converge, or at least run in the same direction. To create the potential for this to happen it is necessary to consider the purposes of environmental education, its relevance to a multicultural society, and its links with National Curriculum.

A definition of environmental education, which encapsulates these points, was created by the International Union for the Conservation of Nature and Natural Resources as long ago as 1970:

> Environmental education is the process of recognising values and clarifying concepts in order to develop skills and attitudes necessary to understand and appreciate the inter-relatedness among man, his culture and his biophysical surroundings. Environmental education also entails practice in decision making and self-formulation of a code of behaviour about issues concerning environment quality. (Neal and Palmer, 1990)

This definition is expanded into the goals arising from the UN Inter-governmental Conference on Environmental Education which took place in Tbilisi, in 1977:

- To foster clear awareness of, and concern about, economic, social, political and ecological interdependence in urban and rural areas.
- To create new patterns of behaviour, groups and society as a whole towards the environment.
- To promote a whole-life philosophy for sustaining the planet's finite resources.
- To provide the necessary knowledge, skills and experience upon which choices can be made. (Manchester City Council Education Department, 1991)

The subjects of the National Curriculum alone cannot deliver these perspectives, and recognition of this led to the development of cross-curricular themes, skills and dimensions. The message is clearly delivered in the NCC *Curriculum Guidance No. 3: The Whole Curriculum* and it is interesting to compare the messages in that 1990 document with more recent attempts to fragment the whole curriculum, especially the statement that:

> the full potential of the ten subjects will only be realised if, in curriculum planning, schools seek to identify the considerable overlaps which inevitably exist both in content and in skills . . . In due course, it is likely that schools will 'throw all the attainment targets in a heap on the floor and reassemble them in a way which provides for them the very basis of a whole curriculum'. (NCC, 1990 a,b)

The challenge is to find ways of re-asserting that statement using cross-curricular themes, skills and dimensions as the framework for a curriculum which meets the needs of all children. The role of environmental education in that process is crucial.

Challenges

Recent politicization and publicity about environmental issues has led to a problem of definition, which in turn leads to the following challenges.

Semantics

It is important to consider the difference between:

- environmental awareness;
- environmental understanding; and
- environmental education.

The importance of this is more than an issue of semantics — it strikes at the heart of stereotyping of environmental concerns. Heightened awareness of environmental issues is apparent in the media and in public conversation. Many television adverts use the environment as a 'hook' to justify why people should use their product. The rich and famous gain publicity from their approaches to local or global issues — or their abuse of them. It is unlikely that this would have been as much the case twenty years ago. Such concern is a healthy starting point, which can lead to a deeper and more informed involvement. It is not always accompanied by an understanding of the issues. The role of environmental education is to turn that awareness into an informed understanding which gives people opportunities to make decisions about their lives and the life of the planet.

Scale and Scope

Linked with the semantic problem is the sheer scale of environmental education when all its layers are identified. The Schools Council's 'Project Environment' of 1974 first presented what has become a popular three-line division:

- education *about* the environment (knowledge);
- education *from* the environment (a resource)
  as a medium for enquiry and discovery
  as a source of material; and
- education *for* the environment (values, attitudes and action).

What this useful model can fail to take into account is the ever-widening nature of the subject. A topic on 'Minibeasts' is environmental, as is one on 'Our school' or 'My surroundings'. The use of the immediate locality is vital, in both urban and rural communities, to counter the belief that environmental education is something that happens 'out there' away from the child's everyday experience. At the same time national, international and global topics need to be considered, either separately, such as 'Planet Earth' or in their entirety, like 'My world'. It is useful in this context to talk of 'macro' and 'micro' topics and to aim for a balance of both throughout the Key Stages.

The Local Environment

Whichever topics are used there are key components which need to be considered if the approach is to recognize the needs, interests and cultures of a multiethnic society. One of these is to value the home environment of the school community. There is as much scope for pupils in an urban environment to learn on their own doorstep, as there is for rural pupils. The old pattern of the school trip to a distant place (like the seaside) had more to do with a patronizing attitude to compensating for the home environment in many cases than the educational potential in such a visit, and devalued the many opportunities in the immediate locality. An extension of this into general attitudes to the school community could create the potential for demotivation, disaffection and action against, rather than for, the environment.

Stereotypes

The challenges presented above include the need for a balance between local and global issues to address two overlapping sets of stereotypes, which may be termed the 'media' stereotype and the 'cultural' stereotype.

The 'media' stereotype arises from the confusion, mentioned earlier, between environmental awareness and environmental understanding. It is typified by statements, often derived from repetition in the media, which are well intended, but not wholly accurate. Examples include confusion between tropical and temperate rainforests in paper production and in people depleting the Earth's resources to deliver a small amount of recyclable material to the local bottle bank. The wider implication is typified by ill-informed intervention in the environment as a response to a perceived need, often to the permanent detriment of that environment and the life forms it supported.

This point leads to dangers inherent in the 'cultural' stereotype. The most graphic example of this involves a mixture of misuse of the media stereotype and a well-meaning but injudicious attempt to relate to the cultural diversity of the school population. In this way the valuable work of OXFAM was undermined by the craze in the 1970s for decorating classrooms with posters representing images of famine as part of a school's equal-opportunities policy. The effect of this on pupils with a cultural link with those areas and the stereotypical attitudes inculcated in other pupils militated against equal opportunities and against the principles of environmental education. The role of education in creating this understanding is demonstrated by the more positive

images of recent times representing Third-World communities as taking positive action for the environment rather than as passive victims, moving environmental education away from a Eurocentric standpoint. At the same time it
should be remembered that the majority of pupils, whatever their ethnic
background, were probably born within the locality of the school and share
the perceptions and interests of their peers as well as their parents. It is important that this is borne in mind in creating a common environmental inher-
itance, pride in community and balanced world view.

First-hand Experience

There is a further challenge inherent in maintaining the balance between local
and global concerns, and that is the impossibility of gaining first-hand experience of world conservation and other environmental issues. Direct contact
with the physical environment is only possible in a certain number of contexts; and it is direct contact above all which creates positive attitudes of care
and responsibility. The challenge is to make the most effective and meaningful use of secondary sources (which do not reinforce the cultural or media
stereotype) to deal with matters like global warming and destruction of rainforests. It is still crucial that this received knowledge is supported by opportunities to experience the issues in their own environment, in order to help
pupils realize the interrelatedness of all environmental factors and the impact
of local issues on the wider world.

Subjects or Topic?

This leads to a further challenge. Environmental education is all embracing
and multidisciplinary. Its roots are in the whole curriculum and its branches
have a spread which is home to thousands of forms of experience and perception. The National Curriculum is by definition fixed in content and made up
of discrete subject areas. It is possible to pick out the various environmental
strands in each subject and throw them on the floor in the way mentioned
earlier. There is a danger that what is picked up again is a fragmented collection of Statements of Attainment rather than a holistic model of environmental education. The way round this is to address the next challenge, which
is to tackle the issue of subject/topic work.

Topic work has already been mentioned as a means of delivering whole-
curriculum matters like environmental education. The waters of topic work
have been muddied by recent debates purporting to reflect state-of-the-art
educational thinking. Many of these have arisen from incomplete evidence
bases or misinterpretation of evidence presented. Most of the arguments in fact
lead to the same conclusion, that good topic teaching is better than bad subject

Table 7.1: Environmental Education: Challenges

Semantics	• Environmental: awareness, understanding, education
Scale and Scope	• About, from and for the environment • Macro and micro topics
Local Environment	• Positive affirmation
Stereotypes	• Media/cultural • Common inheritance
First-hand Experience	• Local action — global issues
Subject or Topic	• Knowledge or skills • National Curriculum
Assessment	• Attainment Targets — or awareness

teaching and vice versa and that a varied diet leads to a healthy curriculum. At the same time teachers are concerned about the impact of the debate on their work in the classroom — and environmental education is not a National Curriculum subject. Instead it is a context for learning which transcends subject constraints and builds on natural experience, drawing together the strands of Attainment Targets in a more meaningful and naturally ordered way.

Assessment

Unfortunately it is also a way which is difficult to assess, arising as it does from areas of experience and growth as a whole person. The biggest challenge facing many teachers right now is the pressure of national assessment and the concept of league tables. There is a concern that anything that deviates from the ten levels of attainment in core and foundation subjects may present a false picture of the achievements of pupils — and their teacher. This concern is reinforced by the combination of external and internal assessment. Is it possible to make a Standard Assessment Task (SAT) that measures human response to environmental issues? The answer to that question lies in the nature of the activity and the school's own policy on assessment and recording of achievement, but the basic line should be that the skills developed by a whole-school approach to environmental education should be transferable to those areas of assessment which are statutory as well as those which inform further planning and form a better judgment on progress and the next steps for development.

Fortunately the Dearing Review of the National Curriculum, its content, delivery and assessment promises greater teacher autonomy (DFE, 1993).

Responses

It is important to recognize the issues in Table 7.1 as challenges and not as obstacles to progress or reasons to give up. The best way to respond to issues and take positive action about them is to analyse what the difficulties are and find positive and practical ways of addressing them.

Semantics

Many attempts have been made to link environmental education with National-Curriculum subjects. This is a valid activity as long as neither becomes watered down. It is also possible to link environmental education with the other cross-curricular themes, ensuring that understanding and awareness contribute to the whole curriculum. The following is adapted from the RSPB policy statement on environmental education, 'The vital link,' and should form part of the school's environmental-education action plan:

Education for economic and industrial understanding
* the impact of economic activity on the environment;
* evaluating evidence from a variety of sources;
* understanding the impact of technological developments on the environment and on lifestyles;
* concern for use of scarce resources; and
* responsibility as a consumer and member of society.

Health education
* awareness of danger and health hazards in:
  the school environment;
  the wider world;
* personal responsibility for care of the school and other environments; and
* concern for health, hygiene and physical and psychological well-being.

Careers education
* awareness of different kinds of work in the local area; and
* the impact of this on the environment.

Citizenship
* understanding the need for, and processes involved in, planning;
* the conflicting demands and pressures on the environment;
* the importance of action to protect and manage the environment;
* how policies and decisions are made about environmental issues; and
* participation in environmental projects. (Elcombe, 1991)

It is interesting that in Northern Ireland another cross-curricular theme covers cultural heritage, aimed at helping pupils to understand their shared and diverse traditions and to develop a critical appreciation of their cultural heritage.

Scale and Scope

To ensure that a proper balance is maintained across each Key Stage in terms of macro and micro topics it is essential that there is a whole-school approach to planning and policy-making. This should also emphasize the strands of environmental education about, from and for the environment. There should be links with those aspects of National Curriculum which are a natural part of the weekly and termly planning, as well as with other school-policy statements and LEA and national guidelines. The School Development Plan should include environmental education as a priority in itself as well as a subtheme in other priorities. The environmental-education policy statement should also emphasize the use of the school building and grounds — the whole-school environment — and the use of the immediate and wider locality. The school's programme of trips, visits and outdoor activities should be clearly coordinated as a matter of policy. Further detail on policy is available in various publications included in the reference section. As a general guideline the following headings should be included:

- aims and objectives;
- methods and timing;
- content;
- resources and their organization;
- assessment, record-keeping and evaluation;
- use of the school grounds and building;
- use of the local environment;
- links with other policy statements; and
- other matters.

Local Environment

The two main opportunities for environmental education within the local environment are those within the grounds of the school itself and those within easy reach. It is very easy, especially within urban areas, for pupils to be given the impression that their community is not to be valued and teachers should be encouraged to balance negative views with approaches that demonstrate the opportunities that are available. Parks and other green areas are the usual starting point but they are just one feature of the urban environment. Streets, buildings and transport networks provide many opportunities for study. Canals and areas alongside them are rich sources for an introduction to industrial archaeology. The urban landscape is rich in exciting flora and fauna and the more derelict the site the more scope there is for discovery. Most schools have a small space where a wild area can be developed as an outside classroom and other features such as hedgerows, bird boxes and bat boxes can extend the scope further. A variety of organizations gives grants for such developments and if pupils are involved from the outset in planning the area and making the project bid they gain much more valuable experience of action for the environment than if they are merely encouraged to say what is wrong with their community.

Stereotypes

Working on a school-environment project also gives vital experience in addressing the media and cultural stereotypes mentioned earlier. Instead of reading about environmental issues pupils will be directly involved in them. Although they will not have first-hand experience of issues like destruction of rainforests they will be able to make the global connection from their work on their own wild area, and they will have a genuine and informed interest. They will be able to use the media as a tool to test their own hypotheses rather than as a provider of stock information. To assist this process it is worthwhile for teachers to video-record the many excellent environmental programmes on television, regardless of original audience, and build up an environmental video library. Pupils should also be encouraged to bring in newspaper and magazine cuttings for analysis and discussion. A useful exercise is to study the way different newspapers approach a particular environment issue, both in terms of presentation and in the amount of coverage given. All of this work can be supported by the many Information Technology (IT) programmes available, especially those simulating action for the environment beyond the home region.

A crucial feature of work arising from the school environment is the opportunity to reinforce the fact that all pupils share that common heritage regardless of where their parents or grandparents come from and that all of us have a shared responsibility.

First-hand Experience

Although there are many common starting points for environmental work in the school locality, every school has its own circumstances which will present particular opportunities and difficulties, especially in the early stages. Again, the first-hand experience of working through these issues will reinforce the link between local and global issues. An audit of current provision, leading to the development of an action plan, is a good way of presenting the pupils with issues that are relevant and important. Pupils can use a variety of research methods and skills to find the answer to questions about:

- the use of peat alternatives and organic methods of cultivation in the school grounds;
- developments to encourage and protect wildlife;
- efficient use of energy in the school building;
- efforts to save water;
- use of recycled paper;
- collection of waste materials: paper, aluminium, glass bottles, old clothes, scrap bottles, even used oil from the minibus;
- use of unleaded fuel in the minibus and staff cars;
- use of timber products from sustainable sources;
- avoidance of wasteful disposables, like plastic cups;
- use of environmentally friendly cleaning materials;
- positive attitudes towards litter control; and
- membership of, and involvement in, conservation groups.

These points can form the basis of an action plan which has the advantage of involving staff and pupils alike in its drawing up and implementation.

Subject or Topic

The issue here is not just whether environmental education can operate effectively alongside, and as part of, the National Curriculum. It is also a matter of finding the most effective ways of teaching to ensure that knowledge, skills, concepts and attitudes support each other in developing the whole curriculum. The place of environmental education in each National Curriculum subject is easy to identify, both in terms of obvious connections and particular Attainment Targets and Statements of Attainment, and it is not the intention here to reproduce those connections as they are readily available in other material. A more important point is the process used to ensure that topic or subject approaches are of the right quality and there is consistency throughout school. The following notes on topic work are adapted from guidelines presented by the Council for Environmental Education and are recommended as a basis for reviewing current provision:

- How do the topics relate to the children's environment?
- How do the children gain access to different environments (past and present)?
- What opportunities are there to investigate current environment issues?
- Can children discuss environmental issues from different perspectives?

- Are children encouraged to begin to understand natural processes in the environment; dependence and interdependence; impact of human activities on the environment; organizations involved in work for the environment; planning and design; effects of past decisions and actions?
- How do you ensure progression within and across Key Stages? (Dorione, 1992)

In that context teaching and learning styles should be typified by:

- variety;
- pupils' involvement in setting goals, organizing and planning;
- opportunities for cooperative work;
- opportunities to empathize with beliefs of others;
- opportunities to retrieve, analyse, interpret and evaluate information;
- opportunities for discussion and presentation of viewpoints;
- action for the environment; and
- enjoyment.

Assessment

Assessment is a vital aspect of National Curriculum work as well as a means of gathering evidence and making judgments which inform the future teaching and learning process. It is easier to assess knowledge than it is to assess skills, and it is easier to assess skills than to assess attitudes. It is important therefore to ensure that assessment of environmental-education objectives involves the following elements:

Discussion with colleagues about what should be assessed in terms of children's knowledge and understanding of the environment focusing on:

- the environmental concepts, ideas and principles we want children to know and understand;
- which aspects of these we wish to assess;
- opportunities to do so within existing practice; and
- planning and coordinating across the curriculum.

National Curriculum requirements, focusing on:

- identification of environmental components within the Attainment Targets; and
- progression through Statements of Attainment.

Development of general skills through environmental education.
Use of the NCC list of six cross-curricular skills plus IT can be a useful starting point, especially with a focus on the environmental context:

Table 7.2: Environmental Education: Challenges and Responses

Challenge	Response
Semantics	• Links: with National Curriculum other cross-curricular themes as part of an action plan
Scale and Scope	• Whole-school approach, considering: LEA and national approach linking with school-development plan leading to policy statement
Local Environment	• School grounds/ locality • Outside classroom: planning and bidding
Stereotypes	• Action for the environment • Positive use of media • Common heritage
First-hand Experience	• Local action — global issues: audit of environmental provision leading to an action plan
Subject or Topic	• Links with National Curriculum: teaching and learning styles following guideline for review
Assessment	• Of knowledge and understanding of: the environment National Curriculum requirements • To develop general skills

Communication skills:
• express views and ideas about the environment through different media; and
• argue clearly and concisely about an environmental issue.

Numeracy skills:
• collect, classify and analyse data about the environment; and
• interpret statistics about the environment.

Study skills:
• retrieve, analyse, interpret and evaluate information about the environment from a variety of sources; and
• organize and plan a project in, and for, the environment.

Problem-solving skills:
• identify causes and consequences of environmental problems;
• form reasoned opinions and develop balanced judgments about environmental issues.

Personal and social skills:
- work cooperatively with others; and
- take individual and group responsibility for the environment.

Information Technology skills:
- enter information about the environment into a database; and
- simulate an investigation in relation to the environment using computers.

It can be seen from this list that well-planned assessment can lead in turn to the development of a learning programme which supports all the requirements of the National Curriculum, but also places environmental education at the heart of a process which values and encourages active learning. As Table 7.2 demonstrates, there are practical ways of responding to all challenges, ensuring access to education for, about and in the environment. It is hoped that the ideas expressed in this chapter have presented a clear picture of the ways that environmental education can meet, and celebrate, the needs and abilities of all pupils in our multicultural society.

References

DORIONE, C. (1992) *Reviewing and Evaluating Provision for Environmental Education 5 to 11*, Reading, Council for Environmental Education.

ELCOME, D.M. (1991) *Environmental Education, the Vital Link*, Sandy, RSPB.

HER MAJESTY'S INSPECTORATE (1989) *Environmental Education from 5 to 16*, London, HMSO.

MANCHESTER CITY COUNCIL EDUCATION DEPARTMENT (1991) *Implementing the Whole Curriculum, Book 4: Environmental Education*, Sheffield, COIC.

NATIONAL CURRICULUM COUNCIL (1990a) *Curriculum Guidance No. 3: the Whole Curriculum*, York, NCC.

NATIONAL CURRICULUM COUNCIL (1990b) *Curriculum Guidance No. 7: Environmental Education*, York, NCC.

NEAL, P. and PALMER, J. (1990) *Environmental Education in the Primary School*. Oxford, Blackwell Education.

SCHOOL CURRICULUM AND ASSESSMENT AUTHORITY (1993) *The National Curriculum and its Assessment: Final Report*, London.

Part 3

Other Cross-curricular Dimensions

Chapter 8

Personal and Social Education

Kanka Mallick

Context

Personal and social education (PSE) are collectively one of the six skills included in the Programme of Study of the National Curriculum. The National Curriculum Council (NCC) is one of three statutory bodies set up under the Education Reform Act (DES, 1988), the others being the Curriculum Council for Wales (CCW) and the Schools Examinations and Assessment Council (SEAC). As from October, 1993, the School Curriculum and Assessment Authority (SCAA) replaces these.

Section I of the Education Reform Act places a responsibility on schools to provide a broad and balanced curriculum which:

(a) promotes the spiritual, moral, cultural, mental and physical development of pupils at the school and of society; and

(b) prepares such pupils for the opportunities, responsibilities and experiences of adult life. (DES, 1988)

The National Curriculum Council's publication, *Curriculum Guidance No. 3: the Whole Curriculum* (NCC, 1990) has identified three cross-curricular elements which have a crucial role to play in helping teachers to provide a curriculum which would fulfil the above requirements. The elements are: dimensions; skills; and themes.

The NCC's view of the whole curriculum and the ways of describing it are different from the view of the Curriculum Council for Wales (CCW).

The National Curriculum Council has issued a series of circulars and newsletters since 1989. Through publications it has stressed the importance of the cross-curricular aspects of the curriculum. It has also made clear that different subjects should be organized and taught in such a way as to contribute to pupils' learning *as a whole*. Furthermore, it has asked schools to keep a distinction between cross-curricular dimensions, skills and themes. The dimensions are: providing equal opportunities for all pupils; and educating pupils for life in a multicultural society. The six skills are: communication; numeracy; study; problem-solving; personal and social; and information technology. The themes are: economic and industrial understanding; careers education and guidance; health education; education for citizenship; and environmental education.

Previously, the only statutory curriculum requirement since the Education Act 1944 was that all maintained schools must teach religious education (RE). However, since 1976, debates and discussions have been going on about the relevance and balance of the school curriculum. Some educationists felt that there should be a more holistic and integrated approach to the 'whole curriculum' within the socially undeniable context of a multicultural society (see Chapter 2).

It is clear from evidence available so far (see Volumes 1–3 in this series) that neither the official NC texts nor debate will determine how schools implement the idea of 'the whole curriculum' in a multicultural context. This obviously will depend on many factors such as the class, gender, and ethnic mix of pupils, the financial constraints imposed by the Local Management of Schools (LMS) and developments in assessment practice. Teachers' awareness of objectives, methods and materials are also central.

The National Curriculum Council (NCC, 1990) states that:

> It is the birthright of the teaching profession and must always remain so, to decide on the best and most appropriate means of imparting education to pupils. (NCC, 1990, p. 7)

The Council's newsletter of June 1989 commented on the interim report (NCC, 1989c), and focused almost entirely on personal and social education as 'arguably the most important of the cross-curricular skills to which schools need to give attention'. Yet, much of the advice reported was not included in the published guidance. Social education was given two brief paragraphs on the final page of Part I of *Curriculum Guidance No. 3* (NCC, 1990). Additionally, there seems to be considerable evidence of ambiguities and contradictions within the two documents.

It should be noted that Circular No. 6 of the Council (NCC, 1989b) has classified cross-curricular provision under dimensions, skills and themes as being 'helpful for review and organisation of the curriculum and the planning of the content'. Cross-curricular dimensions are seen as being 'concerned with the intentional promotion of personal and social development through the curriculum as a whole'. The topics mentioned are personal and social development, equal opportunities, education for life in a multicultural society and positive attitudes towards cultural diversity, gender equality and people with disabilities. Cross-curricular skills named are communication skills (oracy, literacy, numeracy, graphicacy), problem-solving and study skills.

The most extensive section deals with cross-curricular themes which have already been referred to earlier in this paper. It is claimed that these 'enrich the educational experience of pupils'. This does not exclude other potential themes.

But the rationale for the selection of these themes is not made e
beginning of the section on cross-curricular elements NCC sa

> clearly it would be possible to construct an almost infinite n
> cross-curricular elements which taken together make a majc. contri-
> bution to personal and social education. (NCC, 1990, p. 2)

At this point it would seem appropriate to make an attempt to understand what is meant by personal and social education. What is Personal and
Social Education? (PSE). PSE is the area of the curriculum which enables
teachers to concentrate on the needs of the pupils rather than on externally
imposed curriculum requirements. Personal and social education has assumed
a great deal of significance at present owing to the increasing incidence of
antisocial, criminal and offensive behaviours shown by children in modern
societies. Many teachers express a great deal of concern over the discipline and
behavioural problems they encounter not only in junior schools but even in
infant and nursery schools. This paper briefly discusses some aspects of personal and social education in the context of pluralism in society and considers
what teachers can and should do to promote their pupils' personal and social
development.

Few would disagree that schools have always been concerned with pupils'
personal and social well-being. 'Children spend more time at school than
anywhere else except home . . . schools cannot avoid, and no teacher would
wish to avoid, a large measure of responsibility for their pupils' personal and
social development' (Schools Council, 1983, p. 91).

Teachers often help pupils to explore their attitudes, beliefs, moral and
spiritual values through different subjects and/or cross-curricular topics. They
also show concern for pupils' general welfare beyond their teaching commitments. Such concern is implicit in the general philosophy and ethos of the
school and explicit in the organization of curriculum and school policy on
such matters as the pastoral-care system.

Personal and social development is generally seen as forming a significant
but somewhat 'hidden' element in the school curriculum, running through
and across subject areas and other school activities including play. There is
also a general acceptance that any subjects or educational activities that entail
cultural, moral and spiritual aspects may contribute to children's personal and
social education.

It is sometimes thought that personal and social education covers so many
different aspects of pupils' development that it is extremely difficult to consider
it in a coherent manner as a separate curriculum consideration. One writer
aptly comments that PSE 'is truly cross-curricular and the justification of the
personal and social contribution of all areas of the school life has a unifying
effect on the whole school curriculum' (Campbell, 1992). Thus personal and
social development is part of the whole curriculum and needs to be integrated
with the teaching and learning of various subjects and activities.

Many writers have argued strongly that personal and social development should have a more central and explicit place in the curriculum. As early as 1975 when the Assessment of Performance Unit (APU) was set up by the Department of Education, the concept of personal and social development of children formed a significant element of their work. The APU even explored the possibility of monitoring this aspect of pupils' development, because it was recognized that this dimension of education runs through and across subject boundaries, work and play. By 1979 it became apparent that there was no satisfactory way for assessing this area, and the APU decided not to proceed with monitoring pupils' performance in the area of personal and social development (DES, 1981). However, it was generally agreed by the APU that pupils' personal and social development should be given the highest priority by teachers, both in school organization and in curriculum design. Most would agree that at the primary-school level in particular, the personal and social development of the child has a central place in education. During this period the child extends social interactions with an increasing range of adults and other children, and also extends existing, and acquires new, personal and social skills and knowledge. The DES/HMI (1980) report states that

> There are some sorts of knowledge about themselves, about other people, about the nature of the world in which they are growing up — which all pupils need. Personal and social development in this broad sense is a major charge on the curriculum. (DES/HMI, 1980, p. 2)

Despite the considerable importance attached to pupils' personal and social development it is not an easy concept to define or to translate into practice. As is suggested in the secondary-school survey (DES/HMI, 1979):

> There is a need for many schools to reconsider curricula, methods of teaching, use of resources and methods of grouping pupils with regard to their impact on pupils' personal development. (DES/HMI, 1979, p. 218)

Pring (1984) rightly remarks that 'it remains unclear, however, how this general concern can be translated into curriculum practice' (p. 4). According to Pring, any discussion about personal and social development raises fundamental questions as to what are the purposes and effectiveness of schooling. He poses questions such as:

> Can schools seriously affect the attitudes and behaviour of young people towards society and towards one another? Should schools accept this responsibility amongst their many others? If so, what sort of society, informed by what civic and political values, should schools

be helping to form? What sort of personal values and habits should teachers be encouraging in young people and indeed by what authority? . . . some answers to them are necessary if schools are to be encouraged to help with the personal and social development of children. (Pring, 1984, p. 9)

It is clear that difficult and value-laden professional and political issues interact. It is essential to examine briefly the meaning of the concept of PSE. In one sense it can be said that an individual's knowledge, understanding and feelings are all part of his or her personal and social development. But such an all-inclusive description would be too general for practical use. Parents and teachers may find such a description of little value when they talk about the role of the school in assisting with children's personal and social development. It is important to note that this aspect should not be seen in isolation, because it permeates the life of schools. In a broad sense, everything an individual knows, understands, feels and does is part of that individual's personal and social development. And it must always be remembered that no individual is an island.

It is useful to distinguish between PSE as a 'concept' (PSE 'A'), PSE as it is manifest in 'everyday life' (PSE 'B') and PSE as sampled by one of the myriad tests and assessment techniques that exist to measure particular 'facets' of PSE (PSE 'C'). Thus PSE 'A' is an abstraction that can *never* be observed. It is *inferred* from the manifestations of PSE in everyday life. PSE 'C' is a sample of PSE 'B'.

It is clear that what represents a norm of PSE 'B' in one group may not be so for another group in the same society. Insensitivity to such cultural variations is common both *within* ethnic groups and *between* them. Not all individuals or groups enjoy the same foods, the same music, the same conventions for interpersonal relationships, or the same social activities. What can schools do to help children socialize under different value systems within their families and ethnic group, become more accepting of cultural differences?

Manchester City Council (1991) has set out the following as necessary aspects of personal and social development:

- interpersonal skills;
- challenging stereotypes;
- developing self-confidence and self-esteem;
- affirmation;
- assertiveness;
- conflict resolution/negotiating;
- working cooperatively with others;
- taking individual and group responsibility;
- applying critical reasoning skills — constructing; and
- presenting and justifying arguments.

Manchester City Council Education Department offers in its publication (1991) a range of hints and advice to help teachers and schools in their planning and delivery of personal and social education.

Challenges

Personal and social education, as one of the six skills in the National Curriculum, presents a number of challenges to teachers, to schools and to pupils. There is a greater challenge to teachers to explore new materials, some of which may not be readily available and thus they may need to produce their own. They may also need to decide on the most appropriate methods of presentation, given the nature of issues relating to race, culture and ethnicity. Issues concerning personal and social needs of ethnic-minority pupils have been well documented in the Swann report (DES, 1985). It makes quite explicit that:

> A good education must in our view give every youngster the knowledge, understanding and skills to function effectively as an individual, as a citizen in a wider national society and in the interdependent world community of which he is also a member. (DES, 1985, p. 319)

It is clear from this report and the analysis of others (see Volume 2 in this series) that the skills, attitudes and knowledge involved in PSE cannot be restricted to a personal and social education 'slot' in the school timetable or to the pastoral structure of the school. Rather it should feature in the whole curricular area as well as in extra-curricular activities, including play. Personal and social education should provide *all* pupils, through their active participation, with the opportunity to explore attitudes, values and beliefs prevalent in school in particular and society in general.

Within the remit of the Education Reform Act (1988) the NCC has asked all schools and teachers to keep all aspects of the curriculum — not just the National Curriculum and the basic curriculum — under review. It specifically asks them to take account of ethnic and cultural diversity, the promotion of equal opportunity and provision for pupils with special educational needs. The NCC advises schools to consider:

> those cross-curricular issues which should be included in the curriculum of all pupils in maintained schools to assist in securing the purposes set out in section one of the Education Reform Act: in the first instance that advice should cover the Council's views on the extent to which those issues can be reflected in attainment targets and programmes of study for the core and other foundation subjects, and the place and content of personal and social education, including health education in the curriculum . . . (NCC, 1989b)

The above statement provides clear guidance about the named cross-curricular issues. The problem is that there is an implicit assumption that the very general aims stated in Section I of the Education Reform Act point unambiguously towards these particular cross-curricular issues and not others. It is also assumed that, irrespective of class, gender, race, or culture, curriculum breadth and balance will be enhanced through work on cross-curricular skills and themes. Therefore, it is essential that cross-curricular elements should form an explicit and planned part of the school-curriculum policy. The purpose, pedagogy and materials supporting this must be made clear to all those involved in, and concerned with, the planning, development, delivery and evaluation of the whole curriculum.

As pointed out earlier, the two crucial cross-curricular dimensions cover all aspects of equal opportunities, and education for life in a multicultural society (NCC, 1990). In practice, providing equal opportunities for all means:

- treating pupils as individuals with varying abilities, difficulties, attitudes, backgrounds and experience;
- challenging myths, stereotypes and misconceptions; and
- ensuring equality of access to the curriculum implying real opportunity to benefit all.

The second dimension concerned with educating pupils for life in a multicultural society requires:

- extending pupils' knowledge and understanding of different cultures, languages and faiths;
- valuing cultural diversity by drawing on pupils' backgrounds and experiences; and
- offering positive images and role models from all cultures.

These dimensions ought to permeate the whole curriculum. It is a responsibility of all teachers to see that this does happen.

Religious and moral education has always been a controversial issue within the British (and other) educational systems. In the National Curriculum all state schools are required to make Christianity the basis of religious education and provide pupils with a 'broadly Christian' act of daily worship. Given the religious diversity of many of the country's primary schools, teachers feel uncertain as to how this should be achieved. A primary aim in teaching religious education should be to create an ethos where children from differing religious and cultural backgrounds develop self-respect and respect for others' beliefs. Experience of religious beliefs and moral values also contributes to the development of identity which is an important aspect of personal and social development. Therefore the multifaith approach to teaching about religions would seem to be the only strategy that accords with the basic principles of the philosophy of 'Education for All' (DES, 1985) (see Volume 3, Chapter 3).

Responses

Given the challenges outlined in the preceding section, the questions arise as to what schools and teachers can do to achieve the stated aims of the National Curriculum, and how to ascertain that personal and social education is used explicitly within the context of the whole curriculum? Three of the most valuable responses that teachers can make are to rethink their understanding of the importance of friendship and peer relations in children, to update their knowledge of this area and to consider the effects of the models that they provide to pupils, their parents and colleagues both in the everyday work of the school and in their own relationships. Social learning and social development are of the essence and not merely curricular 'add-ons'. To paraphrase Donne, 'No person is an island . . .'.

A recent reappraisal and summary of relevant research that challenges some of the myths concerning friendships between school-aged pupils and infants has been written by a psychologist with a background in counselling and guidance (Irwin, 1993). His book emphasizes the importance of processes of socialisation in the early years and in primary school education, demonstrating connections with other aspects of development and stressing the vital role of relationships with 'significant others'.

Models matter. Teachers (amongst others) can be extremely potent models having profound effects on the social behaviours of children. Of even greater importance, such 'significant others' can help children to internalise constructs concerning interpersonal relationships that accord with the tolerance of diversity and the development of mutual respect on which the social cohesion of any community depends and, *par excellence*, in a multicultural one. In this respect, the importance of teachers (or anyone) modelling the interpersonal relations they wish their pupils to develop is clear. 'Do as I do' provides a far more potent pedagogy that 'Do as I say'.

The work of the National Association for Pastoral Care in Education (NAPCIE) is a continuing tribute to the teaching profession's recognition of the importance of interpersonal communications and relationships in education. Their address is:

> National Association for Pastoral Care in Education,
> Department of Education,
> University of Warwick,
> Wetwood,
> Coventry, CV4 7AL.

Their journal *Pastoral Care in Education* contains a wealth of challenging ideas relevant to all stages of education. A greater input from primary school teachers would, in the writer's opinion, enhance its value.

Whatever the critics say about the weaknesses of the National Curriculum, schools need to consider ways in which dimensions, skills and themes can underpin the core and foundation subjects, and permeate the whole curriculum. The cross-curricular issues play a crucial role in influencing children's attitudes, development, group skills, their understanding of the world, and acquisition of knowledge and skills.

During the primary stage of schooling, considerable changes take place in every area of children's development — social, emotional, intellectual, and physical, including language development. These affect the ways that children experience the world around them, and construct their models of reality. These aspects of development are interdependent and cannot be separated from each other. The Education Reform Act and its emphasis on personal and social education as being a cross-curricular skill has provided a most appropriate and challenging context for the delivery of PSE.

The Metropolitan Borough of Stockport's Education Division published a document in 1988 intended to be a guide for the use of teachers involved in the design and delivery of a programme of personal and social education. According to the document, personal and social development can be achieved by:

> Negotiated activity-based learning involving participation, discussion and questioning. Enabling the student to accept responsibility. The recognition that each individual has a worthwhile contribution to make by drawing on his/her own experience. (MBS, 1988, p. 3)

The document further comments that 'It is important that PSE is seen to be a means of pupil development, *not* containment. Self-esteem and task satisfaction should be the essence' (p. 3). It stresses the importance of the whole-school approach for personal and social development to be effective, and declares that 'care must be taken that messages pupils receive elsewhere in the school are in keeping with the messages they receive in PSE' (p. 4). The development of positive self-esteem is considered vital: 'Indeed the skills, concepts and attitudes developed through personal and social education also enhance the cognitive learning planned by the school and, as such, are of equal importance' (p. 4).

Teachers need to ensure that children have rich, varied curriculum experiences where their personal, ethnic and cultural self-images grow, where pupils' different cultural backgrounds are accepted, explored and valued and where they can feel proud to be 'me' and happy to have children from varying backgrounds as friends, feeling enriched by knowing them, and where they can grow. Helpful materials in achieving these ends have been developed (Lawrence, 1987).

A recent publication by Fountain (1990) on *'Learning Together: Global Education 4–7*, also suggests some interesting approaches to fostering self-esteem in children which help them 'feel positively about themselves, identify their own abilities and strengths; accept their emotions and express them in a constructive way; recognize the positive qualities of their classmates; make genuine affirming statements to others; identify what others might be feeling, and accept the validity of different emotional responses' (p. 20).

An example of such an activity for small groups is given below:

This is My Friend

Materials: None.

Procedure: The children sit on the floor in a circle. One child is chosen to begin. She introduces herself and the person sitting to her right: 'My name is Rima, and this is my friend Sarah.' The friend who has been introduced then continues, introducing herself and the person to her right: 'My name is Sarah, and this is my friend Tim.' Once the children are familiar with this procedure and each other's names, they enjoy introducing themselves and each person who has preceded them, so that the last child in the group has to recall all the names.

Potential: This is a useful game to play at the beginning of the year when children are learning each other's names. It reinforces the idea of friendship and the sense that everyone's name is valued, as well as developing listening and recall skills. (Fountain, 1990)

Teachers can organize many activities, for example, not only for enhancing self-esteem but also for developing communication and cooperative skills in nursery, infant and junior classes. It is possible to do this in three ways:

- by allocating specific time during the day/week for PSE;
- by including the activities as part of cross-curricular thematic work;
- by integrating PSE-based activities as interactive, cooperative aspects in the teaching of core and foundation subjects.

As Lawrence, Fountain and others have demonstrated, it is possible for teachers to include all three approaches in the work of the primary school.

An important aspect of the teaching process is the 'hidden curriculum'. The prescribed curriculum (core and foundation subjects) is supposed to deal with knowledge, facts and competencies, but the hidden curriculum (conscious or unintentional) has a powerful part to play in changing values, beliefs and attitudes in order to further the process of personal and social adaptation. For example, if schools are insensitive to differences between pupils in the principles and practices underpinning their religious and moral development, it may inadvertently damage their self-esteem. Teachers should not only have understanding of such complex contentious issues which may create conflict between the requirements of the home and those of the school, but also require the necessary professional skills to deal with them in a sensitive manner (see Chapter 14).

The fundamental question as to what curricular knowledge and understanding is essential to provide equal chances of success for *all* pupils is still open to debate. Ethnic-minority pupils are presented with an Eurocentric curriculum which tends to undermine their identity, self-esteem and experience. This in turn can adversely affect their educational achievement (DES, 1985).

Teachers should give greater emphasis to the personal valuing of children's cultural backgrounds, beliefs and experiences. In most areas of the curriculum the most immediate and important learning for a child is not the value of the experience to society, but the value to himself/herself. Teachers who are conscious of, and sensitive to, their own values, feelings and emotions are more likely to be able to encourage children to explore the conflicts which pupils feel. The key to this process is listening and responding with understanding. Classrooms and schools with such a 'client-centred' ethos would help many more children to be tolerant of differences between various cultural, religious and social groups.

In the National Curriculum there is an emphasis upon the paramount importance of a commitment to provide equal opportunities for all pupils. As stated in the *Curriculum Guidance No. 3: The Whole Curriculum*:

> The curriculum must aim to meet the needs of all pupils regardless of physical, sensory, intellectual, emotional/behavioral difficulties, gender, social and cultural backgrounds, religious or ethnic origins. All schools whatever their location and intake have a responsibility to promote good relationships and mutual respect.
>
> The ethos of a school should support the school's policy of equal opportunity by countering stereotypes and prejudice, reducing the effects of discrimination and helping pupils to accept and understand social diversity. (NCC, 1990, p. 13)

The National Curriculum Council has identified 'education for a life in a multicultural society' as a cross-curricular dimension, which should permeate all aspects of the curriculum. Permeation does not happen by chance; teachers have to make a conscious effort and schools have to offer support.

The 'Peace Education Programme' described in Chapter 2 is a complementary strategy whereby social cohesion can be developed in a culturally diverse context. Table 8.1 also contains details of helpful sources for teachers.

The National Curriculum can be used in combatting racism as advocated in the guidelines for teachers published by the NUT (NUT, 1992). The guidelines suggest that in English, children should learn myths and legends from around the world. Schools should invite writers from different ethnic groups, though parents and pupils may need to be prepared for these visits in 'all white' schools. In history, it is important that 'it is not just the perspective of the British or European explorer that is given but that of indigenous people in parts of the world to which Europeans travelled and in many cases exploited for their resources and labour' (NUT, 1992). In mathematics teachers should use mathematical games from different parts of the world and teach symmetry through Latin American patterns and tessellations with Islamic patterns. Physical education teachers should point to the success of black athletes, and science teachers to Indian research scientists, 'to combat the stereotypes of science as the product of Western Industrialized Societies alone' (NUT, 1992).

In Volume 3 of this series, experts in each of the NC foundation subjects and RE provide suggestions whereby cultural diversity can be used. Neither the foundation subjects and RE nor the cross-curricular elements can effectively stand alone.

The quality of relationships between schools and parents is another area highlighted in various sections of the ERA. The requirements of the ERA relating to religious education and collective worship are one of the dimensions for community consultation (see Chapter 2 and Volume 3, Chapter 3).

If pupils are to gain from a curriculum which genuinely promotes their personal and social development, careful planning and pluralist strategies need to be developed by teachers. Such an approach must focus on particular themes, competencies and dimensions which go across curricular boundaries. The task is a challenging one, but not impossible!

Table 8.1: Materials/Resources for Teachers on Social and Personal Education

Title:	*Issues: A cross-curricular course for PSE*
Author:	John Foster Collins
Series:	Issues 1. Pupil's Book, £4.95. 0 00 327334 2
	Teachers' Resources, £7.25. 0 00 327339 3
	Issues 2. Pupils' Book, £4.95, 0 00 327334 0
	Teachers' Resources, £7.25, 0 00 327340 7
	Used selectively and flexibly in conjunction with other resources, and carefully coordinated with contributions from other areas of the curriculum, the books do represent, if not the solution to all problems, at least a partial alleviation of resourcing headaches for busy teachers.
Title:	*'Art as Social Action' Project*
Publisher:	News sheet Art and Development Education 5–16 Project top floor Effra School, Barnwell Road, Brixton, London, SW2 1PL (Tel: 01–737–7967 or (project) 01–326–1883).
Media:	Magazine: £2 for 6 issues
	The project aims to explore links between visual arts and development education, examining approaches to issues of gender, race and class and looking at how curriculum extensions can be made from art to other subject areas.
Title:	*Earthrights: Education as if the planet really mattered*
Publisher:	114 Centre For Global Education, University of York, Heslington, York, Y01 5DD (Tel: 0904-433-444)
Media:	Book-illustrated: £4.95 + post and packing (p&p)
	A teacher's handbook exploring the relationship between development, environmental, human rights and peace education and arguing for a global and holistic approach to education. For all teachers — primary, secondary, FE, HE.
Titile:	*Educating the Whole Child*
Author:	Sandip Hazareesingh, Kelvin Simms and Patsy Anderson

Table 8.1:   (Cont.)

Publisher: Building Blocks, Early Years Education, 40 Tabard Street, London, SE1 4JU
(Tel: 071–403–8264)
Media: Book; English: £4.00
Seeks to answer questions such as 'How can we lay the foundations of
children's educational achievement while helping each child take pride in her
cultural accomplishments, care for others, and care for the world in which
she lives?'. . . . and more.

Title: *Issues in Teaching and Learning about Human Rights*
Author: Ian Lister. Centre for Global Education, University of York, Heslington, York,
Y01 5DD (Tel: 0904–433–444)
Media: 10 pages + p&p
Outline of paper for a Council of Europe seminar. Deals with aims, content,
themes and skills of human-rights education; human-rights world studies.

Title: *Racial Justice, Global Development or Peace: Which shall we choose in
school?*
Publisher: David Hicks, Centre for Global Education, University of York, Heslington, York,
Y01 5DD (Tel: 0904–433–444)
Media: 10 pages; 25p + p&p
Considers the similarities and differences of four responses to these issues,
i.e., multicultural education, peace studies, development education and world
studies.

Title: *Teaching Development Issues Section 1 Perceptions*
Publisher: D. Cooke and others. Development Education Project, c/o Manchester
Polytechnic, 801 Wilmslow Road, Manchester, M20 8RG (Tel: 061–445–2495)
Media: KS3 and above. Booklet; 42 pages; illustrated; 1985, £3.50 including p&p
Aims to help motivate and involve pupils in thinking about wider world and
develop skills of empathy; recognize bias and consider their values and
attitudes. Includes teachers' notes and pupils' stimulus materials which can
be reproduced.

Title: *The Human Story — Resource Pack 3 — The Unity of Humankind: An
Introduction to World Studies*
Publisher: Commonwealth Institute, Educational Resource Centre, Kensington High
Street, London, W8 6NQ (Tel: 01–603–4535 Ext. 293/292)
Media: KS2–3. Pack; hire £3 per month, £5 per half-term, £9 per term + p&p
Shows the interdependence of peoples and countries and coexistence of a
diversity of cultures. Contains slides, film-strip, charts, notes, game,
information, resources guide.

Title: *Global Teacher, Global Learner*
Publisher: Graham Pike and David Selby, Centre for Global Education, University of York,
Heslington, York, Y01 5DD (Tel: 0904–433–444)
Media: Book; 312 pages; illustrated; 1988; £12.95 plus p&p; teacher reference
This handbook, which has arisen out of the World Studies Teacher Training
Project, brings together the experience of many teachers and offers a wide
range of teaching approaches and classroom activities for world studies in all
areas of the curriculum.

Title: *Many Faces Many Friends*
Publisher: Advisory Centre, Education Department, County Hall, Glenfield, Leicester,
LE3 8RF
Media: Book; £1.38 (cheques to Leicestershire County Council); teacher reference
Suggestions for the use of stories in primary schools for social, moral and
religious education.

Table 8.1: (Cont.)

Title:	*Religious Studies and PSE materials*
Publisher:	Pergamon Educational Production, Hennock Road, Marsh Barton, Exeter, EX2 8RP (Tel: 0392–74121)
Media:	Books and videos; KS1 and above plus teacher reference
	Pergamon (including religious and moral education press) produce a catalogue of materials for personal and social education and religious studies including various items originally produced by LEA resources centres.
Title:	*Attitude Awareness Pack*
Publisher:	Multicultural Education and Language Service, Broadbent Road, Oldham, OL1 4HU (Tel: 061–665–3734)
Media:	Pack — 3 booklets illustrated in black and white, KS1&2
	A project at primary level about the formation of healthy attitudes towards oneself and others — including affirmation, sharing, cooperation, communications, creative conflict resolution, differences can be good, people from other countries.
Title:	*Myself*
Publisher:	ACER (Afro-Caribbean Resources Centre) Wyvil Road, London, SW8 2TJ (Tel: 01–627–2662)
Media:	Pack — 4 colour books, 8 colour photos, teachers' book; pack £9 (components of pack may also be purchased). 0–KS2
	Designed for the early years to help young children explore ideas about themselves — how they look and feel, and what they do.

References

CAMPBELL, J. (1992) 'A surfeit of themes' in the *Times Educational Supplement*, 25 September, p. 12.

DEPARTMENT OF EDUCATION AND SCIENCE/HER MAJESTY'S INSPECTORATE (1979) *Aspects of Secondary Education in England*, London, HMSO.

DEPARTMENT OF EDUCATION AND SCIENCE/HER MAJESTY'S INSPECTORATE (1980) *A View of the Curriculum*, London, HMSO.

DEPARTMENT OF EDUCATION AND SCIENCE (1981) *Assessment of Performance Unit: Personal and Social Development*, Report by the DES, London, HMSO.

DEPARTMENT OF EDUCATION AND SCIENCE (1985) *Report of the Committee of Inquiry into the Education of Children from Ethnic Minority Groups* (The Swann Report), Cmnd. 9453, London, HMSO.

DEPARTMENT OF EDUCATION AND SCIENCE (1988) *The Education Reform Act 1988*, London, HMSO.

FOUNTAIN, S. (1990) *Learning Together: Global Education 4–7*, York University, Stanley Thornes.

IRWIN, P. (1993) *Friendship and Peer Relations in Children*, Chichester, John Wiley.

LAWRENCE, D. (1987) *Enhancing Self-Esteem in the Classroom*, London, Paul Chapman Press.

MANCHESTER CITY COUNCIL EDUCATION DEPARTMENT (1991) *Cross-Curricular Themes, Skills and Dimensions: Implementing the Whole Curriculum*, Manchester, MED.

METROPOLITAN BOROUGH OF STOCKPORT (1988) *Personal and Social Education: Guidelines for Teachers*, Education Division, MBS.

NATIONAL CURRICULUM COUNCIL (1989a) *Annual Report, 1988–89*, York, NCC.
NATIONAL CURRICULUM COUNCIL (1989b) *Circular No. 6: National Curriculum and Whole Curriculum Planning*, York, NCC.
NATIONAL CURRICULUM COUNCIL (1989c) *NCC News*, June, York, NCC.
NATIONAL CURRICULUM COUNCIL (1990) *Curriculum Guidance No. 3: The Whole Curriculum*, York, NCC.
NATIONAL UNION OF TEACHERS (1992) *Anti-Racist Guidelines*, London, NUT.
PRING, R. (1984) *Personal and Social Education in the Curriculum*, London, Hodder and Stoughton.
SCHOOLS COUNCIL (1983) *Primary Practice: A sequel to 'The Practical Curriculum'* (Working Paper 75), London, Methuen.

Chapter 9

Gender Issues

Val Millman and Sandra Shipton

Context

Most teachers will, in recent years, have engaged in often heated debates about issues of both cultural diversity and gender equality in our schools. These debates may have taken place in staffrooms, playgrounds, at parents' evenings and at teacher-union meetings, on courses and at conferences as well as in our own homes. They have often exposed our personal and professional sensitivities and left us with a range of contradictory feelings and understandings. We believe in equality and justice, we recognize the value and importance of diversity; how can we be sure that the approaches we adopt in our classrooms will bring about greater equality for girls and boys within school and in the world outside?

This chapter has been written by two white European women who have taken part in these discussions over the past twenty years.[1] Although most of our 'on the ground' attempts at bringing about equality have taken place in inner-city primary and secondary schools in Coventry, each of us has also been part of wider debates about equality issues at regional and national level. We are still not 'sure' that the approaches we have adopted are the best ones; but we are glad to have made positive moves in that direction rather than wait for the promise of certainty that probably never arrives! Recognizing that our perspective will be limited by our own backgrounds and experiences we believe we have found ways of making some sense of gender and 'race'-equality issues and of helping adults and children with whom we work not only to understand these but also to take action that will move each of us forward in the direction of greater equality for all.

We start by touching on some of the difficulties and achievements experienced by those of us who have been working to promote 'race' equality and gender equality in recent years. We then consider the relationship between these two areas of development and their current position on the national educational agenda. This leads to an identification of certain principles and assumptions which underlie the examples of practice described in this chapter.

Each example of practice is drawn from a single primary school but has relevance we think to other primary schools which may have very different school populations. The issues we believe are there for all girls and all boys in all schools. The way in which they are approached by teachers may need to differ.

Many of us have at times been tentative in the ways we have tried to introduce equality strategies into our schools. There has been a variety of reasons for this. Despite an increase in educational research into both 'race' equality and gender equality in the 1970s and 1980s, our knowledge base is less securely established than that associated with traditional areas of pedagogy and the curriculum. Many of us have felt more comfortable with one dimension of equality than another. The complexity of incorporating each equality dimension into every aspect of school organization and practice seems overwhelming, especially at a time when school structures themselves are undergoing such radical change. The risk of 'getting it wrong' at times seems too high a price to pay; equality issues have become politically charged and our confidence in handling potentially sensitive issues undermined as a result. Many of us have felt isolated in our attempts to bring about greater equality in schools; we have not succeeded in demonstrating to colleagues that equal-opportunities policies are central rather than peripheral to the performance of the school and the well-being of its community.

Despite these difficulties, many teachers in many schools have shown that it is possible successfully to address areas of inequality through changes to their school curriculum and organization. Although approaches to 'race' equality and gender equality have developed along different routes during the past twenty years, successful change in each of these areas has shared many common features. These include the importance of changing attitudes, both of pupils and teachers, the importance of whole-school approaches in which equality perspectives are central to all new initiatives, the effectiveness of a combined top–down/bottom–up approach to change, the key role played by positive role models and the importance of monitoring progress through the collection of quantitative data (Gerwirtz, 1991). Many children and young people have directly benefited from such changes and from the improved quality of education they have consequently experienced. Indeed, much of the National Curriculum guidance issued by the National Curriculum Council reinforces precisely these aspects of curriculum change (NCC, 1991) although no specific guidance on either cultural diversity or gender has been published. NCC guidance emphasizes that the National Curriculum is an entitlement curriculum and that 'equal opportunities' is a dimension which should permeate the whole curriculum. The 1993 Education Bill has supported this approach by requiring independent inspectors of schools to evaluate the extent to which the particular needs of individual pupils arising from gender, ability, ethnicity and socio-economic background are met within the teaching and life of the school generally. Inspection reports will include an evaluation of the school's policy for equality of opportunity and its effect on the standards of pupils' work; an evaluation of how well the policy is understood and implemented in terms of opportunities and support arrangements for individuals and different groups. (OFSTED, 1993)

We can therefore expect as we move through the 1990s that most primary schools, irrespective of the composition of their school population, will have a written statement or policy that expresses the schools' commitment to equality of opportunity for all pupils. Some of these schools will have developed policy in relation to different dimensions of equality of opportunity ('race' and gender for example) and will have defined precisely what the policy means for each of the constituent groups — their entitlements and their responsibilities for implementing the policy. Few schools, however, will yet have tackled the crucial relationship between each policy dimension; what precisely does equality of opportunity mean for women and men, girls and boys from different ethnic, cultural, religious and social groups?

Challenges

The Relationship Between 'Race' and Gender Issues in Schools

Despite the growing body of research into the areas of 'race' and gender equality, as Gerwirtz (1991) observes 'To date there has been little attempt to integrate "race" and gender into a single theoretical framework.' Heidi Safia Mirza also asserts in her book *Young Female and Black* (1992, p.13) that 'because underachievement has remained the overriding concern of educational research with regard to the black child, . . . the whole matter of gender has been marginalised in academic debate.' Alongside this marginalization Gerwirtz points out that 'correspondingly, there has been reluctance on the part of policy makers to develop practical initiatives which bind them together. On the other hand, evidence is emerging that at the level of actual school practice teachers are employing strategies which engage jointly with issues of race and gender'.

Policy and Practice in a Coventry Primary School

Edgewick Community Primary School has 200 pupils on its school roll with approximately equal numbers of girls and boys in each year group. It is set within an LEA which has maintained a tradition of collaboration both between individual schools and across the LEA as a whole. Most of the pupils' families came to Coventry from outside England, the majority from India and Pakistan, a minority from Bangladesh and Scotland. The most strongly represented religious groups are Sikh, Muslim and Hindu. In the following examples of practice from Edgewick School the broad categories of Asian and white will only be used where, for those pupils or adults involved, there was a discernible difference between the responses of each of these groups. The examples of practice described have been selected to highlight gender equality issues in a range of school-curriculum areas. The term curriculum is taken to include the whole curriculum offered by the school — those planned and unplanned experiences which take place in the course of a child's school day.

The school's commitment to equality is strongly expressed in its aims on the first page of the school brochure:-

> The aim of the school is to create a caring environment in which children are able to develop their full potential at their own pace. We aim for an environment that caters for the individual child whatever her or his needs, ability, culture or background. Further the school is committed to policies of ensuring equal opportunities for all who use it, regardless of race, gender, disability, class or age and to the active participation of both parents and the community in the life of the school.
>
> In adopting Coventry City Council's Equal Opportunities Policy document we, at Edgewick Community Primary School, are committed to the provision of a learning environment for the local community in which each person involved in the processes of teaching and learning is accorded equality of esteem and value.
>
> We have our own equal opportunities policy document in which the principles we adopt and the approaches by which we hope to achieve our aims are set out in full. In brief we intend to promote the policy by our attention to the whole learning environment which we provide (the resources, staff and subject matter which we teach) and by taking active steps to oppose racist, sexist and discriminatory practices and abuse.

The school's equal-opportunities policy is not a static document. Although the principles on which it is based remain constant, there is regular review of the day-to-day strategies involved in implementation. The following assumptions and principles underlie the school's approach to policy-making and monitoring; implementation of equal-opportunities policy; and gender equality in a culturally diverse society.

1. Policy-making and monitoring
   - a policy can only be a framework for action; its effectiveness must be monitored in day-to-day practice;
   - change needs to be planned in the context of policy. Not all change is planned however; a policy can help to guide responses to unexpected situations;
   - all members of the school's community have a part to play in shaping and reviewing school policy. At times members of different groups will have different perspectives. All perspectives must be taken seriously;

each group must learn to handle difference and negotiate resolution of conflict; and

- the concerns of one group of parents usually reflect the concerns of all parents.

2. Implementation of equal-opportunities policy
   - all members of a school and its community have rights and responsibilities in relation to equality and therefore all must play a part in policy development;
   - equality issues are central to the whole curriculum and must remain so in the face of competing external pressures;
   - all pupils are entitled to equal access to the whole curriculum; equality dimensions should permeate the whole curriculum;
   - good practice in relation to gender and race equality is good educational practice for all;
   - the learning environment must be one in which all pupils feel safe enough to take risks, face challenges, grow in confidence, knowledge and skills. The world outside school is both sexist and racist; pupils need to be equipped to be objective, to take decisions for themselves and challenge inequalities successfully;
   - the role of the teacher is to plan, support and intervene; inequalities do not go away of their own accord. Positive action is necessary to redress inequalities arising from past practice; and
   - female and male staff from different backgrounds can offer a range of skills, perspectives and experiences to pupils. Staff need to understand that their own values and attitudes are not necessarily the only 'correct' ones.

3. Gender equality within a culturally diverse society
   - each pupil is different, the product of a particular combination of cultural, religious, educational socialization and of his/her own individuality;
   - education takes place within a framework of human rights based on the equal value of all people; each pupil will need to view this baseline in the context of their own cultural framework and decide on appropriate action.
   - discrimination on the basis of gender is as unacceptable as discrimination on the basis of skin colour or ethnicity;
   - acceptance of different cultural frameworks does not mean an absolute acceptance of male domination within any of them;
   - no culture, including white western culture is homogeneous;
   - there is the potential for intergenerational conflict within all cultures;
   - roles within all cultures tend to be demarcated by gender; this demarcation usually has the effect of subordinating women and girls although the subordination can take many different forms; and

- perspectives and priorities for change will differ from group to group, from culture to culture.

Responses

Equality strategies within the curriculum; six examples

'Sensitive' Issues — Sex Education

Following initial consultation with parents, sex education had been part of the curriculum at Edgewick for some time. It was, however only as a result of a directive from the Department for Education (then DES) in 1989 that the issue was discussed by the school governors and a decision taken that it should become a core element of the curriculum. This decision was taken to a governor's annual meeting for parents.

Initially, it appeared, after explanation and discussion, that there were no objections. The staff therefore planned to include sex education as usual within their curriculum. In years 5 and 6 one member of staff approached sex education within the context of health education, and at one session began to talk to the pupils about puberty and the associated body changes.

The following day the headteacher was approached by the mother of one of the girls. The mother was in an anxious but angry state. She complained that she felt her 10-year-old daughter was too young to talk about such things in school and that she had been very embarrassed during the lesson.

The headteacher listened and realized that perhaps the school had been complacent about the extent to which parents had accepted and understood the school's approach to sex education within the curriculum. The headteacher, with the support of the class teacher met with the parent a second time. The purpose of this meeting was to explain how the issues were being approached in the classroom and to show the mother the range of materials that were being used. It also became apparent that there was a need to communicate with more parents. The parents of pupils in years 5 and 6 were invited to attend a curriculum meeting on health education. During this meeting the parents would be able to view a variety of materials including those used for sex education. The meeting included a translation facility for those parents who required it.

The second meeting with the mother had not changed her views although it was very useful for the headteacher and classteacher as it had enabled both of them to further understand and appreciate her anxieties and sensitivities about the subject. It was therefore with some trepidation that the parents' curriculum workshop was approached. The attendance at the meeting was fairly good. Twelve parents attended, eleven of whom were Asian (including the complainant) and one of whom was white. They were all women. After a general introduction and an examination of materials the discussion that followed was illuminating. All of the women, with the exception of the complainant, welcomed the inclusion of sex education within the curriculum and felt that it was important for both their daughters and their sons. They felt that they had personally suffered because of their own lack of sex education and they shared many of their own disturbing and distressing experiences. Regarding the way that the school was approaching sex education they felt assured by a statement by the governing body on sex education which included the following:-

> Sex Education will therefore take place within the normal classroom structure although there may be occasions when single sex sessions may be appropriate. Children will be taught, as always, at a level that is appropriate to their age and development.

The parent who complained did not change her mind. She did not, however, remove her daughter from any further lessons. Although the school had found it extremely useful to have a statement on sex education to show to parents, staff recognized the need to develop a fuller policy. Initially, having consulted the parents the school had assumed that the consultation was complete. Also at this time there appeared to be more pressing areas of the National Curriculum which demanded time and attention. But, of course, new year groups bring different parents with different view points. On reflection it seems essential to ensure that the demands of the National Curriculum and assessment do not squeeze out work that is to be undertaken in other areas, particularly where, as in sex education, parents have strong views and issues of cultural diversity and gender need to be considered.

Key curricular challenge:
- to gain the support of governors and parents for building sex education into the mainstream curriculum.

Key curricular response:
- consulting through parents and governing body meetings;
- producing a policy statement on sex education; and
- maintaining a dialogue with those involved in sex-education programmes by taking concerns seriously and responding in a positive and open way.

Access to the Curriculum: Residential Education

Although constantly under threat from budgetary reductions, Coventry is fortunate to own an outdoor activities centre in North Wales. Edgewick use this centre annually and the visit to 'Plas-Dol-y-Moch' has become a tradition for the older pupils. Whilst working on the schools equal-opportunities policy various aspects of school life were examined including that of residential visits. It became apparent that although there was always a very high take-up by the boys in the school the response from the girls was not as good. The school was concerned that the girls were missing out on key aspects of personal and social education and skill development.

The staff concerned felt that their responses should be consistent with the way that they would respond to issues of access to any other area of the curriculum. They needed to investigate the reasons why these girls were not taking part.

After talking informally to them the class teacher discovered two main reasons for their non-involvement. Some of the girls had their own anxieties and worries about being away from home and worries about the nature of the activities that they would undertake at the centre. There were other girls however who did want to go but their parents, in particular their fathers, had not given permission. The first group of girls was easier to deal with. Staff set about exploring their fears showing them videos and enabling them to talk to pupils who had previously been to the residential centre. Some were convinced, others not. The approach for the second group needed more sensitive handling. At this time the school was fortunate to have an Asian, Section 11 funded, male teacher for part of the week. He had been very supportive of equal-opportunity strategies and his daughter, who was at university, had been in to school to talk to the pupils about her experiences of travel around the world. He offered to visit the parents to find out about their anxieties. He was then able to assure many of the parents of the safety aspects of the outdoor activities and of the sleeping arrangements. He was also able to discuss with parents the benefits that were to be gained from participating in a residential experience.

At the same time it was felt necessary to develop a school policy on 'outdoor activities'. This was drawn-up in collaboration with the governing body and particularly highlighted equality of access for all pupils.

> Girls should be given the opportunity to participate in activities from which they might otherwise be excluded, i.e., physically demanding or adventurous type activities. It is vital that appropriate and sensitive support is given in this respect.

As a result of this two-fold intervention the take-up of girls increased, although it was still not equivalent to that of the boys.

However, it is the influence that those girls who have participated has had on others which has been important. It was interesting to note their increased confidence both during the residential visit and upon their return to school. Many of them who felt frightened by activities such as rock-climbing and canoeing found that they were able to undertake these confidently and in many cases were as good, if not better than their male counterparts. This posed difficulties for some of the boys but provided an ideal opportunity for the staff to counter the pupils' stereotyped images of both boys and girls through discussion about the visit.

A display of photographs after the visit attracted a good deal of attention from pupils, parents and staff. Upon hearing their own children's accounts of the visit and seeing the photographs the parents recognized the value and worth of such activities. Staff, however, are aware that similar types of intervention will be needed each year to maintain equality of access to this part of the school curriculum.

Key curricular challenge:
- to increase the access of girls to outdoor education in a residential setting.

Key curricular response:
- to increase pupil and parental understanding of the purpose of the visit; and
- to gain pupil and parental confidence in the organized activities and the arrangements for the pupils' safety.

Curriculum Development: Confronting Issues of Racism and Sexism

A priority at Edgewick for many years has been to create an antiracist environment, an environment in which all racist abuse is eliminated. This has worked well within school but following a whole-school visit to a local country park, where some children received racist comments, it was felt that the school needed to do more to equip the children with the skills needed to deal with racist abuse in the 'outside' world. It was interesting that the victims of the abuse had initially asked the adults from school to deal with the matter. The staff did this and discussed their actions with the children both at the time and upon return to school. The incident highlighted the difficulties that we felt some of our pupils could experience upon transfer to secondary school. At the time children were transferring to approximately six different schools in the area, often in groups of twos or threes.

It was as a result of these factors that the staff in years 5 and 6 decided to include racism awareness and gender stereotyping within their curriculum. The topic they planned began by examining migration to England including the historical reasons for this, there being numerous opportunities to develop this within the history and geography National Curriculum. The children then traced their own family backgrounds. They had all been born in England but all of their families had originated from elsewhere, e.g., Scotland, India, Pakistan, Caribbean. The children considered the situations faced by immigrants arriving in new countries, including racism and low pay. Many of them could relate experiences from their own family. They became increasingly interested in experiences of racism and in how black people in particular deal with various forms of oppression. The lives of Martin Luther King, Harriet Tubman, the Rani of Jhansi and Nelson Mandela were studied using materials collected from a variety of sources. The decision to include two black women proved to be successful. The two classes, in particular the girls, became interested in the Rani of Jhansi and this resulted in a full-scale drama production centred around her story which was presented to the school, to parents and to other local schools.

The Rani of this story was an Indian queen who fought against the British when they refused to acknowledge her adopted son as her legitimate heir. Her story was given a present-day relevance by being presented as a play within a play set in present-day Coventry. A Coventry mother told the story to her two children, a boy and a girl, who squabbled about boys and girls roles and duties about the house. As the mother told the story it came to life and demonstrated to the audience that a woman could be a leader and a warrior. Sereena aged 10 who played the part of the Rani, wrote about the play:

> I learnt a lot from the Rani of Jhansi. I thought it was a big experience for me and I think it taught us all that the girls and boys are equal. It is silly to think there are jobs for men and not for women. People say that girls are supposed to stay inside and help their Mums. But No! That can be wrong and I hope all of us understand this. My ambition is to become a lawyer, and some people think to become a lawyer you must be a boy. But if I am affected by this when I grow up I will stand up for what I believe in. I will not take this from anyone so I hope I become a lawyer. But I will have to work hard. But the Rani of Jhansi was an experience I will never forget!

The enthusiasm of both pupils and staff for the project permeated the school and stimulated lively debate and discussion both in the classroom and the staffroom not only about the Rani story but also about other issues including the stereotyped roles that boys and girls are supposed to adopt. In the discussions around migration leading up to the Rani story the children found opportunities to talk about their own experiences of sexism and racism and to work out with their teachers the best way of dealing with it. A good deal of assertiveness training, together with rehearsing how they might behave in different situations, formed the basis of this.

It later became apparent that this project had helped the children understand some of the news stories that were prevalent at the time especially from South Africa. The mother of one of the pupils in Years 5 and 6 called in to see the headteacher one day to tell her about her son who, whilst watching a television news item about South Africa, had been able to challenge some of his grandfather's racist views, providing statistics and evidence to back up his view point. This mother felt proud of her son, was impressed by his growing confidence and wanted the school to know this. This feedback along with comments made by other parents convinced the school that the parents were pleased to know that the school was addressing these issues through the curriculum.

Key curricular challenge:
- to use opportunities within the curriculum to help pupils understand and challenge racism and sexism in appropriate ways.

Key curricular response:
- to ensure that equal-opportunities policy forms an integral part of Schemes of Work planning in relation to curriculum content and learning activities; and
- through recruitment and staff-development policies ensure that staff and pupils are able to develop together appropriate skills and attitudes.

Sexual and Racial Harassment in the Playground

The importance of vigilance in monitoring behaviour outside of the classroom in all schools is essential. Often types of antisocial behaviours come in 'waves' and what might be a major issue one week ceases to be so the next. A judgment therefore needs to be made about high profile, full-scale intervention. It was with this in mind that the following situation was approached. There appeared to be a number of individual incidents of name-calling on the playground accumulating over a period of time. Upon further investigation this name-calling did not appear to be direct but was aimed at other children's families and in particular their mothers. The situation was further complicated for some staff by the fact that this abuse was often taking place in Punjabi, Urdu and Gujerati. The comments of a visiting teacher regarding a similar situation that he had experienced in a primary school in London convinced the staff that action had to be taken in order to prevent the situation escalating further.

Through talking with pupils and supervisory staff, staff with Asian-language skills discovered that the comments were mainly regarding the physical attributes of mothers and their sexuality such as mothers being prostitutes and sleeping with named men, e.g., Salman Rushdie. These comments of course were extremely inflammatory and were the cause of some very highly charged aggression on the playground. It was also discovered that the lunchtime supervisory staff, three of whom were Asian parents of children in the school had also had sexually abusive things said about them and to them but had felt too shy and uncomfortable to report this.

All staff felt that this was a serious issue and had to be met 'head on'. Following a whole-school assembly about name-calling which included abuse of each other's families, class teachers followed the issue up in classrooms giving both the children who had been involved and the perpetrators of the abuse a chance to talk about how they had felt. The children were made aware that this kind of verbal abuse was totally unacceptable and that any further incidents would involve the respective parents. This threat only had to be followed through on one occasion. The parents of the two children involved were seen separately and the school was able to involve a bilingual classroom assistant in translating exactly what had been said.

Through these incidents it became apparent that the lunchtime supervisory assistants not only had a training need but also a need for additional support from one another and the school staff. A course was organized by the headteacher and the schools educational psychologist for these staff which included issues around sexism, racism and confidence building. The whole course was firmly embedded within the context of the school's equal-opportunities policy. These women felt that some of the pupils had perceived their role within the school as being of a lower status than that of other staff and therefore felt at liberty to abuse them verbally. The course was needed to improve their self-esteem and to enable them to further develop their skills in managing challenging behaviours.

Key curricular challenge:
- to stop children harassing each other in the playground by insulting members of their families, in particular their mothers; and
- to prevent this behaviour damaging relationships within the community.

Key curricular response:
- investigating individual incidents by talking with the perpetrator and victim;
- making clear through whole-school and class-based discussions that this kind of harassment was unacceptable; and
- discussion with support staff, directly on the receiving end of this abuse, and how this could be dealt with in the future.

Pupil Groupings

During discussions around the development of the school's equal-opportunities policy a member of staff posed the question of pupil groupings. She said that although she had encouraged mixed sex groupings within her classroom, when pupils were given a 'free choice' they invariably organized themselves into single-sex groups. It became apparent that these groups were also culturally defined. This teacher's experience led to quite a lengthy staff discussion where it was felt that in practice although pupils will usually want to work or play with others who most closely share their personal experiences they also need to learn to work and play with pupils from different backgrounds in order to prepare them for experiences that they will encounter beyond school.

This teacher, together with a male colleague in a parallel Year 1 and 2 class, decided to structure activities and devise strategies which would enable the children to operate effectively in mixed groups. They decided that the vehicle for this intervention should be the use of construction equipment and imaginative role-play. The tasks for each area of activity were very carefully planned with appropriate equipment found or borrowed. The activities devised required cooperation between boys and girls, provided tasks that would not alienate the girls from developing construction skills and illustrated alternative views of gender roles.

The pupils were grouped into threes with two girls and one boy in each group. The ratio of two girls to one boy was a planned part of the strategy but it meant that the remaining few boys were in all boy groups of three. The membership of the groups was changed each week to ensure limited reinforcement of boys working together, especially on construction tasks. The tasks were presented on cards to each group. The teachers' role, whilst moving between groups, was to promote confidence in achievements, support the role of the children as facilitators, ensure that within each group there was a truly shared experience and to ensure that discussion focused around alternative roles. Although initially the groups found the situation rather strange the tasks gradually became the major interest and the hesitancy of working in mixed groups was soon forgotten. The confidence of the girls in using construction toys began to develop and boys also became more relaxed in role-play situations.

This initiative enabled the staff to consider the importance of groupings within school and the importance of the development of skills associated with group work. It was felt to be equally important to give pupils the opportunity to work in single-sex groupings when appropriate. This initiative concentrated on pupil groupings in the classroom. The next step, perhaps a more difficult one is to examine pupil groupings on the playground.

Key curricular challenge:
- for pupils to be able to operate effectively in a variety of groupings and recognize what can be gained from this.

Key curricular responses:
- the use of teacher-directed groups with opportunities for change over a period of time;
- carefully structured tasks for each group, including a clear allocation of roles so that the learning needs of pupils are taken into account, encouraging them to move beyond stereotypical roles; and
- the teacher to act as facilitator, observing and then intervening and supporting as necessary.

Sex-stereotyping in the Early Years

Children's perceptions of both their own cultural and gender roles and those of others are probably more apparent during play than during any other school activity. Play therefore forms an important part of any equal-opportunities work within school. It was therefore disturbing to an early-years teacher when she became aware of the repetitiveness of the children's play and the quite rigid role stereotyping that was taking place within the home corner in her classroom. The girls were continually cleaning, cooking, and looking after numerous babies while the boys frequently disrupted this by being 'bad dogs', 'painters and decorators' and 'robbers'. She wondered whether the boys persisted in this disruptive behaviour because they felt that the girls were in control of the roles they had created leaving the boys without a dominant role to fit into.

The teacher therefore decided to talk to her class about the possibility of using the home corner to create other fantasy worlds. She hoped that this might give the boys more scope for imaginative play. Initially, following class discussion, the home corner became a café complete with male and female cooks, waiters and waitresses and customers. Customers could even telephone the café to book a table. The children were very enthusiastic about the home corner's conversion and despite the fact that it was, on a few occasions, overrun by big 'bad dogs' visited by painters and decorators and burgled, the role-play was most successful. The teacher did notice, however, that the girls found it much easier to take on the new roles than the boys.

At later dates the home corner also became a medical centre with nurses, patients, doctors and administrative support. Again, the girls were better organized and more imaginative but, interestingly, the boys did begin to take on the more caring roles within the centre. Likewise when the corner was a railway station, boys adopted creative roles that contained certain built-in constraints upon their behaviour. Sometimes, when in role as drivers they found themselves having to wait patiently, as passengers waiting their turn, and as guards, having to wait until everything was ready before they could blow the whistle. Through her intervention the class teacher managed to provide both girls and boys with new opportunities for non-stereotypical role-play. She also enabled them to develop skills in sharing and turn-taking as well as having fun.

However the teacher felt that although there were some changes in the pupils' behaviour this was usually when they were aware that they were being observed. At other times they were surprisingly adept at subverting the teacher imposed structure to make the corner become what they wanted e.g., the 'bad dogs' who came into the café. She realized that a one-off strategy was not enough and that sustained intervention and observation targeted at both pupils and parents where possible was vital. She therefore shared her observations with some of the parents who were attending a Women's group at the school. During these sessions they also discussed the development of school policy, gender stereotyping and the influence of toys, using a video that she had made of the children playing in the home corner. This video was such a successful stimulus for discussion with parents that it was also used as a basis for staff discussion during the formulation of the school's equal-opportunities policy.

Key curricular challenge:
• to encourage girls and boys to adopt a wider variety of roles in the home corner; and
• to provide boys with more opportunities to engage in imaginative play.

Key curricular responses:
• to redesign the home corner so that over a period of time it provided a variety of different situations; and
• to share the responses to the work with staff and parents so that they were able to understand the purpose of the activities and would be able to offer their children a similar variety of play activities.

In conclusion, in each of these examples intervention prevented situations within the school becoming crises. The school was able to make decisions based on its knowledge of the local community and its pupils. In some cases by listening to parents and children, decisions were taken as to what form that intervention should take.

Also illustrated is the fact that this is an area of work where a collaborative approach is both essential and productive. This collaboration has included the LEA who, rightly, have kept issues of culture and gender alive through policy formulation and by incorporating issues of equal-opportunities into curriculum training. It may be said, however, that the implementation of ERA has meant that there are now less opportunities for schools to respond to these issues. Pupils are presented with an entitlement curriculum but surely this should be more than just the National Curriculum core and foundation subjects? Increasingly the cross-curricular themes and dimensions as outlined in the non-statutory NCC booklets are being squeezed out and it is not yet clear whether the Dearing proposals for 'freeing up' more Curriculum time beyond the National Curriculum and R.E. will result in teachers choosing to use that time to address equality issues (NCC/SEAC, 1993). This, in turn is set against a background of rapid change, in which staff morale is suffering, equal-opportunity issues in teacher employment become as pertinent as ever with the ultimate responsibility for appointments lying with, sometimes, inexperienced governors and where decreasing resources for staff development focus mainly on the National Curriculum and assessment. It is however, probably more important now than ever before to ensure that schools provide quality opportunities for all their pupils. In this context providing equal opportunities becomes a mainstream issue, needing identification in school-development plans and throughout the curriculum. Involvement of staff, parents, governors and pupils is essential. At the heart of this work is an issue of basic human rights. Just as much an entitlement as maths or science.

References

CITY OF COVENTRY (1993) *Edgewick Community Primary School Brochure 1993/ 94.*

GERWIRTZ, D. (1991) Analyses of Racism and Sexism in Education and Strategies for Change, *British Journal of Sociology of Education,* 12, 2.

NATIONAL CURRICULUM COUNCIL AND SCHOOL EXAMINATIONS AND ASSESSMENT COUNCIL (1993) *Interim Report: The National Curriculum and its Assessment,* London, NCC/SEAC.

NATIONAL CURRICULUM COUNCIL (1991) *Curriculum Guidance No. 3: The Whole Curriculum,* NCC, York.

OFFICE FOR STANDARDS IN EDUCATION (1993) *Framework for Inspection,* London, DFE.

SAFIA MIRZA, H. (1992) *Young, Female and Black,* London, Routledge.

Note

1. We would like to thank colleagues in Coventry with whom we have had discussions about issues raised in this chapter and the pupils, parents and staff at Edgewick School whose support for the school's equal-opportunities policy has been unfailing. Further thanks go to Hazel Taylor for the ideas developed in 'An Open Cupboard Policy' from *The English Curriculum — Gender,* ILEA.

Chapter 10

The Multicultural Dimension in the Primary National Curriculum

Robin Grinter

Context

There is no question about the legitimacy of multicultural education in the National Curriculum. 'Education for life in a multicultural society' is a key element in the dimensions that 'cover all aspects of equal opportunities . . . permeate the school curriculum and are the responsibility of all teachers'. This statement is taken from the National Curriculum Council (NCC) publication *Starting Out in the National Curriculum* (1992), which summarizes and adds to principles already set out in the Education Reform Act (1988), *From Policy to Practice* (NCC, 1989), the guidance documents *Curriculum Guidance No. 3: The Whole Curriculum* (NCC, 1990) and *Curriculum Guidance No.8: Education for Citizenship* (NCC, 1990), and an article on 'A Pluralist Society in the classroom and beyond' in the NCC newsletter of February 1991. It makes clear that multicultural education should be 'an explicit part of the curriculum policy in every school and integral to (its) planning, develop-ment and evaluation', thus creating a curriculum which should, in the words of the Education Reform Act, be 'broad and balanced' and 'ensure . . . cultural development' as an entitlement for all.

Some of the implications of permeation are spelt out in these documents. As the newsletter points out, 'Multicultural Education is concerned with more than the needs of pupils from ethnic minority backgrounds. It seeks to pre-pare all pupils for life in a world where they will meet, live and work with peoples of different cultures, religions, languages and ethnic origins'. The National Curriculum 'contributes to multicultural education by broadening the horizons of all pupils so that they can understand and contribute to a pluralist society'.

Some of the implications of the strategy of permeation are made clear in the documents. *Starting Out in the National Curriculum* (NCC, 1992) states that Education for a life in a multicultural society means: extending pupils' know-ledge and understanding of different cultures, languages and faiths; valuing cultural diversity by drawing on pupils' backgrounds and experiences, and offering positive images and role models from all cultures,' *Curriculum*

Guidance No. 8: Education for Citizenship proposes areas of study such as 'Britain as a society made up of many cultures, ethnic groups, faiths and languages; the diversity of cultures in other societies and a study of human development and culture from different perspectives'. *Curriculum Guidance No. 3: The Whole Curriculum* notes that 'Teachers have a major role to play in preparing young people for adult life; this means life in a multicultural, multi-lingual Europe which in its turn is interdependent with the rest of the world'.

Moreover, the documents go beyond a descriptive approach. All pupils are entitled in the National Curriculum to fulfil their potential, and it is recognized that 'educational outcomes may be influenced by factors such as a pupil's . . . social, cultural or linguistic background'. Since the central factor in underachievement for these reasons is other people's views of pupils' culture and 'race' it is important to note clear antiracist implications in the require-ment in 'The Whole Curriculum' that schools should 'actively promote' positive attitudes to cultural diversity. 'Introducing multicultural perspectives into the curriculum . . . gives pupils the opportunity to view the world from different standpoints, helping them to question prejudice and develop open-mindedness'. 'Starting Out' adds the requirement to 'treat pupils as individuals with their own . . . backgrounds and experiences, challenging myths, stereotypes and misconceptions', to which the 'Whole Curriculum' adds the need to evaluate teaching materials and replace or adapt those shown to be stereotyped or discriminatory. 'Education for Citizenship' includes the proposal for study of 'the origins and effects of racial prejudice in British and other societies'.

Further, the documents stress that proposals must be implemented. 'Equal access to the curriculum means real opportunity to benefit', and the 'Whole Curriculum' states that 'schools need to foster a climate in which equality of opportunity is supported by a policy to which the whole school subscribes . . . reducing the effects of discrimination and helping pupils to accept and understand social diversity'. Three of the documents quoted state the evident implication that 'multicultural education is the professional responsibility of all teachers in all schools'.

Education for all for a multicultural society, effectively permeating the statutory curriculum, with significant antiracist elements that provide its es-sential cutting edge, is now therefore official policy, even if the Swann report of 1985 that first officially defined the need is not quoted. There is no room for additional elements 'bolted on' to an already overcrowded structure.

So far, so good. But in practice there are significant considerations and developments that marginalize multicultural education in the National Curriculum:

1. None of the whole-school cross-curricular themes are statutory.
2. There are real difficulties in fitting cross-curricular skills, five themes and every aspect of the dimensions (which throughout specify gender and special needs alongside multicultural considerations) into the prescribed curriculum, which itself needs reduction to fit into the school week.

3. In this context the NCC's decision not to publish its curriculum-guidance document on multicultural education, but to retain this for internal guidance purposes, has been immensely damaging. It implies that either this field is so straightforward that guidance is not necessary (whereas it is known to be fraught with difficulties), or that it is less important than the other cross-curricular elements. If schools and individual teachers wish to ignore it, they may feel some justification in doing so. Without guidance it has certainly been difficult for schools to make the dimension central to its overall planning of the curriculum, and it will in many cases now need to be developed or reinforced in a less than ideal structure.

4. The prescriptive nature of the various Programmes of Study in many cases reduces opportunities to introduce the most appropriate and effective education for a multicultural society in the first two Key Stages. Here the National Curriculum is the completion of the strategy begun with the abolition of the Schools Council in 1983, to reduce and then remove the opportunities for teacher-initiated curriculum development.

5. Moreover, the evolution of the Statutory Orders and Non-Statutory Guidance (NSG) has been, and in some cases still is, a process of change that has involved a consistent erosion of values and controversial issues from the content and guidance. The subject working group reports varied greatly in their treatment of the dimension, with mathematics for example specifically rejecting the relevance of cultural diversity, but all the others including a separate section on the dimension. This section has not always survived the translation into Statutory Orders and NSG, and normally has been abridged into a briefer statement omitting detailed advice. References and examples in the Statements of Attainment and Programmes of Study have been reduced in number and, particularly in geography's treatment of trade, pollution and conservation issues, frequently been stated much more blandly and uncontroversially. This process is still continuing, with the very positive technology curriculum being revised drastically, and pressure to drop the very relevant though demanding Attainment Target (AT) 2 (interpretation of source material) from Key Stage (KS) 2 in history. Although there is a surprising number of opportunities for the dimension still left in the Statutory Orders and NSGs, and all the positive elements in the Working Group Reports are still applicable, this process means that many of the multicultural and antiracist implications of situations and developments are not made explicit in the statutory elements of the curriculum. Effective permeation therefore depends on the existing level of teacher awareness of these issues, and this has always been the concern of a minority.

6. There are also developments in the primary Key Stages that threaten to make effective implementation of the multicultural dimension more

difficult. Pressure for more subject teaching by specialists is threatening the topic approach by class teachers; demands for more whole-class teaching is putting group work and the benefits of collaborative learning at risk; and the pressure on secondary schools to achieve well in 'league tables' of examination results is translating into pressure on primary schools to concentate on the core subjects of maths, science, technology and English to the detriment of the foundation subjects in humanities and arts where much, though not all, of the most appropriate multicultural education is taught. Cross-curricular elements are therefore also at risk as the concern for the whole child is marginalized. While primary education will doubtless retain its emphasis on working from experience and from the familiar, to the benefit of all non-white pupils, this will not in itself necessarily promote 'Education for All'. Fortunately it appears that the priorities emerging in the evolution of the 'Framework for Inspection of schools' include whole-school concerns for the 'social and cultural' as well as the 'spiritual and moral' ethos of schools — although there is some concern that the second of those aspects may tend to absorb the first to the detriment of multicultural education in its widest sense.

7. All these developments can be understood in the context of the politicization of education as part of the right-wing social and economic ideology of the 1980s. Multicultural education, especially its antiracist component with which many teachers in inner-city schools had identified, was seen as part of left-wing politics, along with other democratic and child-centred strategies.

Two strategies were adopted in essence to subvert these moves. In the curriculum, multicultural education was separated from all concern with the issues of race and class, and associated with an 'equal-opportunities education' now defined in terms of gender rather than the whole range of discrimination and disadvantages. 'Race' and class have been deliberately excluded as concepts and areas of concern. In structural terms, education has been opened up to market principles through the operation of parental choice, the publication of 'league tables' of school examination and assessment results, local management of schools by their own financial affairs and increasingly opting out of LEA control, with governing bodies having the final say in the priorities of the school and therefore its interpretation of the National Curriculum. These developments will all tend to bring about, or confirm, a situation of 'educational apartheid' where multicultural antiracist education will be stressed in multiracial areas and treated in a tokenist fashion elsewhere.

Finally, means of support for multicultural education have been reduced. Local Education Authorities have, with some justification in the case of major metropolitan authorities, been seen as the main source of support for left-wing democratic educational initiatives. In a startling reversal of historic Conservative philosophy, the authorities have now been either abolished, as in the case of the Inner London Educational Authority in 1990, or, as part of the local authority for their area, been 'rate-capped' to restrict their means and freedom of operation. LEAs will therefore have increasingly little opportunity to compensate for the absence of detailed guidance in implementation of the multicultural dimension through advisory work. The opportunities for 'Education for All' in the National Curriculum may well therefore be severely curtailed in practice.

In summary, for the forseeable future the context for multicultural education appears to be one of preservation and retrieval, with an even heavier responsibility on in-service work by those with awareness and commitment to the cause of multicultural education and social justice.

Challenges

The challenges to those with particular responsibility for implementation of multicultural education through the National Curriculum derive directly from the context — both from the responsibilities to promote the dimension and from the difficulties created for doing so. From that analysis it will be evident that they are political as well as academic challenges, and therefore greater than those created by the reorganization of content in academic subject areas, considerable as those have been.

The challenges faced by those promoting multicultural antiracist education have been fundamentally changed by the Education Reform Act and the National Curriculum. Freedom of operation has been reduced drastically. The strategy now has to be one of permeation of a prescribed, subject-based curriculum, whatever the difficulties involved, and however much this may reduce the potential effect. There is now less room for independent curriculum development based on wider educational principles such as relevance to pupils' experience and motivation. The products of this earlier development are now to differing degrees irrelevant, although there may be opportunities to draw on some of them in Key Stage 2: for example, work on migration may well fit into local studies in history, geography or topic work on the local environment or a theme such as 'movement'. Moreover, the work has to be undertaken retrospectively in many schools because of the absence of any curriculum guidance at the early planning stages.

In a more positive light, multicultural education is now a statutory requirement, and at least in theory 'the professional responsibility of all teachers'. It is now consciously linked with issues of gender equality and special needs, and in many schools is the responsibility of a cross-curricular coordinator. Clear links are established with the theme of 'Education for Citizenship', and with cross-curricular skills such as problem-solving and critical awareness which by definition permeate subject curricula.

But it is only the structure here that is really new. In curriculum terms permeation of the traditional subject material always was the real priority for multicultural antiracist educators, and this is now revealed beyond any argument. The real challenge is how to integrate multicultural and antiracist perspectives fully into academic subject thinking, so that they enhance teaching and understanding and thereby improve attainments and examination success. Although this will have, in most cases, to be done retrospectively, the antiracist impact of many of the cross-curricular skills, and the stimulating effect of new perspectives, all carry academic credibility. The real 'road to nowhere' is now the dangers of an *ad hoc* bolt-on approach. Although permeation has its dangers, as shown below, it has to be the main road forward. Success in making the perspectives of the dimension recognized as part of good education will also perform the essential task of persuading parents and governors of its validity through the improved attainment and examination results it can foster.

Part of the challenge here is also to avoid the known dangers and shortcomings of an inadequate permeation strategy. These involve over-reliance on a descriptive and superficial multicultural content, rather than explicitly identifying processes and skills at the centre of subject thinking that promote antiracist purposes. If the two are not held in harness, a superficial multiculturalism may itself be bolted onto the National Curriculum as an illustrative addition that does not influence pupils' thought or understanding. The absence of curriculum guidance for the dimension makes that only too possible. The outcome could easily be that a multicultural approach is taught by teachers who neither understand it nor believe in it.

Advocates of multicultural education have grappled with the problem of the separation of multicultural and antiracist perspectives for many years, and most now accept that the two are not incompatible in practice, even if they are different in nature. Multiculturalism must be associated with a rigorous antiracism. But this underlines the importance of the unending challenge of persuading teachers of the relevance and legitimacy of the dimension's perspectives to academic education. The majority of teachers have always been suspicious of multicultural education, and especially of its antiracist implications. The belief that 'we have no problem here' because a school has few or no black pupils is still very much a reality. The fact that the National Curriculum requires schools to integrate both perspectives into Programmes of Study may persuade teachers that they ought to undertake this task — a point that must be constantly reiterated — but it will not necessarily convince them of its validity or credibility.

A continuing campaign for increasing critical awareness and commitment is therefore still essential, and the pressures of implementing the National Curriculum in core and foundation subjects will not make this any more welcome or easy. Advocates of multicultural and antiracist education will also continue to run up against the familiar obstacles of ethnocentrism, stereotypical thinking and prejudice. Not much has changed in this respect, nor in the problems of finding or creating the materials that convey the required knowledge, understanding and perspectives.

Table 10.1: The Multicultural Dimension: Challenges

- The need to permeate a prescribed and largely ethnocentric National Curriculum.
- The traditional separation of multicultural and antiracist perspectives.
- A lack of academic credibility and relevance for the dimension in the eyes of many teachers.
- Pressures to marginalize the dimension.
- A shortage of relevant and appropriate teaching materials.
- The absence in many schools of a policy and ethos for implementation of the dimension.
- An inegalitarian political climate.

Priorities in meeting these challenges, both old and new, are fairly clear. Coordinators for cross-curricular purposes must establish clear and detailed criteria for the integration of the multicultural and antiracist element of the dimension into the curriculum. Because of the nature of the dimension, this needs to be done in coordination with criteria for gender equality and for ensuring the full potential for pupils with special needs. Work against all forms of unfair discrimination and disadvantage must proceed as a coherent package if it is to be recognized as making an effective contribution to whole-school development, and is to be adopted by subject staff who may not undertake the integration of evidently related elements if colleagues involved in each fail to do so. There is no room for the luxury of separate multicultural and antiracist approaches. The split in practice, if not in theory, between those two related elements has been healed, after much argument and soul-searching; integration of antiracist, antisexist and anticlass discrimination education is now long overdue. The exclusion of 'race' and class as concepts or areas for study in the National Curriculum will create difficulties and perhaps a need for less than an ideally balanced approach, but this integration must be undertaken. Doubtless it will prove a long and recriminatory struggle, but so long as splits continue, so will the work against discrimination and underachievement in schools be delayed.

The first task is to identify and agree guiding criteria using existing work on multicultural antiracist curriculum development, cross-curricular skills such as identification of stereotypes and problem-solving already identified in curriculum-guidance documents, and any appropriate elements that have surfaced at any stage in the evolution of the National Curriculum in subject areas to date — even if they have more recently disappeared. If the guiding criteria are related to National Curriculum materials in this way they will have greater credibility and applicability. A list of criteria in use at the present moment is included in the final section of this chapter as a response to the challenges that have been outlined.

The complementary task is for staff to work as a team to examine systematically the Programmes of Study and Statements of Attainment in the Statutory Orders, the NSG — particularly any sections relating to the dimension, to links between subjects and with cross-curricular skills — and the earlier subject Working Group Reports (WGR), in order to identify opportunities to implement the dimension in subject curricula and/or topic work. This process will indicate both explicit references to multicultural and antiracist elements in the Statutory Orders, NSG and WGRs, and highlight elements that have implications for these perspectives or could be exemplified from them. It is very much a matter of using the National Curriculum for the educational purposes that it should have safeguarded in the first place. This chapter will conclude with a selection of examples from different subjects to indicate how the list of criteria might be applied.

Responses

Criteria

The following list has been drawn-up from two recent publications: the National Union of Teachers' (1992) guidelines *Towards an Antiracist Curriculum* and the very important publication by the Runnymede Trust (1993) *Equality Assurance* drawn-up by a working party set up designed to fill the gap left by the NCC's failure to publish its own curriculum guidance for the dimension. These publications integrate multicultural and antiracist perspectives. The second has been designed to be expanded across the full range of equal-opportunities considerations, where this is not already implied. The criteria in this list are intended to create links and coherence across the curriculum, and guide teachers in the identification and/or creation of appropriate teaching materials.

- highlight achievements, traditions and distinctive values of non-white, non-western cultures and communities, both in their own right and as contributions to human achievement;
- place learning in the global context, exploring links between local, national and global developments;
- increase awareness and understanding of the influence cultures have and have had on one another;
- use pupils' daily-life experiences, and show that their different heritages are valued;
- encourage pupils to explore their own identity;
- explore common elements in human experience in different contexts;
- increase awareness and appreciation of differences in behaviour, values and beliefs in their cultural contexts;
- promote understanding of the value of different interpretations of the world;
- show that recent western cultural tradition and achievement is not superior to that of earlier or alternative cultures;
- identify and challenge bias, stereotypes and racism in the curriculum and in teaching materials;

- promote antiracist and egalitarian attitudes, concerns and skills, such as sensitivity, tolerance, appreciation, independence in views, open-mindedness and critical awareness;
- identify and overcome barriers to learning and achievement, including those relating to language;
- promote concern for justice and human rights; and
- increase awareness and understanding of conflicts of interest and the issues of power relationships that these create.

Implementation of Criteria: Some Examples

The Topic of 'movement' could include the experience of migration and explore many of the issues raised by 'Education for Citizenship'. This would start from pupils' experiences of holiday travel or moving house, drawing directly on any actual experiences of migration. The study would include: exploration of the geographical links between the home region, the nation and an economically developing country of origin, both past and present; study of historical records of the family and recollections of family members; comparison of different accounts and experiences, and similarities and differences between different areas, both now and in the past; calculation of the costs and expenses of the move, and differences in incomes and expenditures in different societies; exploration of the experience of migration through literature, personal accounts and pupils' own writing; discussion of the necessity and justification for the move, and conflicts of interest encountered at all stages. For pupils with their own mother tongues, much of the investigation and some of the presentation might take place in their own language, which would thereby gain respect and status.

Language has featured strongly in the first example, and it is worth here quoting in full the example given in the curriculum-guidance document for 'Education for Citizenship' at Key Stage 2 for the component 'A Pluralist Society'. 'Pupils conduct a survey of the languages spoken by members of the class/school and their families. Follow-up activities are based on the results, e.g., the history of scripts, where words come from, simple relationships between different languages, variety within language — accents, dialects, purpose etc., use of non-verbal language and 'taster' lessons in other languages, including songs.'

A multicultural approach to structures and forces in physics could be illustrated through a study of homes and buildings throughout the world. These could include tent dwellings of nomadic peoples, where, for example, Bedouin structures avoid the need for guy ropes by skilful calculation of fabric tension around the central pole and a low-profile design to reduce wind pressure; Inuit homes create arches from precisely-shaped ice blocks; and, combining this approach with the 'History Thematic Unit' in KS2, 'Houses and Places of Worship', Medieval European cathedrals incorporated a variety

- Establishing academically credible criteria for implementation of the dimension.
- Integrating multicultural and antiracist perspectives in the criteria.
- Relating criteria to National-Curriculum requirements and cross-curricular elements.
- Identifying opportunities for permeation of National Curriculum in Programmes of Study, Statements of Attainment and Non-Statutory Guidance in the core and foundation subjects.
- Creating a whole-school ethos and whole-staff commitment to the concerns of the Dimension.
- Identifying and/or creating appropriate teaching materials.

of arches, and mosques and minarets use different versions of geodesic domes. This provides good examples of contextualization, a very versatile technique for implementation of the dimension across the curriculum, but especially in areas traditionally seen as problematic such as maths, science and technology (see Volume 3). It relates to real-life situations in different cultures, and reveals high levels of sophistication in design and calculations that go a long way towards challenging stereotypes of 'simplicity' and 'backwardness'.

History, where the NSG even includes a statement of the need to help pupils 'identify and thus challenge racial or other forms of prejudice and stereotyping', can undertake this task at many points. However, units such as local, thematic and world history are much richer in potential than the more 'traditional' British history units that dominate the NC, but the former are the subject of very restrictive and sometimes mutually exclusive choice. Nevertheless, immigration features in KS2 units on 'Victorian Britain' (from Ireland and from areas of Jewish settlement in Eastern Europe) and 'Britain since 1930' (from Eastern Europe and the 'New Commonwealth and Pakistan'). Since all these movements of people involved people of different cultures, and very similar experiences of competition, hostility, prejudice, stereotyping and (except for the Irish) exclusion by legislation, aware and informed teachers have the opportunity to examine the beneficial results of cultural mixing and the roots of racism simultaneously.

Even this brief survey will demonstrate that the multicultural dimension has great potential within the National Curriculum, if permeation is tackled using appropriate criteria. The context of educational reform in the 1980s has posed considerable challenges, but a creative and wide-ranging response is possible to educate pupils to become members of a multiculturally harmonious and racially just society.

References

NATIONAL CURRICULUM COUNCIL (1989) *From Policy to Practice*, Department of Education and Science, London, HMSO.

NATIONAL CURRICULUM COUNCIL (1990) *Curriculum Guidance No. 3: The Whole Curriculum*, York, NCC.

Robin Grinter

NATIONAL CURRICULUM COUNCIL (1990) *Curriculum Guidance No. 8: 'Education for Citizenship'*, York, NCC.

NATIONAL CURRICULUM COUNCIL (February 1991) *Newsletter:* 'A Pluralist Society in the Classroom and beyond', York, NCC.

NATIONAL CURRICULUM COUNCIL (1992) *Starting Out in the National Curriculum*, York, NCC.

NATIONAL UNION OF TEACHERS (1993) *Antiracist Curriculum Guidelines*, London, NUT.

RUNNYMEDE TRUST (1993) *Equality Assurance*, London, Runnymede Trust.

Chapter 11

Children with Special Educational Needs

Tony Cline

Context

The 1981 Education Act

Traditionally children who had difficulty with the school curriculum were thought of as 'handicapped' and might have been referred for 'special educational treatment' in a separate school. Their problems were seen as being wholly within themselves: they needed special treatment because of the kind of person they were and the kinds of difficulties they presented. The 1981 Education Act introduced a new concept: special educational needs do not simply reside within the children who show them; these needs arise from an interaction between the children's difficulties and the educational environment in which they are placed. In legal terms children are said to have special educational needs if they require special educational provision because they have significantly greater difficulty in learning than the majority of children of their age or because they suffer from a disability which prevents or hinders them from making use of the educational facilities generally provided in schools in their area for children of their age (DES, 1981).

The Act abolished the practice of categorizing children by handicap in order to plan their education; it increased the rights of parents to have a say in the kind of educational provision made for their children; it set out careful arrangements for the assessment of special educational needs; and, more cautiously, it laid the basis for more children with special educational needs to be educated in ordinary schools with additional support instead of being transferred to separate special schools. The provisions of the Act for the assessment of special educational needs have received a good deal of attention. The assessment of children from ethnic and linguistic minority communities is an important and controversial subject. However, for reasons of space this chapter will focus mainly on the teaching task and will refer to the challenge of assessment only in passing.

The Warnock Committee, whose recommendations formed the basis of the Act, had argued that as many as one in five children (20 per cent) are likely to experience special educational needs at some point in their school life (Warnock Committee, 1978). Just 2 per cent have severe and obvious difficulties of a kind which at that time usually led to them being educated in a special school. The other 18 per cent are a less well recognized group who are likely to continue in ordinary school with or without additional support. The Act paid some attention to this larger group, though much less publicity was given to that at the time and it has often been overshadowed by other developments since. School governors were given new duties. They were required to ensure that children with special educational needs receive an appropriate education, that the children's teachers know about those needs and how they are to be met, and that all staff understand the importance of identifying these needs and providing for them. As a result of these places and of the local progress that has been made in arranging integrated provision in ordinary schools, special educational needs are now better understood and have a higher profile among teachers generally. One outstanding problem that is germane to the subject of this chapter is identifying special educational needs among pupils from ethnic and linguistic minorities.

The Act made it clear that children are not to be treated as having special educational needs simply because the language of the home is different from the language of instruction at school. The problems experienced by all bilingual children in those circumstances are not to be equated with special educational needs. However, the concepts of 'special needs' and 'special educational needs' are often still confused. All pupils may show *special needs* if they come from a social group whose circumstances or background are different from those of most of the school population. In the case of black and ethnic-minority groups, Robson has suggested four areas in which special or additional needs may be identified without any implication that individual pupils have learning difficulties in the same sense that those with special educational needs do:

(a) Language — a particular need for help with English and, if possible, with the development and maintenance of their first languages;

(b) Culture — a particular need for the school curriculum to include reference to, and respect for, a broad cultural range, including their own particular cultural heritage.

(c) Overt Racism — a particular need for support from the school in opposing racist behaviour and in promoting a positive picture of other cultures.

(d) Socioeconomic disadvantage — a particular need, alongside white pupils in the same position, for educational policies and provision that combat the negative effects of socioeconomic disadvantage on school achievement. (Robson, 1989)

All of these sources of special need are *group* phenomena widely shared by children in the same social situation. In this sense they are distinct from the *individual* experience of learning difficulty that is the foundation of 'special educational needs'. (Cline and Frederickson, 1991, Paper 3.1)

The 1988 Education Reform Act

In the years leading up to the 1981 Education Act and more energetically since it was passed efforts have been made in many areas to change attitudes to people with disabilities and learning difficulties. In the early stages the focus was mainly on structural change — developing new kinds of educational provision for them that would allow more integration with other children. More recently greater attention has been given to curriculum issues — how could teaching for children with special educational needs focus realistically on the same curricular goals as teaching for children who did not share their difficulties? In this field the 1988 Education Reform Act introduced a major further change: all pupils, including pupils with special educational needs, would now have a statutory entitlement to a broad and balanced school curriculum that had to include the National Curriculum. This statutory entitlement represented a milestone in the history of special education in this country.

However, sharing an entitlement to something does not in itself guarantee that access will be easy or that it will be possible to make effective use of the benefit that is conferred. In addition, the Act contained provisions for exceptional arrangements exempting some pupils from the statutory requirements or modifying the curriculum for them. For example, Section 18 allows for exceptions to be made to a child's curriculum entitlement if they are made explicit in a statement of special educational needs. Modifications may be made to the Attainment Targets for the child, to Programmes of Study, and/or to assessment and testing arrangements. The child may also be exempted from one or more foundation subjects. These arrangements must be covered in the statement which must give 'details to indicate how it is proposed to replace the exempted programme in order to maintain a broad, balanced programme' (Circular 22/89, Annex 2). There is provision in the 1981 Education Act requiring that the content of any statement, including provisions of this kind, shall be reviewed annually. Thus it might appear that careful safeguards are built into the system. However, many teachers and others expressed scepticism about this section of the Act from the beginning. They argued that with so many other demands being made on schools and with the pressures of delegated funding and greater competition for pupils the fine principles of universal curriculum entitlement would not really be implemented. They speculated that the provisions in the Act for reducing that entitlement would be widely used so that pupils with special educational needs would have their access to a broad and balanced curriculum restricted rather than enhanced.

Critics expressed particular concern about Section 19 of the Act which allows a headteacher to give a 'special direction' modifying or disapplying the National Curriculum for an individual pupil on a temporary basis. This may be for an initial period of up to six months and for up to one year on renewal.

One of the situations in which the DES suggested this may be done is 'where the head is of the opinion that an individual pupil has special educational needs which require the LEA to assess the pupil with a view to a Statement.' The circular emphasizes that 'a temporary exception will not always be necessary when a head teacher refers a pupil for assessment. Head teachers should consider in each case if there is a clear case for a short term exception, and should not assume that this will be the case or prejudge the outcome of the 1981 Education Act assessment procedure. It will remain for the LEA to determine whether there are sufficient grounds for assessment.' (Circular 22/89, par. 10)

At an early stage, the National Curriculum Council (NCC) sought to allay any fears on these points: 'This circular states NCC's full support for the principle of maximum participation in the National Curriculum by all pupils with special educational needs and for the minimal use of the exceptional arrangements that are available through sections 17–19 of the Education Reform Act 1988.' (NCC, 1989a) A few months earlier in one of its own circulars the DES had emphasized that the Act's provisions for modification or disapplication of National Curriculum provisions should be applied sensitively and positively. The pupils concerned should obtain the maximum benefit they can from the National Curriculum. Positive alternatives should be offered in all cases (DES, 1989, par. 59). In the event the formal imposition of exceptional arrangements does appear to be quite uncommon so far. Pressure for it may build up as the results of assessments at the end of each Key Stage begin to be published on a regular basis and affect the public image of individual schools. That has not been seen to happen yet on a substantial scale, but there are warning signals that must give cause for concern — increases in the number of exclusions and in the number of children being referred for assessment as having special educational needs.

Another area of concern in special education in the wake of the 1988 Act was the National Curriculum assessment arrangements. Would the experience of standard attainment testing at ages 7, 11, 14 and 16 prove invalid, discouraging and unhelpful for children with special educational needs and their teachers and parents? Would the prospect of the publication of results make schools more reluctant to admit or include children with special educational needs? What kinds of special arrangement might be made in order to enable children with special educational needs to be involved in the assessment arrangements? Of course, the requirement can be disapplied altogether in a statement of special educational needs, or flexible special arrangements may be made for the assessment process in order to allow children with special educational needs to demonstrate what they have learned. Some of the strategies that can be adopted are outlined below. Two major worries overshadow the explicit commitment of the School Examinations and Assessment Council (SEAC) and other official bodies to ensure that children with special educational needs are not penalized excessively in the assessment arrangements. The trend towards less flexible paper-and-pencil tests sat on fixed dates will be unhelpful to children with special education needs (as it will to bilingual pupils), and the resources available for supporting some of the strategies listed later in this chapter are being reduced as resources are delegated to schools under the Local Management of Schools scheme.

The Intellectual Context

Those working with pupils who have special educational needs are likely to share the intellectual assumptions about education for cultural diversity that are prevalent in their society at the time. The prevalent assumptions in public policy in the United Kingdom have changed dramatically over the last twenty years, and the changes have proved unstable, one trend being rapidly replaced by another. One of the greatest challenges for teachers is that there is no consensus — even about the aims of education. The National Curriculum has been established with Eurocentric and assimilationist aims, but few of those teaching in ethnically mixed areas will accept that this framework must imply the total exclusion of goals discussed fervently in the 1980s such as cultural pluralism and antiracism.

There are also assumptions about the nature of the differences amongst children in a culturally diverse society. Children from diverse backgrounds will have had different cultural experiences before they enter school. In what ways will that enrich their readiness for the school curriculum? In what ways will their readiness be limited? To some degree the answers to these questions depend on judgments about the preparedness of the schools in terms of staff attitudes and expertise and in terms of relevant curricular coverage and resources. But the answers that are given will also depend on intellectual assumptions that are held about the children. For example, if children are bilingual, what assumptions are made about their bilingual language proficiency? Often monolingualism is taken to be the norm and bilingualism is treated as a possibly risky deviation. As Grosjean (1985) has put it, bilingual speakers are seen simply as the sum of two monolinguals. The contact between their two or more languages is treated as if it is accidental and anomalous. No attention is paid to the flexible communicative competence that a speaker of more than one language maintains across a range of different situations, e.g., speaking to people who are monolingual in either language and to other bilinguals. Children who are bilingual require additional social sensitivity to know when to use either of their languages in a particular register and when it is safe and helpful to switch between them in order to communicate more effectively to the person they are speaking to. Approaches to teaching in a culturally diverse society will be influenced by intellectual assumptions about children's abilities and qualities covering such issues.

The Social Context

The social pressures on minority communities appear to be increasing as the world recession deepens and are not likely to be eased very substantially when developed countries emerge from their current economic difficulties. Members of these minority communities suffer most in the recession in terms of increased unemployment and reduced expenditure on public services. They face continuing and increasing pressures from racism nationally and internationally with no reduction in covert institutional racism and a sharp increase in overt racist activity. There is enhanced public concern about new forms and sources of immigration. The status of some refugees is placed in doubt. These trends are inescapable features of the social context in which education for cultural diversity takes place. They affect all pupils from ethnic and linguistic minority communities irrespective of personal factors (such as special educational needs) or communal factors (such as location).

Challenges

This section examines the challenges and opportunities that are associated with the context outlined above. It focuses exclusively on those issues relevant to education for cultural diversity, and it concentrates in particular on the situation of pupils from ethnic and linguistic minorities who experience difficulties in school. Some issues affecting all pupils are also important for this group (e.g., the destabilizing of school management and diversion of adult attention from pupils' immediate needs while staff, governors and parents are debating opting out for a particular school). Because pupils from ethnic and linguistic minorities are especially vulnerable, they may be affected more than others by factors that have negative implications for all pupils. But it is necessary to make the focus here specific in order to highlight the issues that affect this group uniquely. For that reason there is no discussion here of general issues arising from current structural reforms in education and the intellectual and social context briefly described in earlier sections.

The Education Act 1981

It was claimed in Section 1 that one of the medium-term effects of the 1981 Education Act has been that special educational needs are now better understood and have a higher profile among teachers generally. The identification of special educational needs is probably more careful and thorough. It is certainly likely to be helped by the improved arrangements for monitoring and record-keeping associated with the new requirements for teacher assessment at the end of each Key Stage and the new regulations on annual reporting to parents. But there is an outstanding problem of particular relevance to the subject of this book. Identifying special educational needs among pupils whose first language is not English is very difficult. The question arises: Is this child making poor progress solely because of limited proficiency in English or are there underlying learning difficulties that exacerbate the language problem? Teachers have found that question very difficult to answer.

That challenge is often exacerbated because of ignorance in the school about the cultural background and first-language proficiency of a child who is struggling in the classroom. Although there are general improvements in arrangements for record-keeping about the progress of individual pupils, many schools still have inadequate arrangements for the recording and circulation of basic information about bilingual pupils. This can lead to some teachers not appreciating their own lack of awareness of the strengths that children with difficulties can bring to the resolution of their problems. A mismatch between the expectations and efforts of teacher and pupil is much more likely.

In Section 1 a distinction was made between the group phenomenon of 'special needs' and the individual phenomenon of 'special educational needs'. It was suggested that these two concepts are still often confused in schools. When that happens, serious consequences may occur:

- low expectations are held of *all* children from ethnic and linguistic minorities;
- discrimination against such groups is seen to be based on a valid set of assumptions; and
- there is confusion in planning educational support, e.g., expecting the same staff to have expertise in teaching reading to slow readers and in teaching English as a second language.

A significant challenge in schools with a multiethnic population is to minimize the confusion between these two fundamental concepts and to prevent the negative consequences that arise when individual members of staff or parents or governors still confuse them.

The 1988 Education Reform Act and the National Curriculum

The Education Reform Act offers curriculum entitlement to all pupils. The introduction of the National Curriculum has led to a broader curriculum offer in many primary and special schools and has challenged the narrow offer in most special units. As resources allow, it is leading to increases in in-service training provision in areas where teachers in these sectors are least well prepared, and it is stimulating the publication of relevant books and materials. It has already improved arrangements for continuity and progression between schools and between age groups. All of this must be in the interests of children with special educational needs, including those from ethnic and linguistic minority communities. But the proviso about adequate resourcing is an important one: as noted above, the same Act of Parliament that introduced the National Curriculum introduced structural changes in education that place the resourcing of support activities for schools in doubt. This change impinges particularly on minority interests within schools, including the interests of children with special educational needs and those from ethnic and linguistic minorities. There must be anxiety that, once the publication of school-assessment results begin to influence the public image and popularity of schools, pressure will build up for curriculum requirements to be exempted or modified for many more children. It is much harder to tackle the challenge of assuring access to a broad and balanced curriculum for the children with whom this chapter is concerned in the context of declining LEA involvement and squeezed school resources.

Of particular concern, and discussed elsewhere in these volumes, is the ethnocentric character of the National Curriculum as it has emerged from the Orders on individual subjects (see Volume 3). That appears to be the result of a series of political decisions: it is not a necessary consequence of the wording of the Act or the advice of the early subject working parties. In fact, it may be considered that Secretaries of State have defied the spirit of the law as passed in Parliament. The first section of the Act refers to a curriculum that will promote 'spiritual, moral, cultural, mental and physical development of pupils at the school and of society'. In a society that is multiethnic and multicultural it is reasonable to assume that work with children directed to that goal will involve a multicultural curriculum. For the present that assumption is not reflected in the detailed work of the NCC and SEAC or in Dearing's recommendations for reform (NCC/SEAC, 1993). Even so the statutory framework for revision is in place, and it is likely that the slowly growing voting power of ethnic and linguistic minority communities will eventually ensure that the curriculum reflects the shape of our whole society more appropriately. Meanwhile schools must work with curriculum requirements that do not directly encourage cultural sensitivity.

Responses

1. Identifying special educational needs among pupils from ethnic and linguistic minorities

Schools have achieved improvements in the identification of special educational needs following the 1981 Education Act, but teachers still experience difficulty in identifying special educational needs among pupils from minorities, especially linguistic minorities. Often the challenge is seen in terms of a decision between two alternative possibilities — either the pupil's difficulties arise simply from a lack of knowledge or confidence in English, the main language of the classroom, or there are deep-seated and wide-ranging learning difficulties of the kind associated with children of low intelligence whatever their language background. This either-or question may not be the most useful way to think of the challenge. Wright (1991) has listed a range of hypotheses that might be explored: perhaps the ethos and curriculum of the school are experienced as challenging and alien rather than welcoming and accommodating; perhaps the child has a good conversational level of English which has misled teachers into setting tasks too abstract for the child's current language level; perhaps the child has missed many experiences that others in

Table 11.1: Key Challenges and Opportunities

Context	Challenges/Opportunities
Schools have achieved improvements in the identification of special educational needs following the 1981 Education Act and in record-keeping on individual pupils generally since the 1988 Education Reform Act	• Teachers still experience difficulty in identifying special educational needs among pupils from linguistic minorities • Recording and circulation of basic information about bilingual pupils still needs to be improved in many schools
'Special educational needs' and 'special needs' are often confused	• Where this happens, low expectations are fostered for *all* minority children, discrimination is apparently justified, and planning of support is confused
The Education Reform Act offers to all pupils an entitlement to a broad and balanced curriculum, including the National Curriculum	• Entitlement will mean little for pupils with special educational needs without effective support to ensure access and progression • For minority pupils with learning difficulties supporting access may involve special considerations of language and cultural sensitivity
The curriculum in schools must encompass the National Curriculum as laid down in statutory orders	• Pupils with learning difficulties cannot be fobbed off with a 'basic-skills' curriculum • Recent curriculum orders have shown no commitment to education for cultural diversity
All pupils must be assessed at the end of each Key Stage	• This experience could prove invalid, discouraging and unhelpful for pupils with special educational needs, and especially for those from linguistic minority backgrounds

the class have had, is learning at an appropriate rate, and simply needs more time; perhaps the child is subject to considerable environmental stress; and so on. It is likely, in fact, that in most cases the causes of the child's current learning problems will have developed from a complex interaction involving several minor sources of difficulty. Children from ethnic and linguistic minorities face a wider range of alternative possible sources of stress and difficulty than other children. The challenge to the teacher in identifying the nature of any special educational needs can be tackled through (a) clear thinking about each of the possible obstacles to learning (starting with language), (b) working with a speaker of the child's first language who shares the same social and cultural background, and (c) making special efforts to match the level of task demands in the classroom to the child's level of language readiness.

2. Teachers' knowledge of basic information about minority pupils

There has been every encouragement to schools to improve record-keeping on individual pupils following the implementation of the Education Reform

Act. But the recording and circulation of basic information about pupils from ethnic and linguistic minorities has not received the same encouragement and no doubt remains deficient in many schools. The problem exists at two levels: firstly, teachers are unaware of the history and backgrounds of some individual children whose current performance cannot be understood without that knowledge; secondly, school staff often know little of the cultural and communal background of substantial minority communities living in the catchment area. The first problem can be tackled through adapting the record-keeping system to accommodate the requirements of a pluralistic society. The information available to all teachers for particular pupils will need to include any of the following that are relevant to their current functioning in school — the language(s) spoken at a child's home (between adults, between adults and children, between children), religion, periods of residence and schooling outside the UK, changes of school within the UK, opportunities for classroom work in their first language, opportunities for teaching outside school in their first language, experience of a bilingual teaching approach, and arrangements for learning English. Of course, an encyclopaedic record for every child is impracticable and unnecessary. But there should be a key teacher for each child who does have all this information on record, examines its educational significance, and selects what other teachers need to know. All class teachers in primary schools and all form tutors in secondary schools will be key teachers for some vulnerable children. In-service training to meet their needs will valuably draw on the resources of minority communities locally.

3. Confusion between 'special educational needs' and 'special needs'

As noted above, 'special educational needs' and 'special needs' are often confused. At worst, the effects may be that low expectations are fostered for *all* minority children, that discrimination is apparently justified, and that the planning of support in schools is confused. This confusion can be avoided if clear thinking about identifying special educational needs is reflected in the organization of support within schools. The expertise of those who can teach English as a second language or advise on antiracist education and education for cultural diversity has to be clearly differentiated from the expertise of those who can teach pupils with special educational needs or advise on their support. The aims of any support teaching need to be clearly defined, as do roles and duties of additional adults in the classroom (Thomas, 1986; Cline and Frederickson, 1991, Paper 4.5).

4. Curriculum access and progression for pupils with special educational needs from ethnic and linguistic minorities

The Education Reform Act may offer curriculum entitlement to all pupils, but that will mean little for pupils with special educational needs unless there are effective means to ensure access and progression within that curriculum.

For minority pupils with learning difficulties supporting access may involve special considerations of language and cultural sensitivity. The aim is to avoid as far as possible making the formal exceptional arrangements described above in Section 1.

Teachers of children with special educational needs place considerable reliance on the analysis of classroom tasks and activities in order to set inter-mediate goals for those who are likely to find the usual learning goals asso-ciated with a particular task too challenging. This strategy has been advocated for ensuring access to the National Curriculum (NCC, 1989b; O'Toole *et al.*, 1989), and a good deal of work has been done to define intermediate goals of various kinds (e.g., Coupe, 1990). This strategy is not without problems: subdividing Statements of Attainment (SOAs) may fall short of what is required because:

- the sequencing of goals is not logical or not psychologically meaningful;
- inappropriate intervals have been set between goals;
- goals are not defined in sufficiently precise terms;
- there is a failure to ensure clear progression; or
- learning is fragmented unnecessarily (Lewis, 1991, p. 51).

Each of these potential hazards may be more serious when working with pupils whose first language is not English. Many authorities, such as the National Curriculum Development Team for Severe Learning Difficulties, have advocated a focus instead on the analysis of Programmes of Study (PoS) (the 'what' and 'how' of learning, the 'means' towards achievement) rather than on SoAs (the 'ends' of the process). In order to support access for those with learning difficulties it may be possible to adapt for more systematic use strategies that are employed generally with all children, such as matching work to children's levels and areas of interest, varying the presentation of an activity, varying the mode of response available for children, and grouping children in ways that facilitate individual access and mutual support. A list of detailed suggestions relating to one subject, science, may be found in NCC, 1992, pp. 4–5. Two examples of methods that offer specific help for bilingual pupils with learning difficulties are the structured use of peer-tutoring tech-niques to improve the support given to a child with limited proficiency in English (Curtis, 1990) and the analysis of classroom tasks for cognitive de-mand and context-embeddedness (Frederickson and Cline, 1990).

5. The National Curriculum is 'broad and balanced' but ethnocentric

The curriculum in schools must encompass the National Curriculum as laid down in statutory orders. This will happily ensure that pupils with learning difficulties cannot be fobbed off with a 'basic-skills' curriculum, as happened so often in the past. It was quickly recognized that special schools in particular would face a considerable challenge to broaden their curriculum offer and improve deficiencies in provision for science, craft, design and technology, and other specialist-subject areas (NCC, 1989b). For pupils with special educational needs from ethnic and linguistic minorities these advantages have to be balanced against the lack of commitment in recent curriculum orders to any notion of education for cultural diversity. The Non-Statutory Guidance from some of the subject working parties is rather more helpful (Cline and Frederickson, 1991, pp. 125–6), but this cannot entirely compensate for omissions in the central SoAs and PoSs.

The delivery of the curriculum remains wholly the responsibility of schools. Teachers concerned with pupils who have learning difficulties from ethnic and linguistic minorities may employ a number of strategies to offset the narrow aims and content that have been imposed on them. The selection of learning experiences may be designed to reflect the diversity of British society, to counter stereotypes of minority groups, and to enable pupils with a different cultural background to pursue interests relating to that culture in cross-curricular topic work. Considerable use may be made of collaborative learning and problem-solving in small groups in order to promote pupils' commitment and ability to work cooperatively across the spectrum of the school's population. Every effort will be required to maintain high expectations of minority pupils, especially where they have particular strengths that lie outside the national Attainment Targets (such as mastery of a second language or social competence in moving between different cultural domains). Many schools lack adult role models from minority communities. In the medium-term changes in the composition of the teaching staff are required. In the short-term schools need not be discouraged by the Education Reform Act or the National Curriculum from their efforts to improve active parental and communal involvement. The adoption of a Partnership Teaching model for language support is likely to be of value in this context. At the very least schools need to review very carefully strategies for helping children with learning difficulties or limited proficiency in English that involve withdrawing them from work alongside peers for extended periods of time. (A fuller discussion of these issues will be found in Cline and Frederickson, 1991, Unit 4.)

6. National Curriculum assessment arrangements

All pupils must be assessed at the end of each Key Stage, and it is feared that this experience could prove invalid, discouraging and unhelpful for pupils with special educational needs, and especially for those from linguistic minority backgrounds. Special arrangements may be made for SATs and teacher assessment either on the basis of specific mention in the statement under Section 18 of the Act (where a child has a statement) or through a temporary exception under Section 19 of the Act (where a child does not have a statement). Several kinds of special arrangement are possible — additional time may be allowed; the timing of tests may be varied (e.g., for pupils with learning or emotional difficulties who cannot concentrate for long periods); teachers may open sealed test folders early in order to have time to make adaptations for pupils with special educational needs, make audiotapes, etc; pupils may be allowed to use any mechanical and technological aids that they normally use in the classroom; schools may employ an amanuensis or a reader for individual pupils; schools may employ versions of the tests published in braille or enlarged print, or they may employ signing to communicate test tasks to children with hearing impairment (SEAC, 1992).

More generally, it seems likely that bilingual children and others from minority communities will benefit where encouragement is given to parent and pupil involvement in assessment and to developments such as Records of Achievement and profiling. They will also be helped if, in the future, SEAC or its successor body allows a broader definition of the range of admissible evidence of achievement of educational objectives in SATs and teacher assessment. For the present these developments seem improbable for political reasons. But the political pressures on the education service change over time. Educationists concerned for particular groups of pupils such as those with special educational needs must take a long view. The 1988 legislation allows scope for radical curricular reform once the present restrictive interpretation of a National Curriculum and its assessment has been discredited in the eyes of the public The Dearing review has already shown how this may happen (ibid). In the short-term teachers of those with special educational needs from ethnic and linguistic minorities may employ a range of strategies in the classroom to try to neutralize the worst effects of current policies; in the long-term they must be prepared with an agenda for reform of the reforms.

References

CLINE, T. and FREDERICKSON, N. (1991) *Bilingual Pupils and the National Curriculum: Overcoming Difficulties in Teaching and Learning*, London, University College London.

COUPE, J. (1990) 'The National Curriculum and Children with Severe Learning Difficulties', in FREDERICKSON, N. and WRIGHT, A. (Ed) *The National Curriculum and Special Educational Needs*, Section 6, London, University College London.

CURTIS, S. (1990) *Peer Tutoring — Integrating 'bilingual' pupils into the mainstream classroom*, Ethnic Minority Support Service, Northamptonshire.

DEPARTMENT OF EDUCATION AND SCIENCE (1981) *Education Act*, London, HMSO.

DEPARTMENT OF EDUCATION AND SCIENCE (1989) *The Education Reform Act 1988: The School Curriculum and Assessment*, Circular 5/89, London, HMSO.

FREDERICKSON, N. and CLINE, T. (1990) *Curriculum Related Assessment with Bilingual Children: A Set of Working Papers*, London, University College London.

GROSJEAN, F. (1985) 'The bilingual as a competent but specific speaker-hearer', *Journal of Multilingual and Multicultural Development*, 6, 6, pp. 467–77.

LEWIS, A. (1991) *Primary Special Needs and the National Curriculum*, London, Routledge.

NATIONAL CURRICULUM COUNCIL (1989a) *Implementing the National Curriculum — Participation by pupils with special educational needs*, Circular No. 5, York, NCC.

NATIONAL CURRICULUM COUNCIL (1989b) *A Curriculum for All: Special Educational Needs in the National Curriculum*, Curriculum Guidance No. 2, York, NCC.

NATIONAL CURRICULUM COUNCIL (1992) *Teaching Science to Pupils with Special Educational Needs*, Curriculum Guidance No. 10, York, NCC.

NATIONAL CURRICULUM COUNCIL AND SCHOOL EXAMINATION AND ASSESSMENT COUNCIL (1993) *Interim report. The National Curriculum and its Assessment*, London, NCC/SEAC.

NORWICH, B. (1989) 'How should we define exceptions?', *British Journal of Special Education*, 16, 3, pp. 94–7.

O'TOOLE, B. and O'TOOLE, P. (1989) 'How accessible is Level 1 maths?', *British Journal of Special Education*, 16, 3, pp. 115–17.

ROBSON, A. (1989) Special needs and special educational needs, Unpublished paper.

SCHOOL EXAMINATIONS AND ASSESSMENT COUNCIL (1992) *School Assessment Folder (Part 2) for KS3 Science 1992 National Pilot*, London, SEAC.

THOMAS, G. (1986) 'Integrating personnel in order to integrate children', *Support for Learning*, 1, 1, pp. 19–7.

WARNOCK COMMITTEE (1978) *Special Educational Needs*, Report of Committee of Inquiry, London, HMSO.

WRIGHT, A.K. (1991) *The assessment of bilingual pupils with reported learning difficulties: a hypothesis-testing approach*, in CLINE, T. and FREDERICKSON, N. (Ed) op cit., pp. 185–92.

Chapter 12

The European Dimension

Diana Rainey

Context

The idea of a European dimension of education is not new. The Council of Europe have worked on the idea for some forty years and the European Cultural Convention (1954) underlined the need for education for European understanding. The dramatic events which have taken place over the last few years in central and eastern Europe have meant that a Europe with a greater economic and political unity seems just around the corner. At the same time there is considerable debate within each member state concerning just how far they should allow themselves to become entrenched into the new Europe. The concept of unity can be interpreted in a variety of ways and many feel the development of too tight a union conflicts with matters such as national autonomy or regional diversity. Indeed, at the time of writing, words such as sovereignty and federalism are foremost in the minds of politicians and people alike.

During the last forty years the structure and composition of Europe's population has changed and there are more than twenty million citizens who are not living in the country where they were born either through immigration from former overseas colonies or by the migration of workers from nearby countries. There is also a likelihood of an increasing number of migrants in the future together with the escalating social tensions that might accompany any demographic shift. An already culturally diverse Europe is becoming increasingly more so. With unemployment rates high amongst individual member states and workers moving from one country to another in order to find work there may be feelings of resentment amongst unemployed 'nationals'. These are very sensitive and important issues and it is against such a background that we must view the development of a European dimension in our primary schools.

It might be helpful at this point to ask exactly what we mean by the term 'European dimension'? Indeed what do we mean by the term 'Europe'? Do we mean the continent of Europe i.e., the western peninsula of the land mass of Eurasia? Are we referring to the countries of western Europe belonging to the European Economic Community, now through closer political cooperation termed the European Community. Certainly it would seem that Boris Yeltzin and Mikhail Gorbachev before him would see the 'new Russia' as being part of Europe. In fact the term 'Europe' is a dynamic one and perhaps we might accept the view given by Jean Gottman, professor of geography at Oxford, who put forward the idea of a 'tidal Europe' so that a definition of Europe might ebb and flow according to demographic and political change. Until some form of federal Europe emerges, if it is to emerge, and only time will tell, perhaps the idea of Europe as a fluid term should be accepted and this could incorporate a view of Europe which changes according to the action taken upon it. Taking a geographical definition also seems sensible so that Europe can be defined as it was by the Council of Europe in 1981, and reported by Peacock (1982), 'as the continental landmass extending from the Ural mountains to the east and including the British Isles and Iceland.'

Not only is 'Europe' difficult to define but the 'European dimension' itself and its place in education is also a complex concept as Ryba (1992) points out, although the individual states have some common ideas about how the European dimension can be included across the curriculum they differed in how they considered the European dimension could be included in different areas of the curriculum. Most primary-school teachers when preparing learning experiences for children, will view learning outcomes in terms of knowledge to be acquired, skills to be learned and also the acquisition of values and attitudes. Learning within the European dimension must take account of knowledge about Europe, learning the skills necessary for life as a citizen of Europe and also the acquisition of values and attitudes about Europe through living as part of Europe. These values and attitudes are particularly important in the context of cultural diversity. Shennan (1991) gives 'Twenty goals for teaching about Europe' one of which is 'to develop in pupils greater empathy and awareness of the value of living in a multicultural, pluralist society, while drawing strength from those movements, organisations and aspirations promoting unity within Europe.' (p. 37)

If as primary teachers we aim to achieve the above goal, then at the same time we are also improving the opportunities available to various ethnic groups in our society. Sensitively handled nationalism and federalism need not lead to racism but primary teachers do need to be made aware of the issues involved.

During a seminar on 'Europe in primary schools', at Donaueschingen, in November 1985, a group of primary teachers said that in the light of their experience 'A Europe-orientated mentality is possible only if the individual has first become "localised" in his home country. Children must regard themselves as native before they can evolve a European consciousness . . . Later on national feelings will play a smaller role, the emphasis being increasingly laid on attachment to a wider regional grouping, whence it will be easier to impress the notion of a common loyalty to Europe . . . The primary teacher's most urgent task will be to awaken in pupils an emotional approach to Europe: they must become capable of understanding and respecting each other and of living together . . . They should at the same time retain patriotic pride and love of their homeland, while becoming European in mentality.'

Bell (1991) argues that 'attitudes and beliefs are formed in primary schools and in the families of their pupils.' If the development of a European dimension in education is left until the secondary and higher-education phases then Bell feels that this is re-education and could lead to elitism. This author would also argue that there is a need to develop a European dimension early on within the primary school, particularly if we are also to consider the needs of minority ethnic groups.

In developing a European identity or 'European consciousness' as Shennan (1991) calls it, we must make every effort to avoid Eurocentrism. Implicit in the notion of being a European is the idea of being part of a very diverse composition of peoples of all races and ethnic backgrounds. The Bullock report (DES, 1975) stated: 'No child should be expected to cast off the language and culture of the home as he crosses the school threshold, and the curriculum should reflect this.' In the UK pupils of Afro-Caribbean or Asian origin have their own language or culture. In Germany the pupils of east-European origin will also have their own languages and cultures. It is important that these similarities are pointed out, cultural diversity is a characteristic of the whole of Europe. Whenever the diversity of cultures and races from across all the world is considered it is very important that inaccurate stereotyping does not take place.

In May 1988 the European Community Council and the Ministers of Education within the Council adopted a resolution on the European dimension in education (88/C177/02) which aimed:

- to strengthen pupils' sense of European identity;
- to prepare them to take part in the economic and social development of the Community following the Single European Act;
- to improve their knowledge of the European Community and of its member states; and
- to inform them of the significance of the cooperation between those states and the other countries of Europe and the world.

In February 1991 the British Government published a statement of its policy and a report of activities attempted to carry out the resolution. The aims of the European dimension were:

- helping pupils to acquire a view of Europe as a multicultural, multilingual community which includes the UK;
- encouraging awareness of the variety of European histories, geographies, and cultures;
- preparing young people to take part in the economic and social development of Europe and making them aware of the opportunities and challenges that arise;

- encouraging interest in, and improving competence in, other European languages;
- imparting knowledge of political, economic and social developments, past present and future, including knowledge about the origins, workings and role of the EC;
- promoting a sense of European identity, through first-hand experience of other countries where appropriate; and
- promoting an understanding of the EC's interdependence with the rest of Europe, and the rest of the world.

Then in October 1991 the Ministers of Education in the Council of Europe agreed a resolution on 'The European Dimension of Education: Teaching and Curriculum Content'. This states that 'Education should increase awareness of the growing unity between European peoples and countries and of the establishment of their relations on a new basis. It should also help make the younger generation conscious of their common European identity without losing sight of their global responsibilities or their national, regional and local roots . . .'(DES, 1992, pp. 2,3) Has enough attention been given in the previous statement to the cultural heritage and language of ethnic-minority groups within Europe? Britain's minority ethnic groups are not European — they are predominantly Asian, African and Indian, but still European because of their British citizenship. Such communities must not be allowed to feel that their different cultures make them any less European. The resolution continues: 'It should foster understanding of the fact that, in many spheres of our lives, the European perspective applies and that European decisions are necessary. Young people should be inspired to take an active part in shaping Europe's future.' (ibid.)

Schools should encourage awareness of:

- the geographical diversity of the European region, with its natural, social and economic features;
- the political and social structures in Europe;
- the historical forces that shaped Europe, including the development of European thinking on law, the state and freedom;
- the multilingual nature of Europe and the cultural wealth this represents;
- the history of the European idea and the movement towards integration since 1945;
- the tasks and working methods of the European institutions; and
- the need for joint responses in Europe to economic, ecological, social and political challenges.

The British Minister of Education signed the resolution and although the contract made is morally binding it does not constitute a directive and is therefore not legally binding. There was a long delay of almost a year until March 1992 when the DES published 'Policy Models: A Guide to developing

Table 12.1: Challenges for the Primary-school Teacher in Developing European Awareness in the Classroom

Challenges

- To develop a school-curriculum policy statement which includes European awareness
- To link European awareness with the school's policy on multicultural education
- To recognize the potential contribution made by a range of National Curriculum subjects to European awareness
- To identify possible ways of teaching European awareness in the primary school
- To provide resources to enable teachers to teach about Europe

and implementing European Dimension Policies in LEAs, Schools and Colleges'. This addressed some of the relevant issues but failed to give guidance on others e.g., progress towards:

- the introduction of foreign-language learning before the age of eleven;
- increased provision of foreign-language assistants to help introduce foreign-language teaching in primary schools; and
- the requirement of a foreign-language qualification as a condition of qualified teacher status.

The government has provided guidance on implementing European dimension policies. It remains to be seen whether or not it also provides the resources necessary for LEAs and schools to implement any policies that they might develop. This leads to a number of challenges for LEAs, schools and individual teachers. For our purposes these will be confined to the challenges faced by the school and the individual teacher in the classroom as outlined in Table 12.1.

Challenges

In order to develop effectively a European dimension as part of the primary-school curriculum it is necessary to develop a policy with clear aims and objectives that is linked to the school-development plan. There are several reasons why this should take place. Firstly, in developing such a policy the whole of the staff of a school is involved in the initial discussion and the staff are thus involved in asking for themselves the questions: What is the European dimension? Why are we going to develop European awareness in our children? Secondly, as mentioned earlier, the way that the European dimension is handled in school and the way in which it is related to the school antiracist and multicultural policies is very important. It is also important that there is a named person on the school staff who is to coordinate the implementation of such a policy if it is to be effective.

Teachers are extremely busy people and have become under increasing pressure, particularly since the introduction of the Education Reform Act in

Table 12.2: Responses to the Challenges of Developing European Awareness in the Classroom

- Engage the staff in awareness-raising sessions leading to a school-policy statement which includes the European dimension
- Use the above sessions to develop a policy on the Euopean dimension which includes reference to multicultural and antiracist education
- Identify where the European dimension occurs in the National Curriculum and develop links between subjects by using a European topic which embraces all subjects so that the European dimension permeates the whole curriculum
- Celebrating and sharing the 'good practice' of other teachers in teaching about Europe and raising European awareness, through action research, journals and newsletters where the regular reporting of school partnerships can be encouraged
- Acting as a school, group of schools or LEA to identify, budget for and gather the resources necessary to teach the European dimension

1988. Although some might want to argue that the development of the European dimension is so important that it deserves to be a subject in its own right, this would not be practical. The National Curriculum core and foundation subjects can give us an overcrowded, but incomplete curriculum. Unfortunately the National Curriculum was devised by separate working parties, many working in isolation and with little consultation, so full advantage was not taken of some of the obvious links between subjects. In developing a European dimension which goes across all subjects, teachers can help to give balance and cohesion to the curriculum by trying to link the dimension to all subjects, including those subjects such as foreign-language teaching which is currently outside the National Curriculum at Key Stages 1 and 2, at the same time giving adequate consideration to the other cross-curricular skills, themes and dimensions.

There must be opportunities built into the policy document for short, medium and long-term goals to be addressed and achieved. It will also be necessary for the policy to be monitored and evaluated at regular intervals so the development of a European dimension should feature in the school's overall development plan. It is very important that the school investigates whether in terms of the development of values and attitudes the aim of promoting unity within Europe whilst at the same time developing in pupils greater empathy and awareness of the value of living in a multicultural, pluralist society, is being achieved. In the following section ways in which primary teachers can respond to the challenges involved with the development of the European dimension in their classrooms are considered by examining some of the work that is already being carried out by other primary-school colleagues.

Responses

The responses to the challenges posed in the previous section can be summarized in Table 12.2.

The importance of involving the whole of a school staff in the development of a policy on the European dimension cannot be over emphasized. By examining together the question 'What is the European dimension in education?' teachers can come to own a definition based upon a clear understanding of the issues involved. They can then decide what the main aims of developing a European dimension are. To help with this they can look at the EC resolution which can be divided up, in terms of aims, into four broad elements concerned with:

- the development of knowledge and understanding of Europe, the people of Europe and the relationship between Europe and the rest of the world;
- the development, in an analytical way, of positive attitudes towards other people and cultures which are themselves part of the very essence of Europe;
- the development in children of a respect for different ways of life, beliefs, opinions and the ability to view things from another's perspective; and
- the development of another European language so that communication and cooperation with other member states can be promoted more easily.

It is important that the final point should be included. The National Curriculum includes the teaching of modern foreign languages but only at Key Stage 3. This is despite the fact that research suggests that the earlier the learning of a second language is introduced the better. Obviously, if a modern language such as French is taught in the primary school then this may increase the burden of language learning of those ethnic-minority pupils whose second language is English. In the 1960s and 1970s there were several French-language schemes used in British primary schools and many LEAs had teachers to support the teaching of French in primary classrooms. On the whole French-language teaching tended to decline over the last fifteen years due to lack of teachers with the expertise needed. Then with the movement towards closer cooperation in Europe came the obvious question 'Why not teach a second language in the primary school?' In one primary school the reply that it was not included in the National Curriculum was not enough against the arguments that many parents put forward for its inclusion. The school staff later decided to take a small step in this direction by introducing from reception onwards some French songs and some simple French vocabulary. Some LEAs, Stockport and Tameside, for example, have recently revived the teaching of French in the primary school with great success.

As with many schemes however, appropriate resources and funding are necessary prerequisites. If the British government were to introduce the learning of a second modern language in the primary school then it would obviously need resourcing. There is a lack of specialist teachers and if anything current admission policies for post-graduate Certificate in Education courses tend to give precedence to applicants whose first degree is in a National Curriculum subject, a modern language is not part of the NC in the primary school.

The European dimension like other themes and dimensions cannot be viewed as a bolt on addition to the National Curriculum. It is sprinkled generously throughout the 'whole curriculum'. Teachers will see it in many different Programmes of Study and their related Attainment Targets. Examples include the following:

English — In speaking and listening at Key Stage 1 stories, rhymes and songs should include examples from other cultures. At Key Stage 2 they are encouraged to respect their own language and that of others. In reading, books should include those about other countries including the translation of original texts.

Geography — The study of other places takes place during Key Stage 1 but Europe is specifically mentioned at level 5 and above. It is therefore likely that some schools will leave a European locality study until year 6 or even choose not to do one at all if they consider that the children are below level 5. This could have implications for the school's policy on the teaching of the European dimension.

Art — By the end of Key Stage 1, children should be able to identify some of the ways in which art has changed distinguishing between past and present. They should look at, and talk about, the work of well-known artists from a variety of periods and cultures. By the end of Key Stage 2, they should be able to identify work from different periods, cultures and traditions. They should also have looked at and discussed art from early Renaissance and later periods which includes work such as the Bayeux Tapestry, work on Greek vases and the work of European artists.

Music — The Programmes of Study require pupils to perform and listen to music in a variety of genres and styles from different periods and cultures. Examples from European 'classical' tradition should be included. Music from different cultures should be listened to from Key Stage 1 onwards.

Technology — In this subject children should come to recognize a variety of forms resulting from people's different values cultures, beliefs and needs e.g., buildings, style of dress. They also look at the way different cultures have used design and technology to solve familiar problems. They are required to comment on artefacts, systems and environments from other cultures and understand that they have identifiable characteristics and styles.

History — In this subject children are encouraged to suggest reasons why people, including the people of Europe acted the way they did in the past. They are also asked to identify cause and consequences through their understanding of British, European and world history. Core study units related to the European dimension are

- CSU1 — Invaders and Settlers (This provides a historical illustration of the diverse nature of the people of Europe.)

- CSU5 — Ancient Greece (This could be linked to a locality study in modern Greece through the geography curriculum.)
- CSU6 — Exploration and Encounters 1450–1550 (This provides more scope for looking at migratory patterns and the encounters between different cultures.)

Supplementary study units will also provide links between local, British, European and world history over a long period of time.

Science — The discoveries in science were made by people of a variety of cultures and teaching in primary science should reflect this. Science, like mathematics, is a universal subject.

Mathematics — There is plenty of scope within mathematics for 'multicultural maths'. The history of mathematics includes the study of mathematicians from a variety of cultures including Europeans. Particularly in the study of the patterns made by a variety of cultures can the universality of mathematics be demonstrated. This subject cuts across all language barriers.

By pointing out to staff where the European dimension can be found in the various National-Curriculum subjects, it can therefore be seen in a cross-curricular way. This could take the form of a curriculum audit where staff in forming their European-dimension policy, ask the question 'What are we already doing that is about Europe, European awareness, and cultural diversity that we may not have labelled as such?'

The primary curriculum tends to be a holistic one and even when subjects are planned separately, in order to check adequate coverage of National-Curriculum Attainment Targets, aspects such as health education or the European dimension give obvious links. Teachers are far too busy trying to cover everything to ignore these links. In the geography curriculum, pupils need not only have knowledge and understanding of a variety of places in the world but at the primary stage they need to compare their own locality with a locality overseas. Towards the end of Key Stage 2 teachers may have to carry out with children a study of a locality in the EC or Europe. This can be successfully achieved through 'twinning'. Many schools have used this process where a teacher twins with another teacher in another area and the children exchange information, resources, ideas, examples of pieces of work. Children have to study their own area at both Key Stage 1 and 2 and in collecting evidence from their own local area to send to another school abroad, the children have a clear purpose for their enquiry. An advantage of such an arrangement is that there can be an extensive exchange of resources, including large-scale maps, local information etc. Another advantage is that the children are working with resources that are similar to those to which they have been accustomed in the study of their own area.

If the resources appropriate to the needs of one class of children and their teacher are collected then these can be used by other colleagues in the school at a later date. It is important that in making contact with the school abroad the teacher makes it clear that the link is much more than a mere 'pen-pal' system. In such a way the children can cover the geography curriculum and the European dimension in a meaningful way. Many primary children have benefited a great deal from this twinning process and cross-phase links can be enhanced if the local secondary school is used to help with the translation of letters etc. This 'twinning' process has also been termed 'international curriculum linking' and often teachers can receive help through the Central Bureau, or their own LEA — many of these having advisory staff who are able to help in developing a European dimension. It is probably true to say that in the past such agencies have been more concerned with developing the European dimension in secondary education. This is changing and there are now many primary schools who have been involved in projects funded through LEAs and also joint curriculum-development projects funded through the Central Bureau.

There are all sorts of ways that teachers can allow pupils to learn about life in Europe. Books, films, slides, artefacts, and the personal first-hand knowledge of the children, teacher, or an invited visitor to the school can provide starting points. Some primary schools organize visits abroad, and this can be very exciting particularly if the children are able to visit their 'twin' school. A topic such as the Eurotunnel or themes such as food, wine, communications, transport, rivers, flags or even the topic Europe itself can be studied (a locality study would form part of this). Using a topic such as 'Feasts and festivals' can embrace the European dimension and also issues surrounding multicultural education and cultural diversity.

Resources for teaching about Europe need to be obtained and constantly updated. It is very important that any resources used should reflect the cultural diversity of the people of Europe so that the children appreciate that just as there is a substantial number of people of African or Asian origin living in Britain this is reflected in other European countries so that the children appreciate that there are Indian markets in Paris, for example.

Some schools organize 'European events' where the whole school works for a whole day or week on cross-curricular activities with Europe as a central theme. This might include a class assembly where the children act out a scene in a French café using the French language. In learning to converse in a language other than their own those whose first language is English can begin to empathize with those children for whom English is a second language. If this is carefully handled the status of these pupils in the eyes of their peers can be promoted. Board games could be produced with any number of associated European themes. Euro-quizzes, car number-plates, maps of various types, road-signs, shop signs and a host of other Euro-memorabilia could be used. These types of activities can prove useful but cannot replace the sort of experiences provided through a direct link with a school in Europe. The choice of such a school would probably involve considering the ethnic mix of the school. It might seem appropriate to chose a school with a very varied ethnic mix, though if the UK school were all white then the other European school might also wish to choose a school with a greater ethnic mix, for the same reasons.

Table 12.3:   Sources of Information and Advice

British Broadcasting Corporation,
Education Information,
Villiers House,
The Broadway,
Ealing,
London W5 2PA

'Cheshire Twinning',
Langley Education Centre,
Main Road,
Langley,
Macclesfield,
Cheshire, SK11 OBU

Education Officer (Liaison),
Independent Broadcasting Authority,
70 Brompton Road,
London SW3 1EY

The Schools Unit,
Central Bureau,
Seymour Mews House,
Seymour Mews,
London W1H 9PE

In promoting the European dimension in primary education the teacher should always be asking 'What messages about Europe are the children receiving?' Are these messages appropriate in that they are in keeping with the school's antiracist and multicultural policies? If the teacher is satisfied that these questions can be answered in a positive way then through the European dimension can be built a better world for tomorrow where each individual is aware that he or she is a citizen of the world, whose identity includes his or her cultural heritage, family, values, beliefs, nationality and his or her role as a citizen of Europe.

References

BELL, G.H. (1991) *Developing a European Dimension in Primary Schools*, London, David Fulton.

CHESHIRE COUNTY COUNCIL (1992) *Cheshire Twinning*, Chester, Education Services, CCC.

DEPARTMENT OF EDUCATION AND SCIENCE (1975) *A Language for Life* (The Bullock Report), London, HMSO.

DEPARTMENT OF EDUCATION AND SCIENCE (1989) *Science in the National Curriculum*, London, HMSO.

DEPARTMENT OF EDUCATION AND SCIENCE (1989) *Mathematics in the National Curriculum*, London, HMSO.

Diana Rainey

DEPARTMENT OF EDUCATION AND SCIENCE (1989) *English in the National Curriculum*, London, HMSO.

DEPARTMENT OF EDUCATION AND SCIENCE (1990) *Technology in the National Curriculum*, London, HMSO.

DEPARTMENT OF EDUCATION AND SCIENCE (1991) *History in the National Curriculum*, London, HMSO.

DEPARTMENT OF EDUCATION AND SCIENCE (1991) *Geography in the National Curriculum*, London, HMSO.

DEPARTMENT OF EDUCATION AND SCIENCE (1992) *Art in the National Curriculum*, London, HMSO.

DEPARTMENT OF EDUCATION AND SCIENCE (1992) *Music in the National Curriculum*, London, HMSO.

DEPARTMENT OF EDUCATION AND SCIENCE (1992) *Policy Models: A Guide to Developing and Implementing European Dimension Policies in LEAs Schools and Colleges*, London, HMSO.

NATIONAL CURRICULUM COUNCIL (1990) *The Whole Curriculum, Curriculum Guidance No. 3*, York, NCC.

PEACOCK, D. (1982) *Report of the CDCC Symposium on Europe in Secondary School Curricula: Aims, Approaches and Problems*, Neusiedl-am-See, Austria, April 1991, Strasbourg, Council of Europe, p. 31.

RYBA, R. (1992) 'Toward a European Dimension in Education: Intention and reality in European Community Policy and Practice', in *Comparative Education Review*, 36, 1.

SHENNAN, M. (1991) *Teaching about Europe*, London, Cassell, Council of Europe.

Chapter 13

Information Technology (IT): Using Computers as a Tool

Mike Harrison

The computer is a powerful and highly motivational learning tool. Used creatively it can liberate teacher time and enhance primary pupils' repertoires of learning skills. It can increase access to the curriculum for children with a variety of individual needs and from diverse cultural heritages. In primary schools its effective use also poses issues of classroom management, which in their solution can force teachers to confront many of the challenges and issues of cultural pluralism. Such issues include the need for schools:

- to value cultural diversity explicitly;
- to encourage children to value themselves as part of human kind, which celebrates both similarities and differences;
- to allow children the opportunity to stand back and view situations objectively;
- to allow children to express what they honestly feel about themselves, the treatment of themselves and others and their everyday conflict situations;
- to prepare all pupils for life in a pluralistic society characterized by differentiation in language, ethnicity and/or cultural heritage;
- to encourage children to look for strategies for resolving problems, especially conflicts and to capitalize on cooperative communalities;
- to help children to discover aspects of their own culture, particularly those which help them to locate themselves;
- to foster empathy by imagining the feelings of people both in similar and different situations to their own; and
- to use everyday situations to discuss uses and abuses of power and to consider individual and collective rights and responsibilities.

With increasing pressure on schools to demonstrate the rise in children's attainments in academic subjects, there can be a tendency for such important goals to become second order priorities. This chapter illustrates that opportunities can be created to explore these issues, on the way to achievements in subject areas, by using computers as a tool.

Context

As Short and Carrington (1992) argue, primary teachers have traditionally operated within a child-centred ideology which includes a need to protect their innocent charges from pernicious reality allied to a belief that young children are unable to grasp abstract concepts. Thus primary teachers are reluctant to accept that political education, which they rightly see as having to do with conflict and lack of consensus, has a place in their classrooms. An agenda such as that outlined above, which would be viewed as overtly political by most primary teachers, is therefore unlikely to be adopted spontaneously by many. We need, then, a means to facilitate children's growth in these areas, which it seems unlikely will be tackled head on. The collaborative use of a highly motivational tool such as a computer provides us with such means. For 'group work around a computer may be more genuinely collaborative than other group work, thereby enabling more focused group talk' (Davis, Desforges, Jessel, Somekh, Taylor and Vaughan, 1992, p. 20).

There are many who argue that a computer 'is more than a tool because it embodies . . . the capacity to interact with us as a surrogate of its human programmers.' (Somekh and Davies, 1991). Nonetheless it is easier to present to teachers the metaphor of using a tool, especially one so evidently cross-curricular in nature, to achieve movement toward teaching for justice and equality rather than to fathom the mind of the software engineer! After-all a tool can be used:

- to help teachers and pupils analyse some notions presented as common sense;
- to unlock hidden issues;
- in a number of different ways for different purposes;
- to prise open feelings about racism;
- to empower the tool user; and
- to help build ideas about teaching for equality.

The computer is a many-headed tool. In using a computer to produce a class magazine, for example, technology, art and English are all brought together. Data from surveys and numerical information can be accommodated and in the act of editing such an item, cross-curricular themes and dimensions will need to be debated and considered. The editorial team will need to find ways of working together and adhering to agreed principles and styles of presentation.

Many classroom projects outlined in Shan and Bailey's (1991) book *Multiple Factors: Classroom Mathematics for Equality and Justice* can be achieved in primary classrooms with the help of IT. (These include an Indian dance invented by Shobana Jeyasingh to celebrate the work and imagination of the mathematician Sramanujan (1887–1920) and descriptive topics of a multicultural nature.) The requirements of the National Curriculum Programmes of Study in each area can be demonstrated to have firm links with IT, as shown in Table 13.1.

The use of computers to support curricular goals is clearly established in almost all primary schools. However children's expected attainments in the use of computer technology in its own right has also become part of the requirements of the National Curriculum. The Non-Statutory Guidance for IT identifies five strands of IT capability.

- developing ideas and communicating information;
- handling information;
- modelling;
- measurement and control; and,
- applications and effects.

Each of the following software and hardware packages can be presented in such a way that children can be stimulated to express ideas and concerns, seek information to counter argument and debate, establish environments and reflect on situations.

1. Software associated with communicating information: All about me; Caption; Folio; Airbrush; Concept Writer; WRITE; Front Page Extra; More about me; Easel; Phases; Draw; Paint; Pendown; Revelation; Intro tray; Compose; Notate.
2. Software associated with handling information: Graph it; Chartwell; Sorting Game; All about us; Branch; Junior Pinpoint; Animal Pack; Datacalc; Datafind; list explorer; Datashow.
3. Software associated with modelling: LOGO; Moving in; Our school; My world; Landmarks; Granny's Garden; Mallory Towers; Craftshop; Jumbo; Toy Cupboard; Elmtree farm; Crash.
4. Software and hardware associated with measurement and control: Control LOGO; Temperature and light sensors; Mazes and robotic toys such as BigTrak, PIP, Roamer.

How are computers currently used in primary classrooms? In a recent survey teachers were asked about the use to which their class computer was being put at one specified time in a week in January (Harrison, 1994). The types of software which were being used at the time of the snapshot are shown in Figure 13.1 in the form of a pie chart. The most striking feature of the survey is that 29 per cent of all the available computers were not being used at the time of the snapshot. This was in replies by the most interested schools in the district (some 27 per cent replied to the questionnaire). We can safely assume that in those schools which did not reply the percentage in use was not more.

This is an important finding in that, for many children whose lives will increasingly be dominated by computer technology, their only experience with IT is in the classroom. Despite heavy capital investment by LEAs, PTAs

Table 13.1: The National Curriculum and Links with Information Technology (IT)

Nat Curriculum subject levels	Design Technology				English					Mathematics						Science				
	1	2	3	4	1	2	3	4	5	1	2	3	4	5	6	1	2	3	4	5
DATABASES																				
Enter data			■	■								■		■			■	■	■	■
Retrieve data			■	■			■	■	■	■		■		■	■	■	■	■	■	■
Identify appropriate uses				—													□			
Create a database			□				□	□	□		□						□			
WORD PROCESSORS:																				
Manipulate text			□				□	■	□								□	□	□	■
Present information		□	■	■			■	■	■						□		□	□	□	■
SPREADSHEETS:																				
Retrieve data				□					□						■					■
Create a spreadsheet	□		□										□					□		■

■ IT use **explicitly** mentioned in the National Curriculum Attainment Targets

□ IT use **appropriate** to the Attainment Targets

Figure 13.1: *Uses of Computers at One Time on One Day in January 1992*

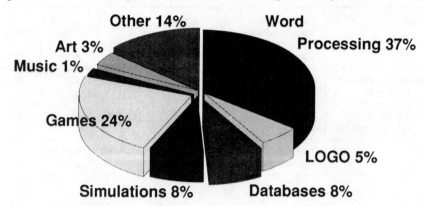

Source: From a questionnaire survey of 1000 primary schools in the Manchester area

(Parent–Teacher Associations) and other sources many children are still not getting that experience. A further survey in three primary schools all in the same LEA carried out by the author in December 1992, asked boys and girls in junior classes if they had a computer of their own at home or access to one owned by another member of the family. As may be anticipated, the percentage of children who claimed ownership of computers varied with economic status of the school population (as measured by free school-meal places).

School A is a Roman Catholic junior school with *less than* 20 per cent of free school-meal places and *less than* 5 per cent of pupils with an ethnic-minority background. School B is an inner-city primary school with *more than* 60 per cent of free school-meal places and *more than* 80 per cent of pupils with an ethnic-minority background. School C is a large estate primary school with *more than* 80 per cent of free school-meal places and *less than* 5 per cent of pupils with an ethnic-minority background.

The claimed ownership of computers was 58 per cent, 40 per cent and 38 per cent respectively. When the survey was analysed by sex some interesting results were noted as shown in Table 13.2.

Bias in attitudes between the sexes toward computers is consistently reported in the literature. Professor Celia Hoyles comments 'It is, therefore, difficult to avoid the disturbing conclusion that girls are learning less than boys about computers and therefore acquiring less understanding as to how they might use computers for their own purposes.' She found a consistent difference in attitude and access to IT between the sexes especially at older ages (Hoyles, 1988). In this survey, if attitude can be equated with claims of ownership, this appears not to be the case in two of the Key Stage 2 populations but is markedly so in the school with a high ethnic-minority intake.

In order to see if family structure and shared ownership would affect this picture the data were further analysed. Children were asked how many brothers and sisters they had living at home with them and later, in a separate section,

Table 13.2: Ownership of Computers

School	School A (mostly white)		School B		School C (mostly white)	
	Boys	Girls	Boys	Girls	Boys	Girls
Claimed to own a computer	51	40	53	30	40	30
Claimed not to own a computer	30	37	50	72	61	54
Chi²	1.96 not significant		10.28 highly significant		0.27 not significant	

Table 13.3: Access to Computers

School	School A (mostly white)		School B		School C (mostly white)	
	Boys with no sisters	Girls with no brothers	Boys with no sisters	Girls with no brothers	Boys with no sisters	Girls with no brothers
Claimed to have access to a computer	29	19	18	9	29	16
Claimed not to have access to a computer	8	7	7	13	12	6
Chi²	0.02 not significant		4.63 highly significant		0.03 not significant	

whether there was a computer in the house which they could use. Replies were then looked for where boys had no sisters and girls no brothers. The results are presented in Table 13.3. It is difficult to generalize from such a sample but this does relate to the research of Smithers and Zientek (1991) who found that gender stereotyping was much higher in Asian groups and amongst those with brothers and sisters than for the population at large. Both of these factors could be at play here. Thus especially for ethnic-minority girls the experiences which they have with computers in primary classrooms are therefore vital.

Four areas of context have been discussed in this first section.

- the cross-curricular nature of primary-school work with computers;
- National Curriculum IT capabilities;
- the current extent of the use of computers in primary classrooms; and
- children's experience in the use of computers outside school.

Each of these have multicultural dimensions which we shall now explore.

Challenges

The influence of IT is wider than just supporting aspects of various Programmes of Study, or debating the best way to use software. Computers can alter the way curriculum content is organized, the sequence and frequency of certain topics, the pace of learning and the way in which learning takes place. In many schools consideration of such curriculum development is some way off. But we may consider advantages of such innovation in the context of this book:

- Work with computers can provide a focus for colleagues to develop a commonly understood policy about the grouping of children including those from diverse cultural backgrounds, for certain tasks.
- Providing knowledge of applications and technical support can encourage confidence and self-esteem in the provider. To whom should such responsibility be given? Can such responsibility be shared to show the value given to skills, knowledge and experience of different children? Can the enhancement of self-esteem be a criteria in choices made?
- Establishing an overview of the use of computers throughout the school can highlight their importance in acting as a tool for expression and communication and give opportunities to demonstrate the respect given by the school to children's mastery of their mother tongue.
- Helping teachers to see where work in IT can support teaching and learning, can re-emphasize the need for meeting individual needs especially those of pupils from ethnic-minority groups.
- Organizing resources so that they are physically accessible forces consideration of the intellectual, cultural and language accessibility of material.

Thus two challenges emerge: The uses to which IT can be put to achieve teaching for equality and justice both in content and in the ways in which it is used; and the ways in which the benefits for children in the use of computers can be disseminated to other members of staff, and thereby help them consider their own best practice.

Responses

Responses to the challenges outlined above include the following:

- the 'twinning' of schools can be enhanced by the use of electronic mail, which can set up a 'colour-blind' dialogue between children from different areas;

- the grouping of children chosen to use the computer may be used as a tool of social engineering;
- using LOGO children learn to split a problem down into smaller elements and solve each independently; and
- the issues exposed when software is selected and evaluated may become a growth point for discussion between staff about classroom purposes and practices.

For example, Meadows (1992) reports on the electronic mail project, EMTENET, which linked students from a variety of countries and cultures, and showed a personal element for many ethnic-minority students taking part. 'Telecommunications allows direct links between . . . school pupils, without the barriers of (possibly out of date) text books or someone else's views coming between the participants.'

An American initiative used electronic conferencing of a more structured kind to provide prospective teachers with opportunities to become aware of their own taken-for-granted assumptions, acknowledge the validity of perspectives different from their own and reflect upon the choices they make (Harrington, 1992). Developments for pupils may follow.

Empowerment is implied here. If 'the purpose of education is liberation . . . not the development of objects' (President Nyerere's 1974 speech quoted in Shan and Bailey, 1991) then it is ironic that the most technical of subjects IT should take us nearer to that ideal.

In the event it will be by reference to standard packages — databases, word processors — that teachers are most likely to see the links with other areas of the curriculum, and teachers can be challenged to achieve the exploration and celebration of cultural diversity set out in the introduction.

Word Processing

Word processing emerged, in the snapshot survey, as the most popular single use of computers in primary schools. It can help children to become familiar with the keyboard in the initial phase. It removes the need for simultaneous concentration on all the aspects of production and encourages drafting, checking for errors, editing and collaborative writing in later stages. 'For some a change in the way text is presented increases its value and provides some "mental distance" from its production both of which encourage re-writing' (Davis, Desforge, Jessel, Somekh, Taylor and Vaughan, 1992). It may help us to convince children to view writing as a culturally mutable entity. In modern 32-bit computers (such as the A3000) fonts in a variety of languages are available and Punjabi and Urdu versions of 'Folio' are produced for the BBC range of computers. 'Full Phases' and 'Penddown' have a speech option whereby words are sounded as text is typed in. Cloze procedures can be generated by

Figure 13.2: Bengali — Keyboard Layout

Note: Bengali and Punjabi fonts are available from Hampshire Micro Centre

using children's own writing and wordbanks are provided to give younger children their first experience of using a thesaurus. The use of different fonts and borders stimulates a sense of audience and the final product can usually be produced in a number of formats (large for the wall display, medium size to accompany a picture, smaller for an entry in a newspaper or collection of works).

Schools need to consider whether a variety of word processors with different facilities are needed to help children to write for various audiences and exploit the rich cultural diversity amongst its pupils. For example different children may want to write:

- newspaper reports about events in different countries;
- an obituary;
- a play script for a puppet show;
- the musings of a famous person;
- a child's record of achievement in his or her mother tongue;
- evidence from a trial;
- the recipe for a relative's favourite food;
- an advertisement for the paper;
- an account of using chopsticks for the first time;
- the tale of Rama and Sita;
- about a holiday in Bangladesh;
- a script for a Diwali assembly;
- instructions (recipe or directions);
- a seventeenth-century version of a modern tale;
- a message in a bottle;
- a doctor's report;
- a poster in two different languages;
- a letter/postcard to a friend;
- a job application;
- a letter of complaint; and
- a conversation.

They might find using only one type of word processor quite limiting. Can expression be encouraged by providing children with the option of a variety of packages?

Collaborative writing can be promoted by the use of word processing. One class of 11-year-olds, where the teacher wanted to encourage the children to discuss their feelings about themselves, the people around them and the world outside in order to begin the process of highlighting similarities, differences and injustices started by getting children to brainstorm 'feeling' words. Typed onto a computer, the list could have been saved each day and when reloaded appear on the screen for all to view. Using these words, groups of children wrote about situations such as: how they felt when someone pushed

Figure 13.3:   *Year 3 and 4 Children Writing in Punjabi Using 'My World'*

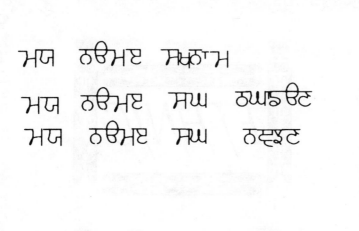

them; how they felt if a friend was ill; and how they felt in the dark. Later children were asked to work in groups and define 'feelings':

Feelings are something inside you and sometimes hurt

Feelings are thoughts. Feelings are things inside you. Things in your brain. They can drive you crazy. They can drive you into dangerous things (Brown *et al*, 1990).

Collaborative word processing was examined by Jessel (1992). He suggests that less redrafting takes place than there might be because the child not only has to have thoughts but must be able to express a rationale for them and this might make intellectual demands, which many 9 and 10-year-olds may find difficult to meet. If this is so, it is even more imperative that such opportunities are provided because the intellectual challenge of working in such a way in a larger group, perhaps under the scrutiny of a teacher, is even more daunting.

Figure 13.4: *Ethnic Borders for Desk Top Publishing from 4mation*

Many word-processing programmes now allow a degree of Desk Top Publishing (even those which do not can be utilized in a 'DTP' process, which also stands for Dab with Tippex and Photocopy). Clip-art pictures can be sized, added to 'Phases' and 'PenDown' and positioned according to need. Scenes from a variety of stories, fables, festivals and cultural traditions will become more and more available as the demands continue to grow, and CD-Roms, which capture images from TV and film and translate them for use on the computer, will become more common in primary schools.

The school's published output will also be enhanced by good quality word processing and printing. A school brochure, especially one which demonstrates the celebration of a variety of festivals, publicly acknowledges the cultural diversity of its pupils. The inclusion of stories and other computer work produced by pupils will enhance the school's reputation within an ethnically diverse community.

Records of Achievement, in which pupils can display their achievements to family and friends can have real effects on the self-esteem and sense of self-worth of pupils. Make sure that the reproduction is the best you can possibly manage (use the school's computer and tell readers that you have done so). With cheap hand-held scanners becoming increasingly more available, schools will be able to create computer images of photographs and art work done in school to place within their documents. With attention paid to the images chosen, this too can demonstrate the value the school places on Britain's cultural diversity.

Databases

Databases are frequently used to show children (and adults) the power of the computer. The speed at which micros can make calculations, sort data, and the graphic capabilities employed to show the results are all impressive.

Two methods can be identified to introduce children to databases:

Method 1

Imagine introducing children to a new concept: books. We would show them a variety of books, picture books, text books, books in foreign languages, books for infants, scientific books, story books and so on. After some time for familiarization they might progress to making their own books closely based on one or more of the examples. We need to approach children's introduction to databases in the same way.

Method 2

The best way to introduce children to the idea of a database is to make one as a response to children's own needs. Thus a sensitive teacher will arrange a project or stimulate a problem to arise from children's own work where the solution lies in the creation and use of a database.

Teachers who want to celebrate similarities and differences will do well to utilize the power of databases. The speed and clarity with which children can present their findings lend immediacy to the issues under consideration.

Figure 13.5: One Cumbrian Junior-school Survey: 'Where Our Grandparents Were Born'

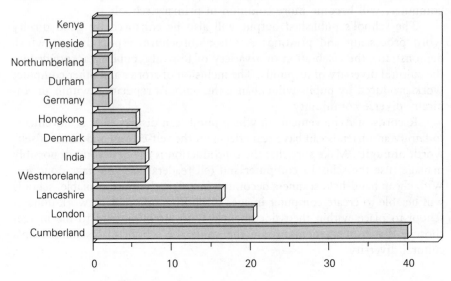

Source: Brown *et al.* (1990), *A spanner in the works*

For example, the graph presented in Figure 13.5 came from data collected by Cumbrian schoolchildren. The interpretation of the data can lead to discussions about the best ways to display such results (Ma,5,4,a — See Vol. 1, Ch. 6 and Vol. 3, Ch. 6)); the purpose of conducting the survey in the first place and the wider issue of how we value such rich diversity.

Drill and Practice Programmes

Drill and Practice programmes are often scathingly attacked as the unacceptable face of computer use. One might argue however, that such programmes often support specific learning objectives; generally give instant reward; they are colour blind; they have appeal to some students; the work can allow for differentiation (the rest of the class being occupied with other matters); and spread the practice of certain skills across a number of media. Such software is occasionally used as an electronic blackboard demonstrating a method to obtain the right answer in an attractive and often tuneful manner. Attention to individual preferred learning styles demands that some opportunities are created for all children to work in this way. The question teachers will need to answer is whether this is the best use of an expensive and scarce resource.

As pointed out in *Children, Computers and the National Curriculum* 'It is more important for children to become skilled in general purpose computer applications than to spend time practising spelling tests. Skilled exploitation of a

Figure 13.6: Islamic Arts and Vedic Maths: Mathematics or Magic?

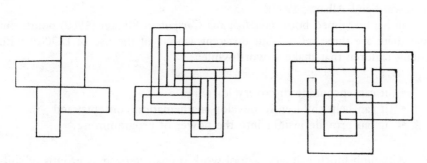

spreadsheet, graphics package or desktop publishing programme . . . can improve personal productivity dramatically and is also transferrable between topics . . .' (Judd, 1991). It could be that some teachers only use IT in this way and may need to be persuaded to use the computer in ways which extend children's skills in using their imaginations by composing written texts, creating graphics, generating and solving problems, devising programmes and investigating data, bearing on cultural diversities and similarities. Catering for individual differences in learning styles and approaches may mean allowing some children to use the computer in different ways to others. Teachers may need to be reminded that technology and its purposes are interpreted differently within different cultures and educational systems, (Verma and Entzinger, 1992).

Islamic geometry and Vedic maths have been brought together in Bunyard and Brine's LOGO programme (available on Micromath Disc 3). This helps to introduce children to exquisite spirolateral patterns drawn quickly and easily by means of the computer. Teachers would do well to remind children that such designs were, and still are, created using only a ruler, compass and protractor. (Shan and Bailey, 1991)

Those of us who react negatively to the idea that children can be taught by computers are more enthusiastic about the concept of children themselves teaching computers routines and procedures. This is the concept behind 'LOGO'. LOGO and turtle graphics are widely spoken of as important elements in work in IT in primary classrooms. Papert (1980) originally designed LOGO to be a language for learning. It was his intention that in this way children could begin to take responsibility for what, and how, they learn. Many references to such work are contained in the National Curriculum (mathematics, technology and science). Teachers who have worked with children in this area report enthusiastically on the benefits for children both in their development of cognition, their confidence and, by the mode of working, their ability to cooperate in problem-solving situations. The author's own classroom experience with young children working with LOGO attests to the cooperation between children evident when acting as human turtles and working with floor robots (such as ROAMERS). More information on early programming and such activities is available in Chapters 3 and 4 of *Making*

LOGO work (Ainley and Goldstein, 1988), and Ready Steady, LOGO (Millward and Albary, 1992).

In her acclaimed book *Children and Computers*, Straker (1989) points out that there are three related but different aspects of the use of LOGO with young children that make it worthwhile:

- it can encourage discovery learning;
- it can help children to develop mathematical concepts; and
- it can provide insight into the power of programming.

Although much primary-school work is characterized as groups of children working together the reality has often been described as a collective monologue. Often there is no evidence of either cooperation nor collaborative learning. Roberts (1985) for example comments 'There is little thought, no research, and the work that is involved is done on an individual basis. This defeats the objective of interaction and reduces group work to what amounts to individual work in the presence of others' (p. 30). It is only by improving the conditions of small-group work that concepts skills and attitudes, such as cooperation, conflict, power and inequality, similarity and differences and rational argument can be developed. Suitable software can help.

Working in flexible groups, exploring and valuing the contributions of others is excellent preparation for life in a complex and culturally diverse society. It has a real role in fulfilling Verma's (1993b) third function of education '[it] sets the patterns and models of behaviour which young people are expected to manifest in group settings in the school, in the world of work and ultimately in the wider social setting.'

Small group work can lead to:

- a secure environment which some less confident pupils need in order to express their ideas;
- some children accepting responsibility to help others;
- full involvement of all the children in the task;
- children recognizing the contributions of others to be as important as their own; and
- children being able to recognize the individuality of others thus breaking down the stereotypes and prejudices often associated with inequality (based upon ideas in 'Working Toward Social Justice' in *A Spanner in the Works* by Brown, Barnfield and Stone, 1990.)

Working with LOGO has been seen to be one of the best ways in which children can be encouraged to work cooperatively on a problem-solving task. They have no choice but to pool ideas, listen to each other and try out a variety of solutions. This checklist might help teachers to consider whether the use of LOGO will achieve their ends.

- What aspects of cooperative work do I want to encourage?
- Where does the IT enhance the curriculum?
- How familiar are the children with LOGO?
- How do I want to group the children?
- How familiar are the children with the problem-solving concepts to be presented to them?
- Do I understand the application myself?
- Can I use the manual to help me?
- What other curriculum areas are being experienced at the same time?
- Will I have access to the computer when I need it?
- How will I carry out any assessment associated with the task?
- What evidence of pupil progress will I need to collect?
- What will I regard as a successful activity?

Arranging for groups of children to carry out a complex task in which they need to cooperate is very demanding. Teachers often complain that, with their limited share of computer time, it takes half a term to get anything done. There are plenty of times, however, when one or two children could be finishing off the analysis of a database or putting finishing touches to a newsletter outside lesson times. Some children love staying in at playtime during cold weather and using the computer can provide a useful occupation.

Careful planning can allow groups or individuals to use the machine at times when they are not involved with the rest of the class.

- during assembly times;
- at playtime and lunch hour;
- after school and before school starts;
- during registration, story time and whilst the class are doing PE; and
- those not going swimming could use the machine at this time.

This will often prompt the use of temporary flexible groupings which can help breakdown some of the more fixed groups which can dominate the organization of such work in primary classrooms. Labelling children according to perceived ability and grouped permanently according to that perception is the antithesis of teaching for equality and justice.

In conclusion, by offering children the chance to interrogate, order and present data teachers can equip children to understand their most valuable lesson namely that 'Facts are always impregnated with interpretations, and although some are more plausible than others, all interpretations are partial' (Verma, 1993).

To achieve our goals we need to put children into situations where they share and discuss ideas, compromise to gain agreements, achieve success and to do this in a safe environment. The overall lesson to be learned from the school and classroom projects so eloquently described by Naidoo (1992), Gaine (1987) and Short and Carrington (1992) is that you have to get close to children to get them to open up and willingly explore their own feelings and pre-judices. Gaine talks of the 'Grange Hill phenomenon' 'school is the backdrop against which [children] act out the important things in their lives . . . friendships/group values . . . The important things happen between lessons in Grange Hill [and in real schools]. Teachers are seldom privy to this world.' Small groups working on computers give a context within which teachers can get closer. Furthermore learning by trial and error, always an aim in primary classrooms, can be a risky business in real life. A micro-world can provide teachers with an opportunity otherwise denied.

For pupils, IT can become an empowering equal-opportunity experience with potential for fostering cultural cohesion. IT is a tool. How it is used, on what content and to what ends its use is directed, are of the essence in a multi-ethnic society.

References

AINLEY, J. and GOLDSTEIN, R. (1988) *Making LOGO work: a guide for teachers*, Oxford, Basil Blackwell.

BROWN, C., BARNFIELD, J. and STONE, M. (1990) *A spanner in the works: Primary school teaching for equality and Justice*, Stoke-on-Trent, Trentham Books.

DAVIS, N., DESFORGE, C., JESSEL, J., SOMEKH, B., TAYLOR, C. and VAUGHAN, G. (1992) 'Can quality in learning be enhanced through the use of IT?', *Developing Information Technology in Teacher Education*, 5, May.

DEVEREUX, J. (1991) 'Using IT, other than computers, to support primary science', in *Primary Science Review*, 20, December.

GAINE, C. (1987) *No Problem Here*, London, Hutchinson.

HARRINGTON, H. (1992) 'Fostering critical reflection through Technology: preparing prospective teachers for a changing society', *Journal of Information Technology for Teacher Education*, 1, 1.

HARRISON, M. (1994) 'Teachers Computers and the Curriculum: The three roles of the Primary IT Coordinator', in HARRISON, M. (Ed) *Beyond the Core Curriculum*, Plymouth, Northcote House.

HOYLES, C. (1988) 'Review of the literature', in HOYLES, C. (Ed) *Girls and Computers*, Bedford Way Papers 34, University of London.

JESSEL, J. (1992) 'Do children really use the word processor as a thought processor?', *Developing Information Technology in Teacher Education*, 5, May, pp. 23–32.

JUDD, J. (1991) *Children Computers and the National Curriculum*, Coventry, NCET.

MEADOWS, J. (1992) 'International collaborations in teacher education: a constructivist approach to using electronic mail for communication in partnership with schools', *Journal of Information Technology for Teacher Education*, 1, 1.

MILLWARD, P. and ALBARY, E. (1992), *Ready, Steady, LOGO*, Essex, Longman.

MORRISON, A. (1988) *Information Technology in Primary Schools*, A research review for the Scottish Education Department, London, ESRC.

NAIDOO, B. (1992) 'Through Whose Eyes? Exploring Racism: reader, text and context', Stoke-on-Trent, Trentham Books.

NCET (1992) *Assessing IT-Curriculum support materials*, Coventry, NCET.

PAPERT, S. (1980) *Mindstorms: Children, Concepts & Powerful Ideas*, Brighton, Harvester Press.

ROBERTS, G. (1985) 'The organisation of learning in primary schools. Memorandum 50', *Achievement in Primary Schools*, London, HMSO.

SHAN, S.J. and BAILEY, P. (1991) *Multiple Factors: Classroom Mathematics for Equality and Justice*, Stoke-on-Trent, Trentham Books.

SHORT, G. and CARRINGTON, B. (1992) 'Towards and Anti-racist Initiative in the all-white Primary school: A Case Study', in GILL, D., MAYOR, B. and BLAIR, M. *Racism and Education: Structure and Strategies*, London, Sage publications.

SMITHERS, A. and ZIENTEK, P. (1991) *Gender, Primary Schools and the National Curriculum*, Birmingham, NASUWT and the Engineering Council.

SOMEKH, B. and DAVIES, R. (1991) 'Towards a pedagogy for information technology', *The Curriculum Journal*, 2, 2, Spring, pp. 153–70.

STRAKER, A. (1989) *Children using Computers*, London, Blackwell.

VERMA, G.K. (1993) 'Cultural Diversity in Secondary Schools: Its Nature, Extent and Curricular Implications', in PUMFREY, P.D. and VERMA, G.K. (Eds) *Cultural Diversity and the Curriculum, Vol. 1, The Foundation Subjects and Religious Education in Secondary Schools*, London, The Falmer Press.

VERMA, G.K. (1993b) 'Cultural Diversity in Secondary Schools: Its Nature, extent and Cross-curricular Implications', in VERMA, G.K. and PUMFREY, P.D. (Eds) *Cultural Diversity and the Curriculum: Volume 2, Cross-Curricular contexts, Themes and Dimensions in Secondary Schools*, London, The Falmer Press.

VERMA, G.K. and ENTZINGER, H. (1992) 'Transferring Knowledge in a Cross-Cultural Perspective', in CERRI, S.A. and WHITING, J. (Eds) *Learning Technology in the European Communities*, The Hague, Kluwer Academic Publishers.

Chapter 14

Initial Teacher Education and Ethnic Diversity

Dave Hill

Context

Since 1984 there have been three major thrusts in government policy on ITE (Initial Teacher Education). All impact on the delivery of the whole curriculum in our multiethnic society and affect both primary and secondary ITE. Firstly, the increased regulation of the ITE curriculum has resulted in a prescriptive and restrictive National Curriculum for ITE.

Secondly, the introduction of new school-based routes into teaching, the almost totally school-based 'Licensed Teaching Scheme', and the two-year overwhelmingly school-based Articled Teacher Scheme for post-graduates. Both started in 1990. By mid-1992 both had recruited around 1,500 new teachers/students (DFE, 1992a), rising to over 2,000 licensed teachers by September 1993 (DFE, 1993a). Circular 14/93 also allows consortia of Primary Schools to set up their own totally school-based ITE from September 1994.

Thirdly, there is the vastly increased school-basing of the two major routes into teaching, the 4-year B.Ed and the 1-year PGCE courses. There were in 1992–3, 16,491 students on PGCE courses and 15,489 new entrants to undergraduate courses (Hill, 1993b, DFE 1993b). For Primary ITE there were 6,300 PGCE students in 1992–3, and 12,100 first-year undergraduate B.Ed (or equivalent course) students. New regulations for more school-based ITE in secondary PGCE and B.Ed courses were set out by John Patten in May 1992 (DFE, 1992b). These were subsequently fleshed out in 1992 by CATE. New criteria for school-basing for primary courses were issued in late 1993 (DFE, 1992e) following a Draft Circular (DFE, 1993c,d) and as a Blue Paper (DFE, 1993b) in Summer 1993. The Draft Circular (and, more obliquely, the Blue Paper) included the 'Mum's Army' proposals for a one-year non-graduate primarily school-based training course for infant teachers. This was, however, dropped from the resulting circular 14/93 (DFE, 1993e).

Two common themes of this tripartite policy are: a move from college-based preparation of new teachers, towards school-based preparation; and stricter control of the college-based coursework, with less theory, less critical reflection, less questioning (Hill, 1989a; Gilroy, 1992). It is contended that issues of race and education already are, and will be, increasingly, squeezed out of the ITE curriculum. This downgrading is occurring both *quantitatively* because less time is available for discrete courses and sessions on race and education, and less time for 'permeating' the ITE curriculum, and *qualitatively* because the *orchestrated* government, media, and ideological attacks on antiracism, and indeed, on multiculturalism are, in effect, frightening off ITE course designers and teachers (Hill, 1992c).

The Radical Right, Teacher Education and Anti-antiracism

I also want reform of Teacher Training. Let us return to basic subject teaching, not courses in the theory of education. Primary teachers should teach children to read, not waste their time on the politics of gender, race and class. (Prime Minister John Major, 1992).

There is justification for dwelling on nationalistic, sometimes visceral hatred of egalitarianism, antiracism, and multiculturalism, propagated by ideologues of the Radical Right. They are more than a noisy and extremist minority. They express, articulate and give form to Prime Ministerial speeches such as the Prime Minister's above, to ministerial speeches such as Patten's blaming 'the 1960's theorists who still dominate the educational world, the trendy left' (Patten, 1992), Kenneth Baker's 'the pursuit of egalitarianism is over', and Kenneth Clarke's attacks on 'barmy theory' in ITE courses are continued by his success.

Within public education, the ideas and personnel of the Radical Right have seized power at national level. Some of these ideologues are now installed at the higher levels of education power. For example, Anthony O'Hear was a member of CATE, (the Committee for the Accreditation of Teacher Education), and is a member of its successor body, the Teacher Training Agency. John Marks, a Black Paper writer and member of the Hillgate Group is a member of the National Curriculum Council. Brian Cox, erstwhile radical writer of the right-wing Black Papers wrote:

Since the general election a persistent rumour has been going round in education circles that the Prime Minister has agreed to a deal with right-wing Conservatives. They will go quiet in their opposition to Maastricht if he will allow them to take control of education. What truth there is in this I do not know, but it certainly fits the situation which has emerged in the last few months. (Cox, 1992; Graham and Titler, 1992; Blackburne, 1992)

The Radical Right operates at three levels of discourse, aimed at three types of audience; they work through ideological pamphlets and books; through the media such as the *Mail*, *Express*, *Telegraph*, *Times* and *Sun*; and through the effect they have on ministerial and Prime Ministerial speeches (Hill, 1990, 1991b,c; Menter, 1992). O'Hear's (1988) *Who Teaches the Teachers?* attacks ITE institutions for 'their obsessions with inequality, with racism and sexism and other passing political fashions'.

The Hillgate Group's (1988) *Learning to Teach* attacks ITE courses for preventing the reproduction of nationalism by 'the constant reform of the curriculum [which] has undermined the attempt to preserve, enhance, and pass the precious heritage of our culture'. The Hillgate Group's *Learning to Teach*, Anthony O'Hear's *Who Teaches the Teachers?*, and Stuart Sexton's *Our Schools — A Radical Policy* all attack theoretical components of teacher education such as multicultural/antiracist education courses.

The first two booklets urge the bypassing of college-based teacher education and its substantial replacement of skills-based learning on-the-job through licensed teacher schemes, or by a two-year school-based post-graduate apprenticeship. Both of these schemes are now in operation. (For critiques of such views see Edgar, 1989; Massey, 1991; Hessari and Hill, 1989; Cole, Clay and Hill, 1991; Clay, Cole, and Hill, 1990; Whitty and Menter, 1990; Gordon 1990; Hill, 1990, 1992b; Hillcole Group, 1993b)

In his seminal work on the new racism, Barker (1981) sets out the new form of socio-biology which has replaced the biological racism in the Conservative Party since the 1970s. On the whole the Radical Right no longer talks in terms of racial superiority and inferiority, it talks instead of 'difference' and how 'natural' it is for people to fear those who are culturally different.

The New National Curriculum for 'Teacher Training'

A major thrust of Radical-Conservative state policy and control over ITE is increased regulation of the ITE curriculum.

1. Prior to 1984 there was no CATE (Committee for the Accreditation of Teacher Education) and no CATE criteria. Courses in 'teacher-training' had very considerable autonomy over the ITE curriculum, although, in practice they offered theoretical courses in 'the education disciplines' (e.g., philosophy, sociology, history, psychology of education and curriculum design). Cultural diversity was commonly viewed as 'a problem' and 'immigrant education' was often slotted into special-needs courses.

The inner-city rebellions of the early 1980s (e.g., in Brixton and Toxteth and the resulting Rampton/Swann, (1981, 1985) and Scarman, (1985) reports caused a major rethink on the implications for policy and practice in relation to cultural diversity.

2. CATE was set-up by the then Minister of Education, Keith Joseph, in 1984. It demanded that 'ITE students should be prepared through their subject

method and educational studies to teach the full range of pupils they are likely to encounter in an ordinary school, with their diversity of . . . ethnic and cultural origins. They will need to learn how to respond flexibly to such diversity and to guard against preconceptions based on race' (DES, 1984).

Of the forces affecting ITE outside the DES and CATE, probably the most powerful was the CNAA, the Council for National Academic Awards, which validated the vast majority of B.Eds and PGCEs taught in higher-education colleges and polytechnics. In 1984, CNAA stated, 'Teachers need . . . to be equipped to prepare all young people for life in a multicultural and racially harmonious society . . . Teacher Education ought to . . . permeate all elements of the course with multicultural and anti-racist considerations . . . encourage a critical approach to cultural bias . . . adopt an approach to all subjects . . . which avoids an ethnocentric view of the world . . . Students ought to be . . . sensitive to the presence of unintentional racism in their own expectations . . . and in curriculum materials'.

In some institutions CATE 1984 and CNAA requirements did have radicalizing effects, for example, in the developments and permeation of anti-sexism, antiracism, — and (more rarely) anti-classism, throughout the curriculum. CATE 1984 facilitated and coincided with the development of courses subscribing to 'the reflective practitioner' model of the teacher, at present (though for how much longer?) the most common model for ITE courses. Courses had to become more holistic. Indeed, some courses aimed at 'critically reflective' models. The previously dominant model of the teacher was the 'technical' or 'technicist' model.

In some institutions the CATE criteria of 1984 gave valuable space and power to those arguing for the discrete 'social context of education'-type courses and rigorous permeation of antiracism (and anti-sexism and anti-classism) throughout B.Ed and PGCE courses. (Whitty, 1991a,b; Crozier and Menter, 1992). However, in many institutions these social-justice criteria were 'tokenist' (Clay and George, 1992; Siraj-Blatchford, 1992; Arten, 1988). Some Higher Education Institutes (HEI) specifically appointed staff as antiracist change agents, setting up equal opportunities and/or antiracist units, resource centres, and policy guidelines. In some institutions they were set out in student handbooks but have now been removed.

3. Some new requirements of the 1989 CATE criteria (DES, 1989), were uncontroversial. However, other criteria have badly squeezed time for studying controversial, social justice, and equality issues (for example more time now has to be spent on technology, maths, English and science). In short, ITE students are to be trained to deliver the National Curriculum and its assessments. With the 'school National Curriculum not only the most prescriptive but also arguably a strongly nationalistic curriculum' there are clear dangers of ITE students accepting a Eurocentric, culturally elitist selection of knowledge (Davies, Holland and Minhas, 1990; Clay and George, 1992).

4. The January 1992 Draft CATE criteria of Kenneth Clarke (DES, 1992) were remarkable. This was the first set of criteria to omit any mention whatsoever of equal opportunities as criteria for accrediting and evaluating ITE courses.

5. The CATE criteria of May 1992 for secondary ITE (DFE, 1992a). Other than criteria of limited reinsertion of equal opportunities, were 1992 criteria, and the draft criteria of January 1992, which they slightly modified, are the most heavily, and most obviously, influenced by the Radical Right, in particular by the Radical Right group on CATE. Following major purges of the membership of CATE they continue to have the Minister's ear (Pyke, 1992).

6. The June 1993 primary ITE Draft proposals by CATE, for the primary PGCE course were to increase course length by two weeks, from thirty-six to thirty-eight weeks, and to increase the number of school-based weeks from a fifteen-week minimum to a eighteen-week minimum (leaving twenty weeks as college-based). The reduced school-based proportion for primary PGCE students compared to secondary 'reflects the fact that students must acquire a large amount of subject knowledge to cope with the national curriculum' (Pyke, 1992).

Draft proposals for primary B.Ed. retained four-year courses with two years spent on academic-subject study, just over one year college-based preparation, and just under one year spent on school-based preparation. Of the two years which are not main subject(s) or academic-subject study-based the minimum number of school-based weeks increase from twenty weeks (1989 criteria) to thirty-two weeks. This would leave around thirty-two weeks maximum for college-based study.

Within the four-year B.Ed the required number of hours to be spent on each of the three core subjects of maths, English and science is increased to 150 hours each out of the 1800 hours of directed time to be spent on 'curriculum and subject studies' in three and four year B.Ed courses. This, indeed, is the first appearance of the notion of directed time on curriculum and subject studies.

7. The Government Blue Paper 'The Government's Proposals for the Reform of Initial Teacher Training' of September 1993, among other suggestions, presented proposals which suggest that 'schools should be able, if they wish, to play the leading role in planning and providing courses' (DFE, 1993b, :2), that 'there will be suitable financial incentives to secure the development and growth of three-year courses in place of four-year courses' (ibid., :5), and that money will be transferred from colleges to schools.

New Routes into Teaching

In 1990 the government introduced two new routes into teaching, the licensed, and articled-teacher routes. In brief, licensed teachers may be non-graduates who have completed two years higher education and can find a school willing to employ them, with minimal guidelines as to teacher education and training. Articled teachers are graduates who follow a two-year PGCE course, 80 per cent of which is based in schools (Both are described and critiqued in Hill, 1989a, 1991a). But the numbers are growing. In January 1992 there were 385 licensed teachers. By July 1992 this had increased to 1481, by September 1993 to 2113. (DFE, 1993b :3) This is actually more than the 1350 articled teachers 'in training' or certificated (DFE, 1992a).

Rather like school opt-outs, the scheme has not (yet) taken off, thanks to professional resistance. The secondary articled-teacher scheme has ended after three intakes following the May 1992 changes to the secondary PGCE (and Secondary B.Ed). The primary articled-teacher scheme may well go the same way shortly.

In June 1993 Minister of Education John Patten's Draft Circular proposed a 'Mum's Army' for infant (Key Stage 1) teaching (DFE, 1993c,d). This new scheme, was for a one-year trained non-graduate 'Mum's Army' for infant and nursery teaching (Key Stage 1 teaching). This proposal, set out by Minister of Education John Patten was to recruit 'mums' with A-level qualifications (that is to say, women who left school at the age of 18 or 19 but who have not had any higher education). Their 'training course would be one academic year of thirty-two weeks of which eighteen weeks would be spent in school and fourteen weeks — a maximum of seventy days in a college. Furthermore the colleges were not to be higher-education Institutes. Instead they would be further-education colleges. In general, these carry out very little degree-level work and have little experience in degree level or postgraduate level or any other level of education and training for schoolteachers.

Circular 14/93, *The Initial Training of Primary School Teachers*, issued in November 1993, is to take full effect for all primary ITE courses, in September 1996. Its criteria will apply to all *new* courses from September 1994. (DFE, 1993e, CATE, 1993). Increased PGCE course length, increased minima for number of weeks in school for B.Ed and PGCE students, 'Directed Time', schools' ability to play a leading role in ITE, transfer of funds to schools wishing to run their own ITE schemes, and financial incentives for three-year B.Ed courses over four-year courses are all retained from the 1993 Draft proposals and the 'Blue Paper' referred to above. Fortunately, the 'Mum's Army' idea was dropped.

The criteria set out in Circular 14/93 list thirty-three 'competences expected of newly qualified teachers' (DFE 1993e, pp. 15–17).

No criteria refer to 'race', cultural or ethnic diversity, multiculturalism — (nor indeed to gender or to social class background). The criteria contain no explicit reference whatsoever, recognizing, theorizing about, or responding to structured forms of inequality.

Four competences which can be utilized for such purposes are that: 'newly qualified teachers should be able to:

- 'identify and respond appropriately to relevant individual differences between pupils;'
  (Competence 2.5.1)
- 'Show awareness of how pupils learn and of the various factors which affect this process;'
  (Competence 2.5.2)

and that 'newly qualified teachers should have acquired in initial training the necessary foundation to develop:

- 'the ability to evaluate pupils' learning, and to recognise the effects on that learning of teachers' expectations and actions'
  (Competence 2.7.5)
- 'vision, imagination and critical awareness in educating their pupils'
  (Competence 2.7.8).

These last two 'Competences expected of newly qualified teachers' are re-legated, however, to those competences established for 'Further Professional Development', competences that 'newly qualified teachers should have acquired in initial training (as) the necessary foundation' for development. (DFE, 1993e, pp. 15–17).

Within the competences, other spaces and legitimation for multicultural and/or antiracist development lies within the National Curriculum itself, as set out in other chapters in this book. Various competences refer to teaching the National Curriculum, and require, *inter alia*, that 'newly qualified teachers should be able to:

- demonstrate understanding of the purpose, scope, structure and bal-ance of the primary curriculum as a whole (DFE, 1993e, p. 15).

However, unlike the 1989 and the 1984 CATE Criteria for Primary ITE overt recognition of ethnic diversity and cultural diversity is absent.

The School-based Training of PGCE and B.Ed Courses

The third aspect of Radical Conservative state policy and control over ITE is to dramatically increase school-basing of PGCE and B.Ed courses. Just as important, for the Radical Right, is the substantial reduction of college-based teacher education. There is no opposition to basing part of undergraduate and postgraduate courses of initial teacher training/initial teacher education (ITE) in schools (Bocock, 1992; Hill, 1992d). Many ITE courses do require students to be in school for more than the minimum time required by the 1989 CATE requirements (Barrett *et al.*, 1992).

Antiracism, Multiculturalism and ITE: The Limits of the Advance

In 1985 The Swann report suggested, that very few institutions offered a core course on antiracism, let alone any cross-curricular permeation (Swann, 1985). This was, however, before the CATE criteria, and the CNAA criteria for validating college and polytechnic ITE courses had had much time to take effect. But it does point to the lack of radicalism, or even of multicultural celebration of cultural diversity, which was actually being developed voluntaristically without these external demands. It is contended that such antiracism and multiculturalism as did happen in ITE courses was, in general, the result of the efforts of individuals, rather than of coherent overall course planning (Hill, 1992c).

By 1989 the CRE suggested that 'What is apparent is that compared with schools, universities and polytechnics have been relatively untouched by the debate on racial equality in education and have not, on the whole, seen the need to develop specific policies in this area' (Swann, 1985, quoted in both Siraj-Blatchford, 1992, and Clay and George 1992). Clay and George (1992) criticize the lack of specificity in CATE guidelines which allowed institutions to implement the criteria in ways that closely mirrored their own levels of consciousness, prevalent beliefs and levels of competence of staff employed. They cite a limited survey of ten HEIs.

> All ten had stated rationales in their courses that committed them to the study of issues relating to cultural diversity. Although, as with the EOC survey, they expressed recognition of the importance of studying 'race' and culture issues, there was considerable variation. The survey found that only two institutions out of the ten stated a clear anti-racist rationale. The rest expressed rationales that were clearly multicultural/multiracial, or as part of general equal opportunities programme. The survey also found that less than a third of the course (8 out of 26) had a core input. Four courses offered an option model, whilst the rest relied on permeation. (Clay and George, 1992, pp. 129–30)

With regard to school-based teaching practice, Crozier and Menter (1992), note that:

> Even on Courses where there is a strong expression of commitment to equality issues, there is evidence that this very rarely leads to effective treatment of these concerns within the teaching practice triad. Research carried out at two institutions indicated a 'stasis' within these relationships. Potentially contentious issues, especially if they might challenge the professionalism of the teacher, were invariably avoided. (Crozier and Menter, 1992, p. 100)

Table 14.1: *Challenges: Issues in School-based ITE and the ITE Curriculum*

School	• Student reflection time
	• Consultation with schools and HEIs
	• School-teacher time
	• Criteria for partner-school selection
	• Responsibility for school selection
	• Support for minority ethnic students
	• School teacher-mentor education and training
ITE Curriculum	• Contextual/social/equality issues
	• Theory and reflection
	• Type of reflection (technical, contextual, or critical)
	• Curriculum organization of theory and reflection

'What has been most striking though, is how often there is a very direct contradiction between the espousal of liberal antisexist and antiracist positions by college staff and the lived experience of students and staff' (pp. 97–8). Blair (1992), and Blair and Maylor (1992) make similar comments.

Finally, ITE institutions have not got far in recruiting ethnic-minority students. A recent survey of black teachers in eight local education authorities has estimated that black teachers make up only 2 per cent of the teaching force compared with a 4.4 per cent black representation in the population as a whole (CRE, 1988). Within ITE, a third of all ITE courses did not recruit any ethnic-minority students, and ninety-eight (out of the total of 270 courses) recruited fewer than 5 per cent of their students from ethnic minorities. (Barrett *et al.*, 1992).

Challenges

Ten Key Issues in School-based ITE and the ITE Curriculum

A number of issues in school-basing and ITE curriculum changes relate to cultural diversity.

School-based ITE
School-based ITE has been criticized for the following reasons.

- It allows too little time for collaborative reflection by students (McLennan and Seadon, 1988; Hill, 1991a).
- There are problems of consultation with teachers and teacher educators about the school–college partnership concerning how school-based ITE will operate.
- Schools in general, and in particular, primary schools, are unprepared to take the lead in ITE, because of fears of overloading teachers. (HMI, 1992; DENI, 1992; NFER, 1992)

- There are dangers in the narrowness of criteria for selecting schools to be used for ITE. These criteria should extend beyond academic SATs results and truancy rates. School-quality audits should include a school's commitment to, and experience of, multicultural and antiracist education.
- Problems exist concerning responsibility for school selection. Who is to do the choosing: the Minister and the DFE? The HEIs? Will all schools, good and bad, effective and ineffective, 'colour-blind' and antiracist be allowed to train new teachers? (CRE, 1992; ARTEN 1992).
- Concerns exist about the relative lack of support for minority ethnic students suffering from racism within the school, and for ITE students wishing to address such issues. ITE HEIs are likely to have a less stasis-bound atmosphere and be able to provide more support than schools.
- Mentors need education and training in such issues (indeed, it can be contended, so do many HEI lecturers).

The ITE Curriculum
Issues arising here include:

- How much emphasis should be placed on contextual issues of education, on the relationship between schooling, society and politics, on social justice and egalitarian issues (such as facts, theories and strategies to combat structural inequalities such as racism?)
- How much college-based theory and theoretical analysis and reflection on practice should there be? Crozier and Menter (1992) are not alone in suggesting that 'recent changes represent the continuing erosion of an intellectual basis for students' preparation as teachers.'
  While there is (considerable) potential for treating the current ITE criteria problematically, intellectually, theoretically and/or ideologically, there is clearly a blazing green government neon light here for de-theorized de-intellectualized technicist 'how-to' ITE courses stuck, at worst, at the technical level of reflection.
- What type of reflection should be encouraged? Should reflection be purely 'technical', about techniques of presentation and 'delivery'? Should reflection extend to 'situational' or 'contextual' matters such as an awareness of issues of race, gender, class, disability, sexuality, stereotyping, teacher expectation within the classroom? Or should it be 'critical, deliberately placing issues such as these, and content and pedagogy themselves, on the ITE curriculum as part of a struggle for democracy, social justice and egalitarianism?
- In course design, how should such contextual and theoretical analysis be organized; by: discrete core modules/elements; course options; permeation; or by a combination? One danger of permeation is the resulting lack of space for theoretical macrosocietal analysis.

Dave Hill

Levels of Reflection in ITE and Cultural Diversity

What do primary-school teachers reflect on in action? What should they reflect on?

Teacher educators in both the USA and the UK suggest three levels of teacher reflection (Zeichner and Liston, 1987; Liston and Zeichner, 1987; Adler, 1991; Hill, 1991c).

1. Technical reflection (level 1)
Reflection on unproblematic technical proficiency at achieving predetermined ends.

> The efficient and effective application of attaining ends which are accepted as given; where . . . neither the ends nor the institutional contexts or classroom, school, community and society are treated as problematic (Zeichner and Liston, 1987)

2. Situational/contextual reflection (level 2)
Reflection on situational, theoretical, institutional assumptions and effects of teaching actions, goals and structures — where the problem is 'explicating and clarifying the assumptions and predispositions underlying practical affairs and assessing the educational consequences towards which an action leads' (Zeichner and Liston, 1987). Adler's summary is that level 2 reflection 'places teaching within its situational and institutional contexts' (Adler, 1991).

3. Critical reflection (level 3)
Reflection on moral and ethical implications of pedagogy and of social structures and concepts — whereby 'the teachers's "critical reflection" incorporates moral and ethical criteria into a discourse about practical action . . . Here the teaching [ends and means] and the surrounding contexts are viewed as problematic'. At this level 'thinking about teaching and learning . . . is guided by concerns about justice and equality' (Zeichner and Liston, 1987). Courses promoting antiracist teacher-education policies, as opposed to courses pluralistically taking a value-free position between assimilationist, multiculturist, and antiracist perspectives are examples of level-3 reflection courses.

Technical Reflection and Cultural Diversity
The technical level of reflection is 'colour blind', ignoring issues of racism, discrimination, prejudice, and stereotyped curriculum materials. It is essentially an assimilationist and individualistic approach. It is also essentially a teacher-based approach. Where respondents (children) fail to give correct responses to teacher stimuli, then (since, by definition, contextual institutional (school) or societal factors are excluded from this technical arm of reflection) those individuals or groups of children 'failing' to give anticipated or desired

responses (in SATs or in behaviour relationships with the teacher) a...
deviant, in need of compensatory assistance or relocation to special u...
schools. This is to say, within the parameters of this technical form of refle...
tion, if the teacher is doing his or her job to technical perfection, and the pupil
is not responding as desired by the teacher, then the pupil can be justly
marginalized or even pathologized as defective — in terms of domestic
culture, child-rearing patterns, intelligence, home-language correctness or
complexity, or whatever . . . (Some similar pathologizing, or hierarchical
differentiation in terms of superiority/inferiority can be applied of course to
social class and to gender.)

This technical level of reflection dominated many B.Ed and PGCE courses
in the 1970s, with the education of 'ethnic minorities' being placed within
'special-needs' courses. It is contended here that it is this type of reflection to
which the Radical Right wishes ITE to return. Their view appears to be that
achievement in schooling is a matter of individual merit, with 'merit' (ability)
being the sum of 'intelligence plus effort'. This individual merit is socially de-
contextualized, and merit, worthiness, and ability, are determined and defined
by a dominating and dominant ideology. That is, 'anyone who is like us can
get on', 'anyone who isn't and doesn't is defective'.

A critical point is, how do ITE students and teachers get to the three
different levels of reflection? What type of theory is necessary for these three
levels of reflection? For technical reflection, trial and error, and mimicry based
on an apprenticeship or licensed-teacher system, or pupil–teacher system could
be enough. Hence, no theory would, at first sight, be required. Rather like an
apprentice butcher, the apprentice teacher could learn her or his cuts and
strokes by copying the 'master' butcher, and by having a go, getting better
through practice. This is a 'tips for teachers' approach, the tip being primarily
related to execution and presentation within a teacher-dominated stimulus–
response framework, with no development or understanding the 'why?' of
teaching, only the 'how to?'

Situational/Contextual Reflection and Cultural Diversity

The second level of reflection, the situational or contextual, enables students
and teachers to depathologize non-elite behaviour (dress, accent, language,
clothes, body language, cultural and subcultural behaviour, food, religion,
family structures) and to become aware of, and accept and (not uncritically)
value, ethnic and cultural diversity. Within the classroom such teachers are
aware of the danger of stereotyping, of underexpectation, of microdiscrim-
ination and prejudice (i.e., within small groups and the classroom, and within
the school). Such teachers are also aware of macrolevel, societal-level prejudice and discrimination. Their classroom behaviour would be non-racist. It
would not simply be colour-blind, it would be aware of, and welcome, the
diversity of colour, and would seek to represent this in a multicultural approach
to teaching, or an approach welcoming ethnic diversity or cultural pluralism.
It would be aware of and combat, within the classroom and school, racial

lages, and interethnic group hostilities. It can,
...tronize cultural diversity.

...ional reflection teachers and ITE students need some
...out attainment levels of different ethnic (and class and
...ne aware of differential attainment, i.e., that there *is* a
...ve to become aware of the ways in which teachers' and
...en curricula, peer group, domestic and societal pressures
can ...an and constrain or enhance and encourage the development of pup... .ests, security, and attainment. They then, within their
own classrooms, and within the school environment, seek to engage in non-
stereotyping, non-culturally exclusive individual and school-wide practice and
behaviour.

The theory required for this level of reflection is that relating to teacher
and school effects, and cultural difference. At this level of reflection, theory
about societal and educational stratification and about its relationship to power
structure and ideology is not necessary. Indeed, it can be seen as dangerously
provocative.

Critical Reflection and Cultural Diversity
At the critical level of reflection teachers, while incorporating the aspects of
multiculturalism listed above, would extend beyond them, seeking to enable
their pupils to develop an awareness of, an understanding of, and a commitment to oppose structural and structured inequalities in society, such as racism
(and classism, and sexism). Such teachers make/take a political stance based
on egalitarianism, the need for political action and a deliberate exposure within the curriculum of racism and antiracism. They represent an egalitarian
activist democracy, as opposed to authoritarian quietist democracy. Such
teachers deliberately and knowingly engage in, for example, antiracist history,
antiracist mathematics and, in varying circumstances, democratic participative
pedagogy.

At this level, macrosociological theories of the role of schooling in a
capitalist society are necessary. Teachers and students need critically to appraise
major analytical theories of power in society. These include the following:

- Structural-functionalist conservative 'meritocratic' analysis (e.g., John
  Major's view of a 'classless' (*sic*) society, by which he presumably means
  socially mobile rather than socially egalitarian.) This theory involves
  social mobility but eschews positive discrimination.
- Liberal-democratic pluralist analyses of power and of the neutrality of
  state institutions in, for example, questions of access and performance
  in relation to different ethnic and social class groups.
- Marxist analyses of the class nature of power in society and the relative (and contested) degree of functionalism of state apparatuses/
  structures, such as schooling, in the reproduction of existing structuring of power in society along lines of a race, sex and class, and resistance to that reproduction.

Table 14.2: Institutional Responses

HEI	• Holistic curriculum
	• Core units plus permeation
	• Institutional policy and monitoring
	• ITE recruitment of minority ethnic students
HEI–School Relationship	• School selection
	• Link teacher/mentor selection
	• Mentor training and education
	• School–HEI contracts
	• Theory–practice partnership
	• Triadic discussions
	• Development of teachers as transformative intellectuals

At this level of critical reflection students need to examine the following, in terms of their validity as responses to the racialized structuring of opportunity and academic and job attainment:

- assimilationism;
- cultural pluralism/multiculturalism; and
- antiracism.

In sum, if teachers and ITE students are to effectively attack racism (and classism and sexism) in the interests of a socially just system of distributing rewards in society, then they need to ask: Whose interests are served by this policy/theory/level of reflection? Who wins? (if only by legitimating the status quo) and who loses? (who has to deny identity in order to join the winners if this is at all possible) and who is likely to have to continue accepting a subordinate and exploited position in society by virtue of their membership of oppressed groups? Such teachers, in short, act as transformative intellectuals (Giroux 1983, Aronowitz and Giroux, 1986; Aronowitz and Giroux, 1990; Giroux and Simon, 1988; Liston and Zeichner, 1987; Giroux and McLaren, 1987; 1989; Sarup, 1986; Cole, 1988; Hill, 1991b,c).

Responses

Table 14.2 sets out eleven aspects of a response by ITE Institutions.

A Holistic ITE Curriculum

Clay and George (1992) argue for 'race' and gender equality to be considered as part of an overall understanding of social justice. They accept that:

> inequalities in practice are multi-dimensional and that their effects
> manifestly impact one upon the other. We therefore question the

desirability of maintaining their separateness. (Clay and George, 1992, p. 125)

Elsewhere, links between antiracism, antisexism, anticlassism have been drawn, suggesting that antiracism and multiculturalism can lead to, and be informed by, anticlassism and antisexism. Many teachers can, and could, substitute the word and concept 'class' (or 'sex') for 'race' in checklists for stereotyping, policies concerning equal opportunities, appointments policies, classroom-activity choices or subject-option choices in secondary schools (Hessari and Hill, 1989). Many other writers examine the interconnections between race, class and gender (Brah, 1992; Cole, 1989b; Williams 1989; Miles, 1989; Antheas, 1990).

At classroom level, in an antiracist or multicultural checklist for stereotyping in books, the word/concept 'race' can be replaced by 'sex' or 'class'. Similarly, just as it is possible to look at the different amount of time and types of response given by teachers to boys and girls in the same class, the same observation techniques can be applied to 'race' and class.

An ITE Core Curriculum and Organization in an Ethnically Diverse Society

A prescribed core curriculum for ITE should include:

- classroom skills and competencies;
- detail and data of racism — many teachers and ITE students are not aware of its existence or of its impact on the lives and education and life opportunities of black, Asian and minority ethnic communities and individuals, or indeed the impact on Whites;
- critiques of competing approaches and ideologies of schooling and teacher education, antiracism as well as multiculturalism or assimilationism, egalitarian anticlassism as well as meritocratic social mobility or elitist stratification and reproduction, antisexism as well as non-sexism or sexism; and
- the ability to 'deal with the incidence of racist remarks, and racial harassment' (CRE, 1992).

As far as ITE courses are concerned, there is virtue in a course-design strategy based on the diagrammatic model set out in Table 14.3. This is content/objectives-based and does not, for reasons of space, refer pedagogically to the need for democratic pedagogy, active and experiential learning.

If multiculturalism is seen as an essential part of antiracism and not as an end-goal, then both strategies are necessary as means to an antiracist end. If, however, multiculturalism stops at celebrating ethnic diversity and does not

Table 14.3: Responses: Curriculum Detail

	Social Class	Race	Sex

What's the problem?
Evidence/data on inequality
Quantitative statistical
Qualitative students' life histories
       children's life histories
in • classrooms
  • school institutions
  • the education system
  • ITE
  • societal structures (e.g., housing, employment, politics, media)			

Why is it happening and why it should or should not
Theoretical analyses explaining, justifying, critiquing/
attacking such inequality, including:
  • biological models
  • conservative structural functionalism
  • liberal democratic pluralism
  • deterministic Marxism
  • voluntaristic neo-Marxism			

Anti-egalitarian policy developments which seek, or have
the effect of increasing *in*equality in:
  • classrooms
  • school institutions
  • the education system
  • ITE
  • society and societal structures			

Egalitarian policy developments which seek, or have the
effect of increasing egalitarianism in:
  • classrooms
  • school institutions
  • the education system
  • ITE
  • society and societal structures			

see itself as a development of a metanarrative of antiracist social egalitarianism and justice, then multiculturalism can be viewed as, in essence, conservative, failing to challenge the social, economic, political, racial power status quo.

Leicester (1992), and Cole (1989b) continue this debate in the UK, as do Gill *et al.*, (1992), Braham *et al.*, (1992) and Donald *et al.*, (1992). US responses to cultural diversity are set out in Sleeter, 1989, 1992). Clay and George (1992) consider that,

> We need to equip students with the intellectual skills critically to examine the nature of the curriculums so that they can in turn consider the challenge the ideologies that underpin the selection of knowledge that they are being asked to acquire and teach through the National Curriculum. (Clay and George, 1992)

Antiracist Core Units Plus Permeation

Despite acknowledging the weaknesses of the permeation model, Clay and George support it because of the increasingly limited time available for such issues (Clay and George, 1992). Permeation can be highly effective, or highly ineffective, but it is not enough. Such issues must be put firmly on the agenda, not just slipped in to myriad spaces within other sessions. Such issues need to be dealt with holistically in two senses. Firstly, it must be done *conceptually*, as part of a holistic anti-egalitarian programme interlinking different forms of oppression.

Secondly, it is necessary *organizationally*, as part of B.Ed and PGCE courses, where the above course outline is presented explicitly as important and with units of study focusing on data, theory and policy in general, at levels larger than a single subject (e.g., primary curriculum music or history) and at levels larger than classroom, school, and education policy.

Institutional Policy and Monitoring

For the newly evolving School Inspectorate system under OFSTED, good practice in ITE institutions with regard to cultural diversity should include the following:

- There is a policy document which heightens awareness, especially if the staff have been involved in its formulation.
- Policies are monitored through qualitative and quantitative indices of good practice.
- Accommodation is provided for focusing resources at the early stages of implementation.
- Tutors have first-hand experience of teaching in multiethnic schools.
- There is a coordinating post, a named person such as an adviser in an LEA, with an appropriate level of seniority.
- Speakers are brought in from the communities.
- There are students from the ethnic minorities in the institution to raise issues bearing on cultural diversity.
- Adequate time is given to allow a proper consideration of multiethnic issues within the core of courses.
- Students are given direct experience of multiethnic schools.
- Multiethnic issues are *not* construed as issues of 'special needs'.

ITE Recruitment of Minority Ethnic Students

ITE HETs should:

- market training courses directly at ethnic minorities, using the ethnic-minority press and broadcast media, and targeting schools and colleges that have a high proportion of students from ethnic-minority groups;

- develop their own public equal-opportunities policies to assure students from ethnic minorities that they will receive fair treatment;
- scrutinize interviewing selection procedures to ensure that direct or indirectly discriminatory practices are not operating to exclude people from ethnic minorities; and
- the DES should collect statistics from institutions providing teacher education, on the ethnic origins of teachers in training. This information should be forwarded to OFSTED and CATE, so that strategically targeted marketing and promotion can be deployed where it is needed. (A number of these points are set out in Carr, 1992, CRE 1992, and Crozier and Menter, 1992).

A Sixfold Plan for Relationships with Schools

The following six points outline a policy for School–HEI relationships:

1. Criteria for the selection of schools

   Schools offering training should be able to demonstrate their ability to offer a good model of equality of opportunity policy and practice, and where appropriate a curriculum responsive to the needs of multi-racial and multilingual communities, in order to be accredited as partnership schools (CRE, 1992).

2. Criteria for the selection of link teachers

   Within those schools, the criteria for the selection of link teachers (teacher tutors, teacher mentors) should include the ability to demonstrate a range of competencies including an understanding of, and/or record of, work in implementing equal-opportunities policies, and/or curriculum development of relevance to multi-racial and multilingual needs (CRE, 1992).

3. Mentor training and education

   As in ITE, schools and teachers currently sometimes lack the expertise to equip student teachers with the skills and understanding required to recognize factors that disadvantage pupils. Mentors need to be provided with full training and support in the issues relating to social justice by the ITE institution concerned.

4. School–HEI contracts

   These should clearly outline the commitments, responsibilities and expectations of HE staff, school staff and students, including a formal commitment to dealing with racism at both an institutional and a personal level.

5. Theory–practice partnership between HEIs and schools

HEIs should provide the opportunity for structured theoretical explorations, and schools should provide the opportunity for students to experience the practical implementation and contexts of those considerations. The matching of theoretical to practical work on this issue is the sort of partnership between institutions that will be most useful (Clay and George, 1992).

6. Triadic discussions

Triadic discussions should take place (while recognizing the stasis usually inherent in such discussions).

Even where the teacher takes major responsibility for supervising and assessing the student, there should be critical discussions within school-experience 'triads' (between teacher, student and HEI tutor) (Menter, 1989, 1992; Crozier and Menter, 1992).

In conclusion, in schools the Conservative National Curriculum seeks ideologically to shackle and determine *what* current teachers teach. The Radical Right and the Education Ministers are also seeking to determine *how* current teachers teach. Appalled at antiracism, at 'relevance', at highlighting and valuing domestic social and ethnic cultures, collaborative, child-centred, interdisciplinary groupwork, they seek to change the hidden (or informal) curriculum in schools along the lines of traditional, didactic, chalk and talk and a return to pre-1960s traditionalist pedagogic and social relationships between teachers and pupils. Such a pedagogy is transmissive rather than negotiated. The content *and* the methodology of training and educating teachers is faced with similar dramatic changes.

This chapter is a critical reflective egalitarian and antiracist manifesto calling for teachers to engage in critical reflection and action as transformation antiracist intellectual practitioners.

References

ADLER, S. (1991) 'The Reflective Practitioner and the curriculum in Teacher Education', *Journal of Education for Teaching*, 17, 2.

ANTHEAS, F. (1990) 'Race and Class Re-visited: conceptualising race and racism', *Sociological Review*, 38, 1.

ANTI-RACIST TEACHER EDUCATION NETWORK (ARTEN) (1988) 'A Survey of Antiracist Practice, in Teacher Education Institutions in the South West and Wales', in ARTEN (Eds) *Anti-Racist Teacher Education, Permeation:*

the Road to Nowhere, Occasional Paper 4, Glasgow, Jordanhill College of Education.

ANTI-RACIST TEACHER EDUCATION NETWORK (ARTEN) (1992) *Response to Kenneth Clarke's Speech and Proposals for the Reform of Initial Teacher Training* (A Consultation Document).

ARONOWITZ, S. and GIROUX, H. (1986) *Education Under Siege: The Conservative, Liberal and Radical Debate over Schooling*, London, RKP.

ARONOWITZ, S. GIROUX, H. (1990) *Postmodern Education*, Minneapolis, University of Minnesota Press.

BARKER, M. (1981) *The New Racism*, London, Junction Books.

BARRETT, E., BARTON, L., FURLONG, J., GALVIN, C., MILES, S., and WHITTY, G. (1992) *Initial Teacher Education in England and Wales: A Topography*, London, Goldsmith's College (Interim Report of the Modes of Teacher Education Project).

BLACKBURNE, L. (1992) 'Government attacked by its old trusties,' the *Times Educational Supplement*, 20 November.

BLAIR, M. (1992) 'Black Teachers and Teacher Education', *Education Review*, 6, 2.

BLAIR, M. and MAYLOR, U. (1992) 'Issues and Concerns for Black Women Teachers in training,' in SIRAJ-BLATCHFORD, I. (Ed) *'Race', Gender and the Education of Teachers*, Buckingham, Open University Press.

BOCOCK, J. (1992) 'Hurdles to be jumped in the schools,' *THES*, 31 January.

BRAH, A. (1992) 'Differences, diversity and differentiation', in DONALD, J. and RATTANSI, A. (Eds) *'Race, Culture and Difference,'* London, Sage publications.

BRAHAM, P., RATTANSI, A. and SKELLINGTON, R. (Eds) (1992) *Racism and Anti-Racism*, London, Sage publications.

CLAY, J., COLE, M. and HILL, D. (1990) 'Black Achievement in Initial Teacher Education — How do we proceed into the 1990's', *Multicultural Teaching*, 8, 3.

CLAY, J. and GEORGE, R. (1992) 'Moving Beyond Permeation; Courses in Teacher Education', in SIRAJ-BLATCHFORD, I. (Ed) *Race, Gender and the Education of Teachers*, London, Sage publications.

COLE, M. (1986) 'Teaching and Learning about Racism: A Critique of Multicultural Education in Britain,' in MODGIL, S. *et al. Multicultural Education, The Interminable Debate*, London, The Falmer Press.

COLE, M. (Ed) (1988) *Bowles and Gintis Revisited: Correspondence and Contradiction in Educational Theory*, London, The Falmer Press.

COLE, M. (1989b) ' "Race" and Class or "Race", Class, Gender and Community: A Critical Appraisal of the Racialised Fraction of the Working Class Thesis?', *British Journal of Sociology of Education*, 40, 1.

COLE, M. (1989c) 'Monocultural, Multicultural and Anti-Racist Education', in COLE, M. (Ed) *The Social Contexts of Schooling*, Lewes, The Falmer Press.

COLE, M., CLAY, J. and HILL, D. (1991) 'The citizen as "individuals" and nationalist or as "social" and, internationalist? What is the role of education?', *Critical Social Policy*, Issue 30, 10, 3.

COMMISSION FOR RACIAL EQUALITY (1988) *Ethnic Minority School Teachers: a supplementary survey of eight local education authorities*, London, CRE.

Dave Hill

COUNCIL FOR THE ACCREDITATION OF TEACHER EDUCATION (CATE) (1992) *The Accreditation of Initial Teacher Training Under Circulars 9/92 (Department for Education) and 35/92 (Welsh Office)*, London, CATE.

COUNCIL FOR THE ACCREDITATION OF TEACHER EDUCATION (1993) *The Initial Training of Primary School Teachers: Circular 14/93 (England)*, A Note of Guidance for the Council for the Accreditation of Teacher Education, London, CATE.

Cox, B. (1992) 'Curriculum for Chaos', *The Guardian*, 15 September.

CRE (COMMISSION FOR RACIAL EQUALITY) (1992) *Response to DES Consultation on Proposals for Reform of Initial Teacher Training*, London, CRE.

CROZIER, G. and MENTER, I. (1992) 'The Heart of the Matter? Student Teachers' Experiences in Schools', in SIRAJ-BLATCHFORD, I. (Ed) *Race, Gender and the Education of Teachers*, London, Sage publications.

DAVIES, A., M. HOLLAND, J. and MINHAS, R. (1990) *Equal Opportunities in the New Era*, Hillcole Group Paper 2, London, Tufnell Press.

DEPARTMENT FOR EDUCATION (1992a) Personal Communication.

DEPARTMENT FOR EDUCATION (1992b) *Circular 9/92. Initial Teacher Training (Secondary Phase)*, London, DFE.

DEPARTMENT FOR EDUCATION (1992c) Teacher Training Circular Letter 9/92, *Reform of Primary Phase Initial Teacher Training (ITT)*, London, DFE.

DEPARTMENT FOR EDUCATION (1993a) Personal Communication to the author.

DEPARTMENT FOR EDUCATION (1993b) *The Government's Proposals for the Reform of Initial Teacher Training*, London, DFE, September.

DEPARTMENT FOR EDUCATION (1993c) *Patten outlines Primary Teacher Training Reforms*, DFE News, London, DFE, 2 June.

DEPARTMENT FOR EDUCATION (1993d) *The Initial Training of Primary School Teachers: New Criteria for Course Approval*, London, DFE, June.

DEPARTMENT FOR EDUCATION (1993e) *The Initial Training of Primary School Teachers: Circular 14/93: New Criteria for Courses*, London, DFE, November.

DEPARTMENT OF EDUCATION and SCIENCE (1984) *Initial Teacher Training — Approval of Courses*, Circular 3/84, London, HMSO.

DEPARTMENT OF EDUCATION and SCIENCE (1989) *Initial Teacher Training: Approval of Courses*, Circular 24/89, London, HMSO.

DEPARTMENT OF EDUCATION AND SCIENCE (1992) *Reform of Initial Teacher Training: A Consultation Document*, London, HMSO.

DEPARTMENT OF EDUCATION, NORTHERN IRELAND (1991) *Teachers for the 21st Century: A Review of Initial Teacher Training, Consultative Paper*, Bangor, Northern Ireland, DENI.

DONALD, J., RATTANSI, A. and SKELLINGTON, R. (Eds) (1992) *'Race', Culture and Difference*, London, Sage publications.

EDGAR, D. (1989) 'Dreams of the Volk', in *New Socialist*, 45, London.

GILL, D., MAYOR, B. and BLAIR, M. (Eds) (1992) *Racism and Educations, Structures and Strategies*, London, Sage publications.

GILROY, P. (1992) 'The end of anti-racism,' in DONALD, J. and RATTANSI, A. (Ed) *'Race', Culture and Difference*, London, Sage publications.

GILROY, P. (1992) 'The Political Rape of Initial Teacher Education in England and Wales: A JET rebuttal', *Journal of Education for Teaching*, 18, 1.

GIROUX, H. (1983) *Theory and Resistance in Education: A Pedagogy for the Opposition*, London, Heinemann.

GIROUX, H. and McLAREN, P. (1987) 'Teacher Education as a Counter-Public Sphere: Notes Towards a Redefinition', in POPKEWITZ, T. *Critical Studies in Teacher Education*, London, The Falmer Press.

GIROUX, H. and McLAREN, P. (Eds) (1989) *Critical Pedagogy, State and Cultural Struggle*, New York, State University of New York Press.

GIROUX, H. and SIMON, R. (1988) 'Schooling, Popular Culture and a Pedagogy of Possibility', *Boston University Journal of Education*, 170, 1.

GORDON, P. (1990) 'The New Right, race and education — or How the 'Black' Papers became a White Paper', The Labour Party, London, New Socialist.

GRAHAM, D. and TITLER, D. (1992) *A Lesson for Us All*, London, Routledge.

HESSARI, R. and HILL, D. (1989) *Practical Approaches to Multi-Cultural Learning and Teaching in the Primary Classroom*, London, Routledge.

HER MAJESTY'S INSPECTORATE (1991) *School-based Initial Teacher Training in England and Wales: A Report by HM Inspectorate*, London, HMSO.

HER MAJESTY'S INSPECTORATE (1992) *School-based Initial Teacher Training in England and Wales — A Report by Her Majesty's Inspectorate*, London, HMSO.

HILL, D. (1989b) 'Teacher Education, Teachers and the attack on Equality', *NUT Education Review*, 3, 2.

HILL, D. (1989c) 'Resisting the Radical Right's Assault on Teacher Education, *Research Intelligence*, 94, Kingston, BERA (British Educational Research Association).

HILL, D. (1990) *Something Old, Something New, Something Borrowed, Something Blue: Teacher Education, Schooling and the Radical Right in Britain and the USA*, London, Tufnell Press.

HILL, D. (1991a) *What's Left in Teacher Education: Teacher Education, the Radical Left, and Policy Proposals*, London, Tufnell Press.

HILL, D. (1991b) 'What's Left in Teacher Education?' in Hillcole Group, *Changing the Future: Redprint for Education*, London, Tufnell Press.

HILL, D. (1991c) 'Seven Contemporary Ideological Perspectives on Teacher Education in Britain Today,' *Australian Journal of Teacher Education*, 16, 2, Perth, Australia.

HILL, D. (1992a) 'What the Radical Right is doing to teacher education: a Radical Left response', *Multicultural Teaching*, 10, 3, Stoke on Trent.

Hill, D. (1992b) 'What's Happened to Initial Teacher Education?', *Education Review*, 6, 2, London, NUT.

Hill, D. (1992c) BERA (British Educational Research Association) Annual Conference Symposium on 'The Left and Teacher Education', Paper by Mike Cole, Dave Hill and resulting discussions, (unpublished), and discussions at the 1992 Conference on Teacher Education and Training: A Response to Kenneth Clarke, King's College, London, organized by the Institute for Education Policy Studies.

HILL, D. (1992d) *'What's it all about? Training Teachers in School and Educating them in College'*, Paper delivered to the BERA (British Educational Research Association) Annual Conference, Stirling University.

HILL, D. (1993a) Personal Communication from DFE, September 1993.

HILL, D. (1993b) 'What Teachers?', *School Basing and Critical Reflection in Teacher Education and Training*, Brighton, Institute for Education Policy Studies.

Dave Hill

HILLCOLE GROUP (1991) *Changing the Future: Redprint for Education*, London, Tufnell Press.

HILLCOLE GROUP (1993a) *Falling Apart: The Coming Crisis of Conservative Education*, London, Tufnell Press.

HILLCOLE GROUP (1993b) 'Whose Teachers?', *A Radical Manifesto*, London, Tufnell Press.

HILLGATE GROUP (1988) *Learning to Teach*, London, The Claridge Press.

The Independent (1992) 'Teacher Training could be switched to schools,' 26 October.

LEICESTER, M. (1992) 'Anti-racism versus New Multiculturalism: Moving beyond the Interminable Debate,' in LYNCH, J. *et al.* (Eds) *Equity or Excellence: Education and Cultural Reproduction*, Lewes, The Falmer Press.

LISTON, D.P. and ZEICHNER, K.M. (1987) 'Critical Pedagogy and Teacher Education', *Boston University Journal of Education*, 169, 3.

MAJOR, J. (1992) 'Speech' to Conservative Party Conference, October (Transcript).

MASSEY, I. (1991) *More than Skin Deep*, London, Hodder and Stoughton.

McLENNAN, T. and SEADON, S. (1988) 'What price school-based work?', Reflections on a school-sited PGCE method course, *Cambridge Journal of Education*, 18, 3.

MENTER, I. (1989) 'Teaching Practice Stasis: Racism, Sexism and School Experience in Initial Teacher Education', in *British Journal of Sociology of Education*, 10, 4.

MENTER, I. (1992) 'The New Right, racism and teacher education: some recent developments,' *Multicultural Teaching*, 10, 2.

MILES, R. (1989) *Racism*, London, Routledge.

NATIONAL FOUNDATION FOR EDUCATIONAL RESEARCH (1992) *Evaluation of the Articled Teachers' Scheme*, London, NFER.

O'HEAR, A. (1988) *Who Teaches the Teachers? A Contribution to Public Debate*, London, Social Affairs Unit.

O'KEEFE, D. (1990a) *The Wayward Elite*, London, The Adam Smith Institute.

PATTEN, J. (1992) 'Speech' to Conservative Party Conference, October (Transcript).

PYKE, N. (1992) 'Longer Primary Training Proposed', the *Times Educational Supplement*, London, 17 July.

PYKE, N. (1992) 'Ministers fuel fear of training overhaul', *Times Educational Supplement*, 2 October.

SARUP, M. (1986) *The Politics of Multi-Racial Education*, London, Routledge.

SCARMAN, LORD (1981) *The Scarman Report: The Brixton Disorders*, London, HMSO (reprinted, London, Pelican, 1986).

SEXTON, S. (1987) *Our Schools — A Radical Policy*, London, Institute for Economic Affairs.

SIRAJ-BLATCHFORD, I. (1992) 'Racial Equality an Effective Teacher Education', in SIRAJ-BLATCHFORD, I. (Ed) *'Race', Gender and the Educating of Teachers*, London, Sage publications.

SLEETER, C. (1989) 'Multicultural Education as a Form of Resistance to Oppression,' *Journal of Education*, 171, 3, Boston, USA.

SLEETER, C. (1992) 'How White Teachers Construct Race', in McCARTHY, C. and CRICHLOW, W. *Race, Identity and Representation*, New York, Routledge.

SWANN, LORD (1985) *Education for All: The Report of the Committee of Inquiry into the Education of Children from Ethnic Minority Groups*, London, HMSO.

WHITTY, G. and MENTER, I. (1990) 'Lessons of Thatcherism: Education Policy in England and Wales 1979–88', in GAMBLE, A. and WELLS, C. *Thatcher's Law*, London, Blackwell.

WHITTY, G. (1991a) *Next in Line for the Treatment: Educational Reform and Teacher Education in the 1990s*, Inaugural Professorial Lecture at Goldsmith's College, London.

WHITTY, G. (1991b) *CATE, Post-CATE and a National Curriculum for Teacher Education*, Paper to the Hillcole Group National Seminar on Teacher Education, Kings College, London.

WILLIAMS, F.C. (1989) *Social Policy: A Critical Introduction, Issues of Race, Gender, and Class*, London, Policy Press.

ZEICHNER, K. and LISTON, D. (1987) 'Teaching Student Teachers to Reflect', *Harvard Education Review*, 57, 1.

Appendix 1

The Race Relations Act and Education

Gajendra K. Verma and Prabodh Merchant

Earlier chapters have provided the ethnic, religious and cultural contexts which should be taken into account if the educational needs and aspirations of all pupils are to be properly fulfilled. Cultural diversity must be made creative in school, by weaving together interrelated principles of cross-curricular dimensions, skills and themes. In an increasingly competitive environment with the ever-present scarcity of resources it is particularly important that those with the primary responsibility of educating society are also aware of the legal context in relation to race and culture within which they need to carry out their work. It will be helpful therefore to look briefly at the development of race-relations law in this country over the past twenty to thirty years resulting from the changing racial, cultural and religious composition of the population.

Background to the Laws

While it is true to say that the UK has always had migrants who have been assimilated into the social and economic life of the country, these have been, up to the mid 1950s, generally of white-European origins. For these migrants difficulties in the main were those resulting from differences in language, religion and those flowing from newness: i.e., lack of contacts, availability of, and access to, goods and services. It was assumed that most, if not all, of the problems likely to be encountered by these migrants would resolve themselves without any special intervention by the state in a matter of a generation or two at most. The differences such as those relating to religion, custom and practice could be accommodated within the existing legal framework. Problems of race discrimination were thought to be virtually non-existent and could similarly be left to be dealt with by the common-sense application of existing public-order legislation supported by the innate sense of fair play on the part of the majority of the British people. The examples of religious and political intolerance involving anti-Semitism and the Catholic–Protestant divide in Christianity are historical facts that cast considerable doubt on such an optimistic analysis.

242

Post-war reconstruction of shattered cities and economies and the scarcity of labour in all the European countries necessitated a wider search for suitable labour. Thus, throughout the 1950s various European countries actively encouraged recruitment of labour from their colonies or from countries newly given their independence. For the United Kingdom the most fruitful sources of labour were the islands of the Caribbean, and the newly independent countries of the Indian subcontinent. People from these countries were already familiar to the British and, as members of the Commonwealth, were free to enter the mother country without any restrictions.

Throughout the 1950s people came to work and mostly returned to the countries of origin to visit the families whom they supported. As their prime concern was to obtain work, they were attracted to towns and cities offering opportunities for unskilled and semi-skilled work. Again, with the responsibility of supporting their families in their country of origin, it was important that living expenses in this country were kept to a minimum. This typically meant living in Victorian terraced housing shared with friends and relatives in the cheapest areas of town, close to mills, factories and transport depots where they worked. Inevitably, differences in priorities, culture, language, religion, and so forth caused friction between these newcomers and the white working-class residents.

Towards the end of the 1950s, in response to public clamour, the government made known its intention to introduce restrictions on the entry of Commonwealth citizens. This intention was translated in 1962 into the Commonwealth Immigrants Act. Commonwealth citizens entering the UK for work after the passing of the Act in mid-1962 needed vouchers. Dependents of those already in the UK were, however, allowed to come without vouchers. This had a significant impact on the nature of immigration and the pattern of their settlement in the UK. Initially there was a rush to beat the deadline of unrestricted entry. This was followed by a need for entrants of both the pre and post-period of the 1962 Act to take up permanent settlement and make arrangements for their families to join them here in the United Kingdom. Thus, by introducing an element of sponsorship, the voucher system reinforced bonds of friendship and kinship and provided a further incentive for the new entrants to settle among existing communities and into similar work areas. This change in the composition and pattern of migration had, in its turn, implications for various services including the education service. The arrival of families with school-age young people into areas which were already the poorest in terms of housing, education and social and environmental amenities created further tensions and friction.

The 1962 Act was followed in 1965 by the first of the three Race Relations Acts. The 1965 Race Relations Act created a Race-Relations Board with powers to take up individual cases of overt discrimination in a very limited sphere of public life. The emphasis of the Act was on conciliation, with the reserve power to take those few who behaved in an illegal way to court. As yet there was no official acceptance of racial discrimination as a significant factor in the continuing disadvantage and harassment suffered by those who were now being euphemistically referred to as 'New-Commonwealth immigrants'.

The task of helping the newcomers to adjust to British society was largely left to the newcomers and voluntary groups such as the Joint Council for the Welfare of Immigrants, the National Committee for Commonwealth Immigrants and concerned individuals. However, the extra burden on local authorities with substantial populations of migrants from the new Commonwealth was recognized. Section 11 of the Local Government Act 1966 therefore provides that the Secretary of State may pay grants towards expenditure on additional staff to those 'local authorities who in his opinion are required to make special provision in the exercise of any of their functions in consequence of the presence within their areas of substantial numbers of immigrants from the Commonwealth whose language or customs differ from those of the community'.[1] Up to 75 per cent of salary costs of approved posts was payable. By far the largest proportion of this grant was used to fund posts in education. Thus, in 1986–7, of the estimated £100 million Section 11 expenditure, 79.5 per cent went towards funding posts in education mainly as generalist teachers, ESL school-based peripatetic teachers and classroom assistants.

By 1992/93, Section 11 expenditure had risen to £129 million covering around 800 projects and 10,500 posts. In November 1992, the Home Office announced its intention to phase out Section 11 funding. Its original proposals were to reduce the maximum level of central support from 75 per cent down to 50 per cent by 1995/96. Although the proposals were subsequently modified, with local authorities being required to submit bids for funding projects meeting tighter criteria, the net effect has been an incremental reduction in the monies available to local government for meeting the needs of its ethnic communities.

Returning to the race-relations legislation the next substantial piece of legislation covering race relations was the second Race Relations Act in 1968. This act extended the powers of the Race Relations Board to cover employment, housing, education and the provision of goods, facilities and services, and the publication or display of discriminatory advertisements and notices. The Board was also given the power to investigate suspected unlawful discrimination where there was no individual complainant. However, due to inadequate resources and the absence of any provision to tackle indirect discrimination, in practice the Board's investigations were largely confined to individual complaints. The 1968 Act also established the Community Relations Commission and charged it with the responsibility for creating better understanding and harmonious relations between peoples of different races and cultures. The CRC in turn provided funds to local voluntary committees to employ officers to undertake work in pursuance of these objectives. Both the Race Relations Board and the Community Relations Commission did some very valuable work in tackling the difficulties experienced by new Commonwealth migrants.

However, by the early 1970s, it was apparent that the law needed widening to include indirect discrimination and strengthening to allow a proactive rather than a merely reactive approach to be taken to counter the continuing high levels of direct and indirect discrimination based largely on colour. It was also recognized that equality of opportunity and treatment could not be made conditional upon the total abandonment of cultural and ethnic identity by racial minorities, increasing proportions of whose members were either born here or had been substantially brought up in the United Kingdom (See Chapter 2 for the demographic context).

The Current Law

With these considerations and the experience and lessons learned from the 1965 and 1968 Race Relations Acts, a new Race Relations Act was enacted in 1976. The Act merged the Race Relations Board and the Community Relations Commission to form a new body, the Commission for Racial Equality, with new and stronger powers for the creation of a society based on equality of opportunity for all racial groups. The Commission has a duty of:

- working towards the elimination of discrimination;
- promoting equality of opportunity and good relations between persons of different racial groups generally; and
- keeping under review the workings of the Act and, when required by the Secretary of State, or when it otherwise thinks it necessary, drawing up and submitting to the Secretary of State proposals for amending it.

The 1976 Act gave a wider definition of unlawful discrimination to include traditional practices and procedures which, although they may not be intended to discriminate or disadvantage, nevertheless had that effect on ethnic minorities. A requirement or condition which although applied equally — or which would be applied equally — to all racial groups constitutes unlawful indirect discrimination if:

- a considerably smaller proportion of persons of a racial group can comply with it as compared with the proportion of persons of another racial group;
- which cannot be shown to be justifiable irrespective of colour, race, nationality or ethnic or national origins of the person or persons to whom it is applied; and
- which is to the detriment of the person who cannot comply with it.

Thus unnecessarily demanding educational qualifications for jobs which do not require such high qualifications could be indirectly discriminatory. Similarly, unjustifiable dress or language requirements could constitute unlawful indirect discrimination. The 1976 Act also enables measures to be taken to meet the specific needs of particular racial groups in regard to their education, training or welfare, or any other ancillary benefits. Additionally, the Act allows provision to be made for training and encouragement to apply for work in which particular racial groups are underrepresented. Actual selection for a job must, of course, be on merit.

Section 1 of the Act distinguishes two types of discrimination: direct and indirect. Direct discrimination refers to treating a person less favourably than another on racial grounds. For example, to refuse a student entry to a college because he or she was black would constitute direct discrimination. Indirect discrimination involves applying a requirement or condition in a way that a smaller proportion of a particular ethnic group can comply with it. It has also to be established that failure to comply with the condition or requirement is detrimental and that the requirement is not justifiable on non-racial grounds. It is important to note that discrimination need not be conscious; it may be discrimination by effect, rather than by intention.

The two basic objectives of the Race Relations Act 1976 can therefore be stated as follows: firstly to regulate behaviour by laying down minimum acceptable standards which should govern relations between groups and individuals in any civilized society. The second objective is to encourage behaviour and actions necessary to overcome the effects of discrimination and disadvantage and thereby help to create a society in which groups and individuals enjoy genuine equality of opportunity. As both objectives aim to bring about qualitative changes in society, their importance to educationalists cannot be overstated. This then, is the broad legal context in terms of race relations, within which the education service has to operate. Detailed guidance on the implementation of the Race Relations Act with specific reference to every section is, of course, available from a variety of sources. Thus, for example, the Commission for Racial Equality's Code of Practice for the elimination of racial discrimination in education sets out the implications of every relevant section of the 1976 Act to help those involved with education to provide it without discrimination made unlawful by the Act. Other publications provide detailed guidance on important issues relating to the encouragement of awareness and initiatives necessary for the creation of an education service which is capable of meeting the needs and aspirations of a multiracial, multicultural and multifaith society.

The Race Relations Act 1976 is the most important piece of legislation so far passed in Britain to combat racial discrimination. In 1977 the National Association of Head Teachers published a Council Memorandum on racial discrimination. A revision was published some nine years later (NAHT, 1986). Very few would disagree that the Act has given Britain the most comprehensive laws of all the EC countries. However, there is still evidence of discrimination in employment, housing and other areas. It is also clear that much work remains to be done in outlawing discrimination on grounds of ethnicity. People from ethnic-minority groups still do not have the same opportunity as the mainstream of the population in employment, social services and education. It is useful to consider, albeit very briefly, one or two important avenues for making progress towards achieving these objectives within the framework of the Race Relations Act.

Multicultural Education

Clearly this has been, and continues to be, important in disseminating information relating to the culture, traditions and beliefs of various groups within society. The need is to build on the understanding and tolerance which will result from greater awareness of other ways of living by ensuring that the more positive aspects of different systems and values are identified and respected. As noted elsewhere in this series of four books, such aspirations are more readily expressed than achieved. Despite this caveat, there are many ways in which a multicultural education can be developed.

Antiracist Education

A careful and sympathetic review of teaching materials and methods is necessary to ensure that they are as free as possible of cultural and racial bias based on negative and/or stereotypical images and assumptions. Their replacement by appropriately based materials and methods will be helpful in promoting self-development and mutual respect amongst students and teachers. Encouragement can also be given to underrepresented groups to apply for work in the Education Service, especially in teaching posts. This would not only provide much needed role models, but may also be an additional cultural resource.

The National Curriculum

Implementing some of the initiatives discussed above within the constraints of the National Curriculum is inevitably going to pose challenges in respect of both resources and commitment. As far as may be practicable, attempts should be made to ensure that teaching materials and methods in various subjects within the National Curriculum are such as to enable the various minority groups and the majority group to understand and value their particular ethnic identities.

Finally, there are also other Acts which impose various duties and obligations on those involved in providing education. For example, the Education Reform Act 1988 with its provision for the Local Management of Schools opting out, the National Curriculum and the character of religious worship. All of these issues have racial as well as cultural and religious dimensions.

Similarly, the right of parents to a school of their choice for their children poses challenges, which sometimes may be in conflict with obligations under other legislation.

Consider, for example, the recent test cases in Dewsbury and Cleveland. In both, the High Court upheld the right of parental choice under the 1988 Education Reform Act, even though such judgments appeared to undermine the 1976 Race Relations Act. Under the terms of the latter, LEAs are not allowed to act in any way that would constitute racial discrimination. The parents won the right to have their children transferred to other schools from the ones to which they had been originally allocated. The parents were white and the schools had a high proportion of Asian pupils.

Section 18 (I) of the Race Relations Act 1976 as originally enacted made it unlawful for a Local Education Authority (LEA) to discriminate racially in carrying out those functions under the Education Acts 1944 to 1975 which do not fall under Section 17 of the 1976 Act. The Education Acts of 1980 and 1981 updated Section 18 so that it covers functions under those Education Acts also. There is no similar reference in the 1986 or 1988 Education Acts. There is a suggestion that the words in Section 235 (7) of the 1988 Act that it 'shall be construed as one with the 1944 Act' are intended to deal with this point. But the position is not clear.

In addition to the requirements and expectations embodied in the Education Reform Act 1988, there is legislation relating to race equality in the Children Act 1989 as well as that contained in the Race Relations Act 1976. A number of the implications for practice have been set out in *Lessons of the Law: a casebook of racial discrimination in education* published by the Commission for Racial Equality in 1991. The formal relationship between the Race Relations Act 1976 and the requirements of the Education Reform Act 1988 and the Children Act 1989 presents a number of issues that will require legal clarification concerning the rights and responsibilities of individuals and institutions. The complexities of these three pieces of legislation will almost inevitably create considerable work for members of the legal profession.

A test case, brought before the High Court in September 1993 by Asian parents living in Bradford, involved both the Race Relations Act 1976 and the Education Reform Act 1988. The parents complained that the LEA's school catchment-area policy revised to reduce overcrowding at some oversubscribed secondary schools, discriminated against them in that it systematically excluded their children from entry to the best schools in the area. They argued that 31.4 per cent of Asian applicants from their district did not manage to gain admission to a school of their choice, as compared to 5.3 per cent of non-Asians elsewhere in Bradford. The judge argued that a proper comparison was with non-Asians living in the same district: among them 37.5 per cent failed in their choices. The judgment went against the Asian parents on the grounds that the LEA policy, even if geographically discriminatory, was not so racially. (*The Times*, 11 September 1993)

It should be mentioned that what we have learned as a result of twenty years' experience is that the law is a necessary but not a sufficient condition for addressing the problems of race relations. The aims of legislation have to be translated into practice by various institutions in our society (e.g., courts, industries, universities, schools, politicians, employers and all citizens).

As with all laws, race-relations legislation must be kept under review to ensure that it addresses contemporary concerns adequately. The Commission for Racial Equality (CRE) undertook a review of the Race Relations Act 1976 in 1985, and made recommendations to which the government made no formal response. In the light of subsequent events, the CRE undertook a second review and published in 1992 the *Second Review of the Race Relations Act 1976*. This calls for improvements to three-core parts of the Act: (a) *the coverage of the Act* — the CRE argues that equal opportunities should, as a matter of principle, apply to the whole of public life. The Race Relations Act 1976 as currently exists is not of general application, (b) *a framework for equality* — the CRE calls for a new legal framework for achieving equality which emphasizes achieving equal opportunity beyond the basic elimination of unlawful race discrimination which is all that is required under the present Act, (c) *racial discrimination cases* — the Commission is concerned about the standard of adjudication in race cases, people's access to justice, the failure of the system to get to grips with the group nature of discrimination and the inadequacy of remedies. The CRE proposes a number of remedies in this area. The Second Review of the Race Relations Act 1976 published in September 1992 is available from:

> Lavis Marketing,
> 73 Lime Walk,
> Headington,
> Oxford,
> OX3 7AD
>
> Price £5.50 (including p&p)
>
> Telephone: 0865–67575

The CRE sets out proposals for changes in the legislation which it considers will improve the effectiveness of the law-enforcement process. The document also reflects on issues closely related to race relations and on ways in which society might better manage the many and varied tensions that occur across the boundaries of race, religion and sex, bearing in mind the implications of the move towards a more integrated Europe. The CRE has stressed that unless the law is significantly sharpened and strengthened, and as a matter of urgency, the rate of progress towards racial equality in Britain will be dispiritingly low.

Notes

1   For a scrutiny of grants under Section 11 of Local Government Act 1966, see Appendix 3.

Gajendra K. Verma and Prabodh Merchant

References

COMMISSION FOR RACIAL EQUALITY (1991) *Lessons of the Law: A Casebook of Racial Discrimination in Education*, London, CRE.

COMMISSION FOR RACIAL EQUALITY (1992) *Second Review of the Race Relations Act 1976*, London, CRE.

NATIONAL ASSOCIATION OF HEAD TEACHERS (1986) *Council Memorandum on Racial Discrimination* (Revised), NAHT, Haywards Heath.

Appendix 2

Sources and Lists of Recent Education and Curriculum-related Publications

Peter D. Pumfrey

Educational Publications

Over 700 official documents concerning education were published in England in 1992 alone. The Department for Education (DFE) produces a monthly guide to these entitled *Education Publications*. A concessionary rate of £17.50 for an annual subscription was available in 1993 to schools, colleges and LEAs. The contact address is:

Department for Education,
Library and Information Centre,
Sanctuary Buildings,
Great Smith Street,
LONDON, SWIP 3BT.

National Curriculum Materials

All maintained schools in England are entitled to a free allocation of the majority of official curriculum and assessment-related publications. The establishment of the Schools Curriculum and Assessment Authority (SCAA) as from 1 October 1993 will lead to the creation of new and more efficient channels of communication.

'Schools' Update'

If the reader wishes to maintain an overview of ongoing work by the DFE, NCC and SEAC (the latter two to be integrated under SCAA, as from 1 October 1993) a helpful free publication is available entitled *Schools Update*. It is published termly and briefly indicates current proposals for, and current developments in, the curriculum, its content, pedagogy and assessment. Prior to the establishment of the Schools Curriculum and Assessment Authority (SCAA), *Schools Update* included order forms for selected publications from the DFE, NCC and SEAC.

At the time of writing, schools can request the curriculum and assessment materials to which they are entitled using the DFE/NCC/SEAC joint order form issued termly with the newsletter 'Schools Update'. Many schools have already adopted the far more efficient means of obtaining such information by registering on a scheme which entitles schools automatically to receive a free allocation of all future publications as they become available. Arrangements also exist for individuals, independent schools and overseas customers to purchase these curriculum and assessment materials.

From the viewpoint of schools, there are nine key documents bearing on the cross-curricular themes, elements and dimensions discussed in Chapter 2. They are published by the NCC under the heading 'Curriculum Guidance Series'. Details of each are given below.

CURRICULUM GUIDANCE SERIES

1	*A Framework for the Primary Curriculum* July 1989	ISBN 1 872676 07 3	£4.00
3	*The Whole Curriculum* March 1990	ISBN 1 872676 14 6	£3.00
4	*Education for Economic and Industrial Understanding* April 1990	ISBN 1 872676 19 7	£5.00
5	*Health Education* July 1990	ISBN 1 872676 23 5	£5.00
6	*Careers Education and Guidance* August 1990	ISBN 1 872676 24 3	£5.00
7	*Environmental Education* October 1990	ISBN 1 872676 25 1	£5.00
8	*Education for Citizenship* November 1990	ISBN 1 872676 30 8	£5.00
9	*The National Curriculum and Pupils with Severe Learning Difficulties* March 1992	ISBN 1 872676 50 2	£6.00

The National Educational Resources Information Service (NERIS)

In the writer's opinion, to the detriment of all involved, we are seeing the death of a phoenix of educational information. In the era of information technology, at a time when the potential and use of networked computers within and between schools and other sources of information are both increasing exponentially, it is staggering that a most promising educational development has been effectively 'killed off' by government policy. Fortunately, the phoenix characteristically arises in the fullness of time. The growth potential in the ashes of the electronic-information system is unlikely to remain dormant for long. Readers need to know what has happened to a system that could have been helping them now in delivering the National Curriculum by providing a ready source of information.

The National Educational Resources Information Service (NERIS) was established in 1987 to help teachers and others efficiently locate information concerning teaching materials and other resources. It is an electronic database, run by a non profit-making trust. Initially it was supported by the Department of Trade and Industry through its industry–education unit, the then DES, NCC, SEAC, CCW (Wales), NICC (Northern Ireland), SCC (Scotland) and the Training Agency. At the time of writing, NERIS is based at:

Maryland College,
Leighton Street,
Woburn,
Milton Keynes,
Buckinghamshire,
MK17 9JD
(tel: 0525290 663)

At one time, NERIS used commonly available educational computers, a modem and some specially written software that enabled users to locate information on learning materials and the curriculum using on-line searches. Institutions using Prestel. Prestel Education and Campus (the successor to the Times Network System) could, at one time, access the NERIS database. Discs containing the database, or sections of it, could also be obtained. The NERIS database includes copyright-free materials that can be reproduced or adapted for use in schools.

Initially the system was subsidized both in respect to both the network charges and overheads and was grant-aided by the DTI. In June, 1990, it was reported that some 5,700 schools were using the database which comprised about 33,000 items at that time. By June 1992, the number of items on the database had risen to 53,000 and was continuing to increase. Unfortunately, the number of schools subscribing to the service had fallen to about 3,000.

In Volume 2 of this series, a series of searches were carried out to identify references to resources bearing on cross-curricular elements (10pp.), themes (13pp.), skills (16pp.) and dimensions (4pp.) of the curriculum. As NERIS was then being continuously extended and updated, we had intended to present similar but updated information of materials particularly relevant to cross-curricular elements, themes, skills and dimensions. For the reasons given above, that approach has been modified.

A variety of searches were carried out for documents related to cross-curricular elements within the National Curriculum i.e., themes, skills and dimensions. The flexibility of the NERIS database was one of its great strengths. Another was that additional curriculum-related resources were continuously being added. In combination, these attributes allowed subscribers to search the database efficiently and rapidly for materials related to particular curricular concerns, whether these were related to specific subjects or cross-curricular themes, skills or dimensions at any specified Key Stage. This is not to say that the system is perfect. In a changing and complex field such as education, any database is limited by the amount of new information that is fed into it and the means whereby the database can be accessed.

Ten *examples* of the type of educational information that can be obtained from NERIS are presented below. The entries are based on a search of a NERIS CD issued in May 1993. The entries cover a search restricted to the NC cross-curricular theme of equal opportunities. The items have been de-liberately selected to have a focus on cultural diversity, rather than on other areas of concern about equal opportunities. Other searches can rapidly be carried out in relation to all the NC cross-curricular elements listed in Chapter 2, at both primary and secondary-school levels, by schools having access to the NERIS CD-ROM.

NERIS Ref: 1037066139
Title: *The world of equal opportunities*
Media: Resource pack; set of four modules; teacher notes; photocopiable activity sheets, literary extracts, audio-cassette
Series: South East Region Flexible Learning
Publisher: Croydon TVEI
Published: 1992

NERIS Ref: 1037070627
Title: *Cross-curricular themes and dimensions — the primary perspective*
Media: Booklet
Publisher: Wiltshire County Council
Published: Undated

NERIS Ref: 1037063219
Title: *Learning about racism: an introduction for use in schools*
Media: Booklet; 8pp.
Publisher: Runnymede Trust
Published: 1989

NERIS Ref: 1037063218
Title: *Race and immigration*
Media: Periodical
Publisher: Runnymede Trust
Published: Ten issues per year

NERIS Ref: 1037060950
Title: *Race, education and society* (E208)
Media: Multimedia pack; books; audio cassettes; videos
Publisher: The Open University and Sage Publications
Published: 1992

NERIS Ref: 1037073530
Title: *Ethnic minorities*
Media: Book 104pp. A5; col. photos.; tables, reading list
Publisher: HMSO
Published: 1991 (December)

NERIS Ref: 1037068398
Title: *Involving parents in schools*
Media: Book; hardback 160pp.
Author: Wolfendale, S. *et al.*
Publisher: Cassell
Published: 1992

NERIS Ref: 1037066139
Title: *The world of equal opportunities*
Media: Resource pack; set of four modules; teacher notes; photocopiable activity sheets; literary extracts; audiocassette
Series: South East Region Flexible Learning
Publisher: Croydon TVEI
Published: 1992

NERIS Ref: 1037063491
Title: *Equal opportunities and computer education in the primary School: guidelines of good practice for teachers*
Media: Book
Author: Ellis, J.
Publisher: Equal Opportunities Commission
Published: Undated

NERIS Ref: 1037059447
Title: *Education for citizenship in a multicultural society*
Media: Book; hardback 144pp.; bibliography; indices
Author: Lynch, J.
Publisher: Cassell
Published: 1992

Currently, NERIS information is only available on CD-ROM. Even this service is to be discontinued by 1994.

Access to Information on Multicultural Education Resources (AIMER)

AIMER is a database, similar to NERIS, but of even greater importance to those concerned with cultural diversity and the curriculum. With the support of the Commission for Racial Equality, a project was established at Bulmershe College, Earley, Reading. It is known by the acronym 'AIMER' (Access to Information on Multicultural Education Resources). It offers 'students, teachers, advisers and others information on multicultural antiracist teaching materials'. By virtue of the importance of this aspect of the curriculum and the interest then shown by LEAs, schools and teachers, the Department of Education and Science made a three-year grant covering the period 1987–1990. This enabled a full-time resource development officer to be appointed. In 1989 the amalgamation of Bulmershe College with the University of Reading Faculty of Education and Community Studies took place. The address of the project in 1994 is:

AIMER,
Reading and Language Information Centre,
Faculty of Education and Community Studies,
The University of Reading,
Bulmershe Court,
Earley,
READING, RG6 1HV

Eighty-six LEAs became major users of the AIMER service. The AIMER database was available to institutions with access to NERIS either online or by CD-ROM. AIMER also established a postal inquiry service. Details of the postal service can be found in Volume 1 of this series, together with details of the 'Topics' included in the AIMER database.

Sadly, the withdrawal of central-government support for NERIS and the failure of potential users to subscribe to the service means that NERIS is, as noted earlier, currently only operating using CD-ROM. Even this limited service is likely to end in 1994. If the 'market forces' currently operative in education result in the collapse of both NERIS and AIMER, it will represent a considerable medium and long-term national educational loss to set against whatever short-term and minor financial economies are effected.

Fortunately, AIMER, under the direction of Dr Vivienne Edwards, is continuing its activities. The AIMER database still represents the most comprehensive and up-to-date compendium of information on multicultural materials available in the UK. In addition to the postal-inquiry service, AIMER can provide a wide range of resource lists on topics central to the multicultural dimension of the National Curriculum. Of even greater value to practising teachers is the AIMER Yearbook. The 1993/4 was published in June 1993. It costs £45.00 including postage and packing. The edition includes *photocopiable* resource lists on:

- professional development and in-service;
- home–school links;
- assessment and testing;
- materials for beginners in English;
- materials for second-stage learners;
- language-support materials;
- materials in Bengali, Chinese, Gujurati, Punjabi and Urdu;
- oral and written literature;
- arts and crafts;
- dance;
- music;
- maths;
- technology;
- life-sciences;
- physics and chemistry;
- geography;
- history;
- economics;
- development studies;
- beliefs;
- race awareness;
- home economics;
- business studies; and
- games, sports and toys.

Additionally, information concerning the names and addresses of many of the recently reorganized Section 11 teams are included (see Appendix 3 for further information concerning Section 11).

Bilingual Pupils and the National Curriculum

Britain is a multicultural, multiethnic society. It is becoming increasingly so (see Chapter 2). It has been estimated that pupils in schools speak a range of over 200 different languages other than English. The following question summarizes an important educational concern. How can the values of ethnic and linguistic diversity, and the social cohesion represented by a common language, be reconciled within the context of the curriculum?

Two qualified and experienced teachers and educational psychologists with longstanding and continuing involvements in multicultural education have coordinated the production of a most valuable resource pack centred on systematically addressing such questions. The loose-leaf format of this photocopiable compendium is extremely 'user-friendly'. The full reference to this resource is: Cline, A. and Frederickson, N. (1991) *Bilingual Pupils and the National Curriculum: Overcoming Difficulties in Teaching and Learning*, London, University College, pp. 242.

To be bilingual is to be fluent in two different languages. At its highest level, the individual is able to think in each language. There is no need laboriously to translate from the less familiar language into the one in which one is competent. In this publication, the term 'bilingual' is used to refer to 'individuals who have to alternate between the use of two languages, *whatever their level of proficiency* in each of the two. Pupils whose parents are not native speakers of English 'face particular challenges at school because they are exposed to a variant of English at home and in their community' (p. 2).

Communication is central to community. Verbal-language matters. The building of the Tower of Babel was not a success. Readers who have visited a country and were either ignorant of its language, or had only an elementary knowledge of it, will well appreciate the increasing difficulties that can arise as verbal communication between individuals reduces. Isolation and alienation of the individual unable to communicate effectively in the majority language, is likely to increase. In Britain, not to be able to communicate effectively and efficiently in English carries high social and economic costs.

Is this no more than an expression of an Anglocentric linguistic imperialism, or is it a legitimate concern in a democratic society? The aspiration of building a multicultural democratic metaphorical equivalent of Jerusalem in this green and pleasant land, including its less than salubrious deprived urban areas, is facilitated by the use of a common language. It is a necessary, but not sufficient, condition for achieving the greater objective of social cohesion.

The two largest minority ethnic groups in Great Britain are from India and Pakistan. The third largest minority ethnic group is pupils of parents of Afro-Caribbean origins. The issue of non-standard dialects is different from that facing bilingual children. For those concerned about the former, an annotated reading list on 'British Black English' is provided at the end of the Cline and Frederickson materials (pp. 241–2).

Do many British-born bilingual children of parents whose mother tongue is not English fail to fulfil their potential in the educational system? If this is the case, is it, at least in part, a consequence of the demands of bilingualism and of perceptions of the minority culture and language held by members of the majority native English speakers? What are the implications for that subset of bilingual pupils who have learning difficulties?

On the positive side, the benefits of bilingualism can be considerable. 'Additive' and 'subtractive' bilingualism are interestingly explored (p. 55). Understanding the nature of bilingualism amongst minority ethnic groups and its educational and social implications are crucial to the development of a multicultural democracy.

The above set of learning resource materials has drawn on the experiences of a wide range of educational psychologists, teachers and other professionals working mainly in LEAs in London, the Home Counties and the North of England.

The organization of the materials is based on the following three assumptions.

- Institutional racism can affect the educational achievements of many pupils from minority ethnic and linguistic groups.
- The needs of bilingual pupils and their families would best be served by teachers and educational psychologists who share the clients' first language.
- Current professional practice has many weaknesses, but there are promising practices that can be developed and disseminated.

The materials have been developed for use by local study groups. The initial focus is on the individual's learning objectives in joining a study group. Such groups can be either professionally homogeneous or multidisciplinary. The purpose of the materials is to help teachers and educational psychologists improve their knowledge, understanding and skills in relation to work with bilingual children in general and with those considered to have learning difficulties, in particular. The system is extremely flexible. This is exemplified in the three examples of study-group plans that were developed by different groups (pp. 8–10).

A distinction is drawn between such children's *special needs* and their *special educational needs*. The former are construed as existing in any social group whose 'circumstances or backgrounds are different from those of most of the school population' (p. 89). This is an extremely broad concept. Language, culture, overt racism and socio-economic disadvantage are given as examples.

The authors list three aims.

- To 'raise awareness of current thinking and practice in the education of bilingual pupils'.
- To 'inform the selection of methods and material for assessment and teaching when children with limited English proficiency appear to show learning difficulties'.
- To 'assist staff in devising suitable methods and materials in response to individual needs' (p. 1).

The materials come in a sturdy ring folder. They comprise an introductory chapter on how to use the materials, plus a 'menu' of six substantial units on:

- language and community;
- language development;
- cognitive development and learning difficulties;
- the National Curriculum in multilingual schools;
- multiprofessional assessment of special educational needs; and
- additional resources.

What a cornucopia! Each of the six units has a similar structure. Each begins with an overview and a coordinators' guide. Then follow a number of discussion papers, plus group exercises. The number of words in each of reading provided, plus and estimated reading time, are stated.

The materials will be helpful in both initial teacher training and in-service training and professional development. The structure is clear and the contents coherently presented, focusing on an important series of issues. Suggestions presented for group and individual activities are neither conceptual nor ideological straightjackets. The illustrative situations used as stimuli to discussion have the 'ring of truth' in that the vignettes presented are recognizable, professionally challenging and to which there are no straightforward or simple answers.

The approaches to assessment presented in Unit 5 draw on the work of Cummins, a Canadian psychologist, concerning the nature of bilingualism. A hypothesis-testing model developed in Surrey and the use of curriculum-related assessment are two helpful and complementary papers.

The authors are to be congratulated in providing this most helpful publication. It merits widespread use.

Appendix 3

Section 11 of the Local Government Act 1966: Background and Current Administrative Arrangements

Peter D. Pumfrey

In each of the three preceding volumes in this series, Appendix 3 has provided information and comment concerning developments in various aspects of government policy and practices related to Section 11 funding in general and to the implications of these for LEA services in particular. This theme is continued here. Growing concern, contingent on changes in government policy and increased financial restrictions on provision in relation to Section 11 activities, has been expressed by LEAs and other groups concerned with the 'Education for All' exemplified in the philosophy underpinning the Education Reform Act 1988 and the whole curriculum. Such restrictions are likely to impact adversely on education during the period up to 1996.

In November, 1992, local authorities were informed of proposed reductions.

> the level of financial support which the Government is able to pro-
> vide by means of Section 11 grant crucially depends upon the eco-
> nomic circumstances of the country. The general economic situation
> has changed markedly since local authorities were invited, in October
> 1990, to apply afresh for all Section 11 funding with effect from the
> 1st. April, 1992 . . . the Government, with much regret, can no longer
> afford, throughout the whole of the 3-year period, the level of finan-
> cial help to local authorities . . . which the Home Secretary has earlier
> planned to provide by means of Section 11 grant. (Home Office, 1992)

On the basis of 'current best estimates', the Home Office provided the following figures for the rate of Section 11 grant likely to apply until March 1996.

Present to March 1994:   75 per cent (no change)
April 1994 to March 1995: 57 per cent
April 1995 to March 1996: 50 per cent

Education has always been a major beneficiary of Section 11 funding. In education, the majority of such funds go to areas with a high incidence of minority ethnic-group families. For understandable financial and cultural reasons, these groups tend to form in geographical locations where socio-economic deprivation is relatively high (see Volume 3, Chapter 2 and Volume 4, Chapter 2). In these areas, the LEAs are typically already under severe financial pressures. If the National Curriculum as an 'entitlement' curriculum and the cross-curricular theme of 'Equal opportunities' are to mean anything, LEAs' concerns about Section 11 funding are of national rather than solely of local importance.

According to the Home Office estimates, the 1992/1993 allocation was expected to fund 800 projects with 10,600 posts. This showed an increase in posts, but a Local Authorities Race Relations Information Exchange (LARRIE) survey indicated that 'This increase may be explained by an overall decline in the number of posts in higher grades' (LARRIE, 1992). According to the LARRIE survey, some 32 per cent of youth projects and 81 per cent of projects supporting E2L in schools were supported. 52 per cent of education projects designed to support children and young persons of Afro-Caribbean heritage were also approved. As a result of the impending cuts in Section 11 grant support listed above to projects in the first year of up to three years, 'thousands of teachers and community-worker jobs will be lost over the next three years' (*Education*, 1992). Some projects involving Curriculum and Parental Support Assistants (CPSAs) were funded for five years as from April, 1992. 'At the end of each year there will be reviews of all the individual posts as well as the overall project' (Bhogal, 1992).

It is appreciated that between the writing of this appendix and its publication in Volume 4 of this series, there may be some moderating changes in government policy concerning Section 11 grants. In late 1993, the country's current account deficit suggests that any changes that may take place are unlikely to lead to increased funds.

LARRIE is a registered charity originally established in 1984 by LEAs in England and Wales. It provides a free information service designed to help local authorities 'initiate, develop and monitor their race equality strategies' (LARRIE, 1993). LARRIE has a database which, in 1993, is described as containing over 6,000 abstracts of committee reports, policy statements, action plans and research reports covering all aspects of local-authority service provision and employment practices. Its address is:

Local Authorities Race Relations Information Exchange,
81 Black Prince Road,
LONDON, SE1 7SZ

On 12 June 1993, a national conference was held at Whalley Range High School, Manchester. The conference was entitled *Changes in Section 11 Funding: The Impact on Education*. The conference attracted widespread and high-level professional representation, including senior officials from the Home

Office with responsibility for the administration of Section 11, LEA Section 11 administrators, Section 11 teachers and research workers. Additionally, lay members of various minority ethnic groups also attended. Deliberations drew extensively on Home Office documentation, on the research and publications of LARRIE and the varied professional Section 11-related experiences of those taking part. The conference was jointly organized by the Northern Association of Section 11 Authorities (NASA) and the Centre for Ethnic Studies In Education (CESE): the latter organization being based in the University of Manchester School of Education. As one of the organizers and Head of the CESIE, Professor Gajendra K. Verma chaired the sessions at the conference. The following notes concerning Section 11 funding draw on information presented and issues considered at that conference. The conference considered a range of strategies whereby the concerns of interested parties over the impending reductions in Section 11 grant could be disseminated and communicated to various branches of government.

What is 'Section 11' funding? Since 1967, local authorities have been helped by a discretionary grant through Section 11 of the Local Government Act 1966. The resource was targeted at 'Commonwealth immigrants'. This term was interpreted as a person, adult or child, born in another country of the Commonwealth, who had been ordinarily resident in the United Kingdom for less than ten years, or the child of such a person. This grant originally covered 75 per cent of staffing costs (excluding running expenses such as accommodation, etc.). Subsequently, in 1986, the term 'Commonwealth immigrant' was officially construed as including all those born in another country of the Commonwealth (or Pakistan before it left the Commonwealth in 1972) however long they have been resident in the UK, and their immediate descendants.

The tables in Chapter 2 indicate the numbers of adults and children of non-Commonwealth origins. The absence of additional funding, similar to that covered by Section 11 grant, available to local authorities to assist members of minority ethnic groups and their children from non-Commonwealth countries, is a matter of considerable concern. This major criticism has been addressed in the Local Government (Amendment) Act 1993 which came into force on 20 September 1993. Section 11 funding is now extended to cover 'ethnic minorities whose language or customs differ from those of the rest of the community'.

In 1992, the principle that Section 11 funding was designed to assist in supporting was stated as:

> the reduction of racial disadvantage which inhibits members of ethnic minorities from playing a full part in the social and economic life of this country . . . by helping local authorities to meet the costs of employing additional staff required to overcome linguistic or cultural barriers and thus gain full access to mainstream services and facilities. (Home Office, 1992)

Where the needs of ethnic-minority pupils are 'either different in kind from, or the same as, but proportionately greater than those of the rest of the community', the Home Office is empowered to reimburse local authority expenditure on special provisions designed to address such needs.

> The Government believes that Section 11 has an important role to play in assisting ethnic minority communities to enter fully, and benefit from, the mainstream of national life. The government's aim is to help the members of such communities to benefit fully from opportunities for educational, economic and social development. To this end, the grant has provided and will continue to provide support in the teaching of English, in strategies aimed at improving educational performance, and in tackling particular needs which arise where economic, social or cultural differences impede access to opportunities or services.

> The Government fully recognises the benefits that derive from the maintenance of religious, artistic, cultural and linguistic traditions among ethnic minority communities. It does *not*, however consider Section 11 grant to be appropriate for initiatives aimed at such purposes. (Home Office, 1992)

In connection with education, the government intends that Section 11 funds be used to achieve particular ends, including the following:

1. General
   - To remove barriers to true equality of educational opportunity for ethnic-minority groups.
   - To assist education services in equipping ethnic-minority groups with the knowledge, skills and understanding they require to participate fully and on equal terms in all aspects of British life while maintaining their own cultural identity.

2. Specific
   - To give school-aged children whose mother tongue is not English a command of English which, as far as possible, is equal to that of their peers.
   - To help school-age children from ethnic minorities to achieve at the same level as their peers in all areas of the curriculum.
   - To strengthen ties between schools and the parents of ethnic-minority pupils, where those ties are hard to establish because of the parents' lack of English or because of cultural or social factors, so as to enable parents to become more fully involved in the education of their children and in the work of the schools.
   - To offer ethnic-minority pupils pastoral support in school which meets their needs.

Inevitably, since 1967, there have been various criticisms of the Section 11 grant. These included its low take-up by certain LEAs and the quality of the monitoring of the management and effectiveness of the projects. A helpful summary of the history of changes was presented at the 1993 LARRIE Manchester conference.

The most recent review of the administration of Section 11 grant began in October 1988. It led to the publication of a detailed examination of the administrative efficiency and monitoring procedures involved (Home Office, 1989). This scrutiny found that improvements were required in order that the grant was more effectively used within a more clearly defined framework. The following major changes were proposed in connection with Section 11.

- Funds will be cash-limited.
- Applications must be for projects.
- Projects must be 'needs'-led with need based on a case supported by statistical evidence.
- Posts must be integrated into projects which will be time-limited, usually for three years. For language projects, approval may be given in the first instance for five years.
- Applications must be made in accordance with a prescribed annual timetable (see Appendix 3, Volume 3).
- Provision must fall within the new criteria for grant as set out in the policy accompanying Circular 78/1990.
- Approved projects must be monitored regularly against recognizable performance targets.
- Targets have to be set which are 'achievable and measureable'. Empirical evidence must be produced in order that the effectiveness of the project can be evaluated.
- LEAs are required to monitor the performance of ethnic-minority pupils in the schools against the National Curriculum Attainments Targets.
- Local authorities to be required to identify within their bids a proportion of provision for the voluntary sector.
- Section 11 grant to be paid quarterly in arrears.

Home Office Circular 78/1990 set out the new arrangements for the administration of the grant.

References

BHOGAL, P.S. (1992) 'Section 11 Funding — History', Paper presented at the Conference on *Changes in Section 11 Funding: The impact on Education*, Whalley Range High School, Manchester, 12 June.
EDUCATION (1992) *Education*, 4 December.

Peter D. Pumfrey

HOME OFFICE (1989) *A Scrutiny of Grants under Section 11 of the Local Government Act. Final Report December 1988*, London, HMSO.
HOME OFFICE (1990) *Section 11 of the Local Government Act 1966: Circular No. 78/1990*, London, HMSO.
HOME OFFICE (1992) *Letter to Chief Executives*, London, HO, 26 November.
LOCAL AUTHORITIES RACE RELATIONS INFORMATION EXCHANGE (LARRIE) (1992) *Guide to Section 11 Funding: Research Report No. 3*, London, LARRIE.
LOCAL AUTHORITIES RACE RELATIONS INFORMATION EXCHANGE (LARRIE) (1993) *Section 11 Survey Report: Part One*, London, LARRIE.

Notes on Contributors

John Bennett was, until March 1993, health-education coordinator in Coventry LEA, a post he had held for 4 years during which work was done with schools to implement 'Curriculum Guidance 5, Health Education'. Previous to this he had held teaching and community-education posts in Coventry and Birmingham working in a variety of settings with different groups. The ending of the health-education coordinator's post has meant redeployment and he is currently employed half-time to develop home–school links in one area of Coventry and the other half post is to continue work on certain health issues and overview HE in the curriculum.

Contact address: Elm Bank Teachers' Centre, Mile Lane, Coventry, CVI 2LQ.

Tony Cline has been codirector of training in educational psychology at University College London since 1986. Previously he taught in primary and secondary schools in London and Hertfordshire and worked as an educational psychologist in two London authorities. His last LEA post was as principal educational psychologist to the Inner London Education Authority.

Contact address: Department of Psychology, University College London, Gower Street, London, WC1E 6BT.

Margo Gorman, having completed a B.A. Hons degree from Queen's University, Belfast, moved to England where her interests and involvement have focused on the broad issue of discrimination and inequality. She has worked on children's rights with Save the Children as development officer with gypsies and travellers in the North of England. Currently she is principal officer for Save the Children's work programme in Merseyside. She conducted a small research project for Save the Children in Northern Ireland in 1986 and has been involved in writing up some of the experience of her work with gypsies and travellers. In 1992, she completed her research on 'A Framework for Interculturalism' and obtained the degree of M. Phil from the University of Manchester.

Contact address: Save the Children Fund (Merseyside), Ground Floor, Toxteth Annexe, Aigburth Road, Liverpool, L17 7BN.

Robin Grinter is senior lecturer in the Arts and Humanities Department of the Didsbury School of Education of the Manchester Metropolitan University, and coordinator for equal-opportunities education. He has published numerous chapters in books and journals exploring the relationship between multicultural and antiracist education and the opportunities for implementing these educational dimensions in the National Curriculum.

Contact address: Didsbury School of Education, the Manchester Metropolitan University, 799 Wilmslow Road, Manchester, M20 8RR.

Mike Harrison, director of the Centre for Primary Education at the University of Manchester, was formerly a primary teacher and headteacher. He has worked and researched in the use of computers to support the primary curriculum and promote learning with young children in school. He currently leads the primary PGCE course and teaches mathematics.

Contact address: Centre for Primary Education, School of Education, University of Manchester, Oxford Road, Manchester, M13 9PL.

David Hill is course leader of the Crawley Primary B.Ed for Mature and non-standard entry students and is centre head of the Crawley Centre for Teacher Education at Crawley College. The course is run by West Sussex Institute of Higher Education. His recent publications include *What's Left in Teacher Education?* (1992) (Tufnell Press). He is a cowriter of the June 1993 Hillcole Group booklet *Whose Teachers? — a Radical Manifesto* (Tufnell Press), and of the book *Changing the Future: Redprint for Education*. He was an advisor to the Labour Party on teacher education prior to the 1992 general election.

Contact address: Crawley Centre for Teacher Education, Crawley College, College Road, Crawley, West Sussex, RH10 1NR.

Pushpa Jhingan graduated and trained as a teacher at Punjab University, India, where she began her teaching career before coming to England in 1962. In England, she worked in a number of primary and secondary schools prior to joining the Advisory Service in Manchester where she worked as a senior advisory teacher with the Education Development Service and latterly as a coordinator at the Language and Learning Support Service (Section 11) with additional responsibility for staff development and training. Since taking early retirement in 1993, she now works as a freelance consultant and trainer specializing in equal opportunities, language and curriculum development and ethnic-minority issues.

Contact address: 62 Woodlands Road, Handforth, Wilmslow, SK9 3AV.

Jo Jolliffe is head of the Section 11 funded Language and Learning Support Service in Manchester. She was formerly deputy head of Dick Sheppard Comprehensive School, Lambeth. Her research includes the language and learning needs of black and ethnic-minority children; the education and careers of Muslim girls and antiracist policies in schools. She is currently working on her Ph.D research concerned with 'A Study of History and use of Section 11 funding (under the 1966 Local government Act) for the development of educational provision for ethnic-minority pupils, with particular reference to Manchester'.

Contact address: c/o Language and Learning Support Service, Palmerston Street, Ancoats, Manchester M12 6PE.

Kanka Mallick is senior lecturer in psychology of education at the Didsbury School of Education, Manchester Metropolitan University. Her main research interests include personality and self-esteem. She has written and researched into the area of ethnicity and educational achievement, and cross-cultural psychology. She is an associate fellow of the British Psychological Society and a Chartered Psychologist.

Contact address: Didsbury School of Education, The Manchester Metropolitan University (*v.s.*).

Val Millman trained as a primary-school teacher and taught in primary and secondary schools before taking up her current post as education adviser with Coventry City Council. Her current responsibilities include advice and training for teachers on equal opportunities, careers education and teacher appraisal.

Contact address: c/o Elm Bank Teachers' Centre Mile Lane, Coventry, CV1 2LQ.

Peter Pumfrey is professor of education and head of the Centre for Educational Guidance and Special Needs at the University of Manchester. His research and teaching interests include inter-ethnic relationships, multicultural education, social psychology, specific learning difficulties (dyslexia), and children's reading attainments. He has published widely in these areas. He is author/ editor/coeditor of fifteen books. *Educational Attainments: Issues and Outcomes in Multicultural Education* (1988) and *Race Relations and Urban Education* (1990) were edited, and contributed to, in collaboration with Gajendra K. Verma.

Contact address: Centre for Educational Guidance and Special Needs, School of Education, University of Manchester, Oxford Road, Manchester, M13 9PL.

Diane Rainey taught for several years in primary schools before becoming a lecturer in primary education at the University of Manchester. Her major responsibility is in work with PGCE primary students on the Curriculum and methods of teaching geography.

Contact address: Centre for Primary Education, School of Education, University of Manchester (*v.s.*).

Sandra Shipton has worked in Coventry for nineteen years as an early-years class teacher and with the Minority Group Support Service. She is currently head of Edgewick Community Primary School in Coventry. She has also served on the National Union of Teachers, National Advisory Committee for Equal Opportunities (Gender) and has been involved locally and nationally in the delivery of personal and professional courses for women teachers.

Contact address: Edgwick County Primary School, Cross Road, Soleshill, Coventry, CV1 2LQ.

Ian Smith has been a district inspector with Manchester City Council Education Department for four years. He has a phase responsibility for primary education and is also responsible for primary humanities. For eleven years he was headteacher of a large Manchester primary school. He has developed a range of National Curriculum planning materials which are used throughout the country and is the principal author of the *Cross-curricular Humanities Topic Planners* published (1991) by Folens Ltd.

Contact address: Greenheys Centre, Upper Lloyd Street, Moss Side, Manchester, M14 4HZ.

Gajendra Verma is professor of education and director of the Centre for Ethnic Studies in Education, School of Education, University of Manchester. He is also dean of the Research and Graduate School in the Faculty of Education, University of Manchester. Over the last fifteen years he has been responsible for directing over fourteen national and regional research projects concerned with education, social and occupational adaptation of ethnic-minority groups. He has researched and published widely in the field of race and education, self-concept, identity and curriculum evaluation; and was a member of the Swann Committee of Inquiry into the Education of Children from Ethnic Minority Groups. He has also served on a number of national committees concerned with the education of ethnic-minority adolescents. He is author/coauthor/editor of over twenty-four books.

Contact address: Research and Graduate School, Faculty of Education, University of Manchester (*v.s.*).

Name Index

Subject Index

ability, 177, 229
academic, 83, 106, 167, 168, 171, 199, 222
access to curriculum, 9, 10, 61, 137, 150, 152–4, 163
  and computers, 199, 203, 215, 230
  special educational needs, 175, 180, 182–3
Access to Information on Multicultural Education Resources (AIMER), 83, 256–7
accountability, 62, 111
achievement, 10, 103, 105, 121, 141, 199, 129
  difficulties, 106–7, 169, 170, 259
adult
  life, preparation for, 33, 73, 131, 163
  as role model, 47
advisors, 104, 107, 165–6
AIMER
  see Access to Information on Multicultural Resources
All-Parliamentary Group for Racial Equality, 6
'all-white' areas/schools, 106, 167
alternative schools, 18–19, 85
Anglocentric Curriculum, 9, 12
antiracism, 108, 177
  and ITE, 219, 221, 224, 225–6, 228, 230, 231, 232, 233, 234, 236
antiracist
  aspects, 154, 191
  curriculum, 163, 164
  education, 5, 165, 166–9, 247
  teaching, 13, 47, 167, 168, 256
antisexism: and ITE, 221, 226, 232

APU
  see Assessment of Performance Unit
Art, 142, 194, 200, 203
Articled Teacher Scheme, 218, 220, 222, 223, 224, 229
assessment, x, 10, 47, 49, 132, 134, 152, 165, 179–80, 215
  environmental education, 121, 123, 126–7
  ethnic minority children, 7, 9, 78, 79, 82–3
  materials/resources, 160, 252, 259, 260
  special educational needs, children with, 173, 175, 176, 178, 181, 184–5
Assessment of Performance Unit (APU), 134
assimilation/-ism, 4, 6, 177, 228, 231, 232, 242
ATs
  see Attainment Targets
attainment, 9, 10, 167, 199, 230, 231
Attainment Targets (ATs), 11, 47, 111, 112, 121, 125, 126, 136, 175, 194, 265
attitudes, 5, 35, 74, 100, 102, 133, 136, 140, 147, 175, 204
  antiracist/multicultural, 36, 62, 67, 70, 170
  curriculum, 60, 73, 116, 117, 118, 125, 126, 139, 163
  formation/development, 15, 60, 61, 116, 117, 118, 125, 126
  and Europe, 188, 192, 193
  and the teacher, 15, 156
  see also adult; awareness; positive